Groundwork of
Science and Religion

Groundwork of Science and Religion

Philip Luscombe

EPWORTH PRESS

To Laurel and Benjamin

0 7162 0535 1

First published 2000
by Epworth Press
20 Ivatt Way
Peterborough, PEP3 7PG

Typeset by Rowland Phototypesetting Ltd,
Bury St Edmunds, Suffolk
Printed and bound in Great Britain by Biddles Ltd,
Guildford and King's Lynn

Contents

4 What is Science? – The Philosophy of Science

5 Making Science – Sociology and the claims of 'Truth'

6 Scientific Views of the World

9 Creation Waits: Making a Theology for Today

Preface

Any attempt to discuss science *and* religion is fraught with dangers. The author is liable to offend two different camps of opinion at the same time. At the start of the twentieth century, Sir Oliver Lodge, the first Principal of Birmingham University and a distinguished physicist, began to write extensively about the relationship of science and Christianity. His critics were quick with their scorn:

> If this is Christianity, Lodge has assuredly the honour of being the first Christian and it is not improbable that he will have the additional honour of being the last.[1]

was the comment of a rationalist critic who was equally dismissive of Lodge's science. Lodge's local bishop agreed and refused to allow permission for him to preach in his parish church.

One of the recurring themes of this book is of the importance of synthesis and the holding together of large pictures drawn from across as many of the fields of human endeavour as possible. As we shall see, however, it has become increasingly difficult to be an expert, or even to hold a reasonable competence across a variety of disciplines. We are each experts in our own narrow sphere, and there is not enough time for us, or even capacity in our brains, for any of us to fulfil the old ideal of the polymath.

Here is an issue to which we shall return again and again in the course of this book. The attempt to understand across narrow subject boundaries may be impossible but it must be made. It is not my hope that science and religion will eventually merge into some new synthesis. Neither the religious nor those whose first language is science would recognize such a product. Much as I admire his attempt, another of Sir Oliver Lodge's critics was probably correct when he wrote that 'Sir Oliver's theism is of a kind which would make the hair of a Christian stand on end.'[2]

We should have learnt by now that neither science, if science can be described as a single entity, nor religion, which certainly cannot be described in monolithic terms, will ever succeed in gaining complete dominance over the other. Regrettable as the continuing battle over so-called Creationism is, it can at least teach us this truth. However dominant science appears the strength and raw power of the religious impulse is unlikely to be entirely subsumed under a scientific world view. Equally the simple success of science in explaining and taming the world over the last few hundred years means that it is unlikely that science will ever cease to be a major player both as a force to be explained and in its impact on the popular imagination. The fragmentation and tolerance of postmodernism may be a passing trend, or the next great worldview, but it will still have to make its accommodation with science.

To enter into more detail now would be to anticipate my argument throughout the book. Our subject matter is the rise of science to its present, not unchallenged, position of dominance, and the inevitable encounters along the way between different branches of science and religion and their representatives. What does science understand about the world in which we live, and how does our Christian proclamation of the world as the creation of God relate to our scientific perception? Should traditional Christian understandings be modified in the light of scientific knowledge? And if so, how? And if not, why not?

My own initial education was in physics, or natural philosophy as the subject was labelled at my somewhat traditionalist university. Later, as I was completing my training in theology, I was persuaded to begin to examine how the two subjects might relate to each other, and I have continued to study the relationship through the past twenty-five years. I owe a deep debt of gratitude to Professor Dan Hardy who first suggested this study to me, and who through his own encyclopaedic knowledge continues to provide an example of the best kind of synthesis between different branches of knowledge. In asking me to deliver the Fernley-Hartley Lecture at the Methodist Conference in 1993, the Trustees forced me to think systematically about the subject once again. My Fernley-Hartley Lecture ' "The Silence of their Equations":

The Study of Science and the Practice of Theology'[3] underlies this book, although my ideas have been much changed and expanded since then. The published version of the lecture won a Templeton Foundation Exemplary Papers award, and I am grateful for the Foundation's support.

During the time that I was writing this book, I was teaching in Durham, and the students and staff of both the Wesley Study Centre and Cranmer Hall, St John's College, have helped me to refine my thoughts, especially on the effects of scientific knowledge on our understanding of theology. Professor Brian Tanner, of the Department of Physics in Durham, has been a constant source of up-to-date information about current science and also the source of innumerable hard questions about the relationship between science and religion. Professor Tanner shares my fascination with the relation of different branches of knowledge, but of course the errors – scientific and otherwise – in the current book are my own.

Chapter 1

A Large Map – The Relation of Science and Religion

Canon William Tristram ought to be better remembered. His portrait dominates the finest room in St John's College in Durham. From time to time I have taken groups of students studying science and religion out of their lecture room to stand in front of Tristram's picture. He is the epitome of a Victorian cleric. Dressed in dark clothes, his MA hood prominent over his shoulder, he holds a book in his left hand, the index finger carefully marking his place, as if he is impatient to get the sitting over and return to his reading. His right hand rests gently on a table on which lie the usual bric-a-brac of a Victorian gentleman's study including the reassembled skeleton of a fairly substantial bird. William Tristram sports a full and flowing white beard and could almost be mistaken for Charles Darwin. Two Victorian gentlemen similar in looks, and no doubt in class and attitude.

Like Darwin, Tristram was a serious scientific naturalist working at the middle of the nineteenth century. The bird Tristram's Grackle is named after him, which may explain the presence of the skeleton. More importantly to students of the relationship between science and religion, Tristram was the first person to go into print to use Darwin's theory to explain the scientific results he was collecting. Observing birds in the Sahara, Tristram used the theory of evolution by natural selection to account for the resemblances and differences between different species.

The first scientific use of Darwin's theory was thus made by a clergyman of the established church, in support of his own scientific work. That alone deserves a footnote in the history of science, but what happened next is more striking. Within a year of using Darwin to explain his scientific results, Tristram had rejected Darwin's theory on the basis of the famous debate at the British Association in Oxford in 1860. This was when Thomas Huxley (Darwin's Bulldog) clashed with Samuel Wilberforce. The popular myth is that an overbearing bishop was thrashed in public debate by a well-informed young scientist. In fact the debate was inconclusive, and contemporary reports suggest that the supporters of both Wilberforce and Huxley went away thinking that they had won.[1] The way in which new scientific theories are evaluated by the scientific community is complex. Hard evidence for new theories is often lacking; the older and well-established theories have often done good work in explaining the world and can usually be modified to take account of new results. The relative claims of new and old are difficult to determine, as we shall discover.

Was Tristram converted back to the old – scientific – orthodoxy on the basis of Bishop Wilberforce's science? Wilberforce certainly possessed a fine mind, and had been advised before the debate by Robert Owen, the leading expert on fossils, and the coiner of the word 'dinosaur'. Or did the Anglican canon defer to the bishop, and fall back into old certainties? Was his scientific judgment fatally undermined by non-scientific factors? As with the outcome of the Oxford debate itself, our judgment here may well depend on the presuppositions we bring to the case. The relationship between science and religion is more complicated than we usually imagine.

A debate that will not go away

To reassure you that this debate is not simply a historical curiosity let me quote some more recent authors. Peter Atkins' book *Creation Revisited* is published as a 'Penguin Science' book. Towards the close of the book Atkins writes:

> That is really the end of our journey. We have been back to the time before time, and have tracked the infinitely lazy creator to his lair (he is, of course, not there).[2]

Atkins, who lectures in physical chemistry at Oxford, makes the claim that by understanding the basic building blocks of the universe, we can explain everything and understand everything. There is nothing else. In a similar vein, the physicist Steven Weinberg has written about scientific progress towards the so-called TOE, the Theory of Everything, linking all our physical theories into one great unified theory explaining the physical condition of the universe, both what is out there now, and how it got there. He is also dismissive of the possibility of anything beyond matter and the simple laws which govern its behaviour:

> News that nature is governed by impersonal laws will percolate through society, making it increasingly difficult for people to take seriously astrology or creationism or other superstitions.[3]

Brian Appleyard, who is a perceptive commentator on science, if a rather sceptical one, doubts that Weinberg is correct. We need and cling on to our superstitions:

> [W]e cannot be talked out of our magical dialogue with reality. There is, within us, some indefatigable determination to place meaning outside ourselves, to invent strange and scientifically meaningless patterns and, in some part of our mind inaccessible to scepticism, to take them seriously.

What are the implications of this? Does it provide a comforting suggestion that religion will survive whatever science may prove? 'Our magical dialogue with reality' has some positive overtones. There is the suggestion that religion can add colour and depth to the monochrome world of science, keeping alive whole worlds of possibility. On the other hand 'magical' is somewhat disconcerting. Does it line up Christianity with astrology (the main subject of Appleyard's article) and flat-earthism? 'To invent strange and scientifically meaningless patterns and, in some part of our mind inaccessible to scepticism, to take them seriously.' Is that how we want to defend our beliefs?

Reading Peter Atkins, or listening to Richard Dawkins speaking to large and enthusiastic audiences, the overwhelming feeling is not so much of their hostility to Christianity, though that sometimes slips out, as in Dawkins' famous: 'Theologians don't do anything, don't affect anything, don't achieve anything, don't even mean anything.'[4] The overwhelming feeling is of their exasperated tolerance. When the light of knowledge has spread sufficiently widely then Christians will pack their bags, and theologians find more useful employment.

Some fundamental questions

Christianity claims to be an incarnational religion and to speak of God as creator. Appleyard's talk of 'scientifically meaningless patterns', although not intended to be hostile, ought to present us with a problem. If we do truly proclaim the God who both created the earth and walked upon it, then the real world ought to matter to us. Do the 'assured results' of science affect Christianity in any way, and if so how? According to Appleyard, beliefs are 'inaccessible to scepticism' which may give some comfort in the face of sceptical criticism, but most Christians will be uncomfortable with the idea of retreating beyond argument into some secret ghetto.

It is certainly true that science is under attack today. Charles Kingsley, best known now as the author of *The Water Babies*, was a contemporary of Canon Tristram, another Anglican clergyman who was also a naturalist. One hundred and twenty-five years ago, Kingsley defended Darwin's work by claiming that no one could show him anything that science had done that wasn't for the good of humanity. We would be rash to make such a claim today. The shorthand of Hiroshima, Chernobyl and Bhopal reminds us of the darker side of science. Whatever the reasons, society has also begun to loose confidence in the scientific claim to direct and comprehensive knowledge about the world. There is no longer an automatic deference paid to science and scientists. For all their ability to generate publicity, Dawkins and Atkins are in some ways remarkably old-fashioned figures. This raises a question for the religious observer of science: are such developments to be welcomed or regretted?

It is true that Christianity is no longer under the cosh of science, but do we really want to live in a world where anything goes, and where there are no agreed standards? For the two hundred years since the Enlightenment, it has seemed as if there would be a future where society lived under an agreed code of knowledge and ethics demonstrably true by common sense and needing no further justification. Such a view is now crumbling. Does the postmodernism that is replacing it mean that anything goes? Christianity is once more intellectually acceptable, but no more so than belief in talking rocks, or aromatherapy.

Does Christianity want to be one cult among others, or should it once more claim to be 'queen of the sciences', or may the neutral reason of the Enlightenment turn out to have been a friend rather than an enemy?

Discussion of these wider questions inevitably brings us into the sphere of philosophers and theologians. In the more philosophical companion volume to his best-selling *On Being a Christian*, the liberal Catholic theologian Hans Küng retold an old story:

> Some time ago, an English Nobel prize-winner is supposed to have answered the question whether he believed in God: 'Of course not, I am a scientist.' This book is sustained by the hope that a new age is dawning when the very opposite answer will be given: 'Of course. I am a scientist.'[5]

In one sense, of course, any book such as this will seek to affirm Küng's answer, but part of our task will be to examine the very different responses of different philosophers when faced with the question. One example here will set the scene.

The gospel and contemporary culture

In the early 1990s a group of churchpeople who were concerned to build bridges between the church and the world founded the Gospel and Contemporary Culture project. Inevitably they saw 'science' as one of the main subject areas which they must seek to understand and test. However, when they invited the philosopher Mary Midgley to discuss the relevance of science to religion, she wondered what all the fuss was about. Why should science and religion seek to struggle for a single position? To use her title, this would be a 'Strange Contest':

> We are used to the idea that *religion* is logically insecure, and people who say this tend to have the unspoken feeling 'Why can't it be more like science?' But should an elephant try to be like a concrete-mixer? And are we clear about just what kind of a concrete-mixer science is meant to be anyway?[6]

The point Midgley wishes to emphasize is one which everyone who seeks to discuss the relationship of science and religion needs always to keep in front of them. She claims that society has set a ridiculously high value on knowledge. Ridiculous, because scientific knowledge is defined in a very narrow way: 'exact information about the physical world, acquired professionally by experts using experimental methods'. Other writers have made a similar point by reasserting the distinction between knowledge and wisdom. An abundance of brute facts is much less significant than knowing something of value. What is useful is not always true, and the 'whole truth is usually something so large and complicated that we will never have stated it properly'.[7]

We must learn not to be overawed by the ability of science to assemble vast arrays of facts and to measure detail ever more precisely. If such knowledge is to have value, it is essential to make the attempt to assess its significance. The success of physical science has led many people who should know better to believe that all successful explanations will look like the answer to a physics exam. As we shall see later, in her Gifford lectures *Science as Salvation*, Midgley has great fun attacking the pretensions of modern physicists to envisage secular forms of salvation – from science-fiction-inspired escapes from a dying earth to the storage of human brain waves within the fundamental physical construction of the universe.

The significance of this is that far from demonstrating a creative enlargement of science, all such harebrained schemes show is the lack of training of most of today's scientists in any field outside their own disciplines and, to use Midgley's characteristically acerbic words, the barrenness of their imagination. So, religion should no more try to look like science than an elephant should try to behave like a concrete-mixer. Is there a simple overall scheme into which all our knowledge and ways of trying to understand it can be arranged? One of the tasks of this book will be to wrestle with this question. Midgley certainly suggests that we shall need a large map, but it will not be a simple one.

We need to avoid the kind of discussion in which 'science' and 'religion' appear as sole protagonists, confronting each other in a vacuum.[8]

Religion needs to gain confidence. There is no need to mimic science. The most important question is no longer 'How securely do we know this?' Instead, we must not be afraid to ask, 'Is this worth knowing?'

A large map

The previous section suggests that we shall need a large map in to order to understand the relationship between science and religion. In the previous few pages we have sketched out some of the history of the relationship and its complexity. We also glanced at the opinions of some modern sceptics, partly to question whether their uncompromising assertion of the superiority of science over the non-sense of religion and theology still made sense in the postmodern world.

Contemporary challenges to the superiority of science may be welcomed as supporting the cause of religion, or feared as leading us into new dark ages where anything goes. Hans Küng looking towards a future rational, scientific status for Christianity may now seem as old-fashioned as his opponents. Mary Midgley thus asks an urgent and difficult question as to how we are to make sense of different forms of knowledge or wisdom.

In attempting to understand the relationship of science and religion, a number of different starting points are possible. History is obviously important – the great set pieces of Galileo and Darwin must be discussed as well as the less well-known interludes. Warfare, co-operation, armed neutrality and total indifference can all be discovered in the history of the relationship as we shall see.

Philosophy cannot be ignored. *What is this thing called science?* is the title of one popular text on the philosophy of science. Philosophers claim to cut through our prejudices and preconceptions in order to ask the simple questions which others fail to address: What is science and how does it work? What are its limitations? Are the claims of science to possess a reliable method for discovering the truth about the real world correct? How can different branches of human knowledge relate to each other? Indeed, is it reasonable to claim that both science and religion are valid and valuable branches of knowledge?

In recent years, the claim of philosophy to possess a unique role in examining and categorizing all branches of knowledge has faced a new challenge. From humble beginnings sociology has gained experience in analysing the behaviour of society and groups within it. More recently, sociologists have begun to examine our human claims to knowledge, and the ways in which people seek to build their systems of knowledge. Religion was an early target for investigation, but eventually the spotlight was turned on science. Why do scientists work in a particular way? Why do they make these absolute claims for science and the knowledge accumulated by science? Who benefits from these claims? Have scientists become a new secular priesthood, the guardians of society's wisdom? This sociological probing has extended into a critical examination of both the ways in which scientists work, and the status of science itself – in textbooks of sociology, science is often discussed in the section on 'belief systems', much to the dismay of scientists. We shall examine the importance of these relativizing claims.

Can the central assertions of modern science be compressed into a few pages? Before turning to more directly theological issues, we shall attempt briefly to outline some of the major theories of modern science and their consequences. How does the scientific community understand itself and the world?

All of this has great consequences for religion and theology. We shall need to consider how people have understood the relationship between religion and science – does any single scheme do justice to the rich complexity? Finally we shall work through some examples of the ways in which theologians working today have made use of modern science, both its methods and particular theories.

Does the way in which we understand religion, the way in which we do theology, need to change in the light of the vast enterprise which science has become over the last two hundred years? This central question will follow us as we seek to understand the implications of the rise of modern science.

I have attempted to take the widest possible view of the relation between science and religion, taking the study of the philosophy of science and the sociology of science as seriously as its history, which is unusual in discussions of the relationship of science and religion. I have not attempted to discuss the implications of technology or the ethics of science in any detail. Such topics would require a separate book to themselves.

Living in a scientific culture

What is the value of the study of the relationship between science and religion? All parts of humanity's intellectual history are in themselves important, but has the subject a greater relevance than that? One of the themes of this book is that science – its factual results, the use of those results to change society though technology, and the influence of scientific ways of doing things – is probably the most powerful single influence on us today. It is obvious that the practical consequences of science shape our lives, from the six-year-old, and therefore two generations out of date, word processor on which this is written to my worries about genetically modified food. Just as importantly, however, scientific ways of thinking have changed our mental map. The relentless scientific demand for more facts, and for very particular ways of demonstrating those facts has deeply influenced our thinking. We shall explore the claim that fundamentalism, for example, and the various versions of religious literalism only took shape, and indeed may only make sense when proclaimed *within a scientific culture* with its repeated demands for proof defined in a specialized, scientific way.

Equally we shall explore whether theology, and hence the shape of our Christian belief, is affected more directly by science. The phenomenal success of Stephen Hawking's best-selling *A Brief History of Time* is well known. The majority of its readers probably skipped over the physics in favour of the more easily understood philosophical implications:

> So long as the universe had a beginning, we could suppose it had a Creator. But if the universe is really self-contained, having no boundary or edge, it would have neither beginning nor end: it would simply be. What place then for a creator?[9]

One of our tasks will be to evaluate such statements. Do scientific discoveries have any effect on the doctrine of creation? Theologians, even if they know some science – and they should – cannot possibly be experts. How are they to evaluate the importance of theories such as Hawking's? Is the theory good science? Will it take its place as a part of the 'established results' of science? How does it relate to other parts of science? How does the language of science relate to the language of theology? When Hawking talks about 'a Creator' does he mean the same as a Christian means when reciting: 'I believe in God, the Father almighty, creator of heaven and earth'? If there is a potential conflict between the apparent meaning of a scientific theory of 'creation' and Christian doctrine, how can the difference be dealt with? Perhaps we must learn to live with an apparent ambiguity until in time we come to perceive a deeper unity. It may be that there is a genuine conflict between the two disciplines. In this case must we alter our previous, perhaps very ancient, perhaps even apparently biblical, understanding? In the course of this book we shall see that all of these situations have been faced by Christians in their meeting with science.

Breaking apart and bringing together: relating science and religion

To help us understand the task, an analogy may be helpful. The biblical scholar and Anglican priest John Drury has written of the work of scholarship as a taking apart and a putting together. Drury compares the work of the biblical critic with that of the Christian minister celebrating the communion service. The minister breaks apart the bread, which is the body of Christ, in order to make it available to everyone. In a similar way, the critic breaks apart the text in order to make it more readily available:

> In both [tasks], something holy and whole is taken apart. That is how it is made available to other people as food for the mind or soul. The holiness is not annihilated but digested. Holy bread and holy texts are transformed into holy living. The truth is our bread . . .[10]

But it can sometimes be forgotten that the task of the scholar involves not only a taking apart, but also, crucially, a putting together. Drury writes of the scholar as being like the host at a party introducing 'texts to texts which had not met before, or, if they had, not quite like this'. He quotes a story from the *Midrash Rabbah* about one of the old Jewish rabbis, not expounding the visions of Ezekiel ('the secrets of the chariot') or any of the seemingly more exciting passages of the Hebrew Bible, but simply doing his ordinary daily job of reading the Law of Moses:

> Once as Rabbi Ben Azzai sat and expounded [the scriptures], the fire played around him. They went and told Rabbi Akiba saying 'Sir, as Rabbi Ben Azzai sits and expounds, the fire is flashing round him.' He [Akiba] went to him and said to him 'I hear that as you were expounding, the fire flashed round you ... Were you perhaps treating of the secrets of the chariot?' 'No', replied Rabbi Ben Azzai, 'No, I was only linking up the words of the Law of Moses with one another and then with the words of the prophets, and the prophets with the psalms and wisdom writings, and the words rejoiced as when they were delivered from Mount Sinai, and they were sweet as at their original utterance.'

Drury comments that at a party people must first be prepared to leave their homes in order to enjoy themselves, to be refreshed by new meetings, and so give enjoyment to others. In bringing the separate parts of the scriptures together, the Rabbi's skill 'in making an apt guest list, full of happy possibilities of conjunction, [resulted] in a good time, with all lit up.'[11] We shall see later that one of the more recent developments in the study of science is that people have begun to understand the importance of the human contribution to science. The skill and personality of the individual scientist, as well as the vitality of the community of scientists, have all been necessary in allowing the progress of science to take place.

The importance of breaking apart and bringing together; the uniqueness of individual effort brought into harmony with the values of the community. Beyond the real disagreements, many of which are unresolved, the practice of science and of religion share many important values. It is this conjunction which we shall hope to demonstrate and affirm in the following chapters.

Chapter 2

Religion and the Rise of Science

We have no scope here to write a history of science, or even a history of the relationship between science and religion. Indeed, John Brooke, one of the most thorough and respected of recent commentators on the relationship suggests that a history is not possible anyway, all the historian can do is to provide a series of sketches, because '[t]here is no such thing as *the* relationship between science and religion. It is what different individuals and communities have made of it in a plethora of different contexts.'[1] In this chapter we shall make extensive use of Brooke's magisterial work, *Science and Religion*, to highlight some of the most suggestive questions raised by the long history of interaction between science and religion.

Beyond warfare

Our hesitations were not shared by a number of influential Victorian writers on science. They knew what must be the proper relationship between science and religion. The mathematician William Kingdom Clifford had been an enthusiastic Christian, but had been converted away from the religion of his youth:

> These sickly dreams of hysterical women and half-starved men, what have they to do with the sturdy strength of a wide-eyed hero who fears no foe with pen or club? This sleepless vengeance of fire upon them who have not seen and have not believed, what has it to do with the gentle patience of the

investigator . . . that will only ask consideration and not belief for that which has not with infinite pains been solidly established.[2]

Similarly, J. W. Draper's *History of the Conflict between Science and Religion* (1875) charted an inevitable struggle between the forces of progress and reaction in which there could only be one outcome. Andrew White was only a little more subtle. His *A History of the Warfare of Science with Theology in Christendom* (1895) claimed only to take issue with dogmatic theology rather than with religion as such, but for many of his readers the distinction was not obvious. And something of this attitude perhaps remains in the popular mind. White's book was being reprinted well into the second half of the twentieth century and his thesis of the warfare between science and religion has entered into the popular consciousness.

White's book is a catalogue of extremes. It is really no surprise that some religious people opposed the changes that science seemed to threaten, but it is much more dubious to paint a picture of total opposition from the work of a few extremists. It has been pointed out that apart from the committed propagandists, many of the specialist writers and historians who have continued to use the warfare motif use it *outside* their own particular period of study. Warfare is always on the horizon, about to erupt, but never actually happening during the period under discussion. This may suggest that the idea of the warfare between science and religion is a pervasive myth, but a myth nevertheless which fades away under detailed study.[3]

Many writers since White have successfully demonstrated just how interconnected science and religion have been until at least very recently. Detailed study of the rise of modern science has led several scholars to propose that Christianity in general or Protestantism in particular was essential to the rise of science. Others make a more specific link to the Puritan ethic, whilst yet others claim a positive role for Catholicism, or for the importance of the doctrine of Creation in helping to form the scientific world view. We should probably be hesitant about trying to draw specific conclusions. It is easy for historians to project their own views back into the period under discussion:

When the history of science is hijacked for apologetic purposes, it is often marred by a cultural chauvinism. The realization that religious beliefs were relevant to the rise of science
is transformed into the more parochial claim that a particular
religion, or religious tradition, was uniquely propitious.[4]

What are 'science' and 'religion'?

It is hardly possible to write about the history of the relationship
between science and religion without first defining the terms used,
but where are we to start? The story is often told of the Oxford
philosophy undergraduate, expecting to be initiated into the
mysteries of the cosmos, who spent days sitting in despair
on the staircase outside his room after his first tutorial,
because his tutor had only been concerned to make him define
the word 'the'. The 'and' of science and religion is also a decep-
tively simple conjunction: does it link two similar entities, both
of which share the same sort of characteristics, and both of which
are equally important? Or are 'science' and 'religion' very different types of things which are misunderstood by being yoked
together?

Our problems multiply with the words 'science' or 'religion'
themselves. By 'religion' do we mean Christianity, or all the
organized religions (or even all religious yearnings within humankind)? The relation of science to other religions than Christianity
does raise a host of fascinating questions: Can Fritjof Capra
possibly be correct in *The Tao of Physics* when he claims intimate
links between the theories of modern sub-atomic physics and
Eastern mystical religion? Are 'New Age' movements reclaiming
an organic view of the universe pushed out centuries ago by
Christian theologians to the detriment of the environment? Does
the recent renaissance in Christian *Trinitarian* theology and its
relevance to creation make a common science and religion dialogue, involving the great world religions, even more difficult?
Reluctantly we shall be forced to limit our discussions to Christianity in order to keep our task within bounds.

Returning to Christianity, just what do we mean by *Christianity*? Should we consider the organized dogma of the scholar
(science and *theology*), or the popular belief of the person in the
pew? The beliefs of one particular group or denomination, or

some common denominator (if we could ever agree upon such a concept)? Our historical studies will demonstrate that some historians believe that particular branches of Christianity may have been uniquely placed to help science at crucial turning points in its history. An important part of our task will be to ask whether such optimism can be justified.

It is almost as hard to define what we mean by *science*. Do we mean the best science of today? Such an approach would tend to judge the past history of science according to whether the results of a previous age matched up to those of our own time. In the past, scientists have been notorious for the way in which they were selective about the history of science. To them, it seemed self-evident that contemporary science had replaced that of a previous generation because of its superiority, and that therefore the history of science consisted more or less of searching for the roots of contemporary orthodoxy in the work of previous generations of scientists. Historians of science today tend to speak instead of the best science of a particular age as it seemed to those living and practising science then. This inevitably raises difficult questions of judgment and discernment. In fact even to look back in this way is misleading. The 'science' of previous generations is composed of a rich mixture of those studies which we would unhesitatingly recognize as science and what one study labels 'Rejected Knowledge': alchemy, astrology and psychical research, to name only a few.[5]

Among the historians, David Knight defines science as an intellectual, social and practical activity, whereas Hooykaas sees the necessary building blocks of modern science as logic, mathematics and the use of observation and experimentation to form the beginnings of a rational interpretation of the world.[6] An important recent change is to emphasize the importance of the scientific *community*, as the place where theories are tested, gain credibility, are preserved and may eventually be overthrown. Such a concept would not have occurred to earlier writers who simply saw scientific theories as self-evidently true, at least until replaced by a more general theory. In this context we can appreciate the value of Brooke's comments that definitions are inevitably difficult, because what we mean by science changes. Brooke highlights Newton's remark that it was part of the business of natural philosophy to discuss the attributes of God and his relation to the physical world; today few scientists would consider that their *science* involved such a direct study of theological issues.

It should by now be apparent that the very boundaries of science and religion shift with time, whilst both science and religion belong in their social contexts, and can only be properly defined within those contexts.[7]

The failure of early science

Science as we understand the word is generally taken to begin with the ancient Greeks, although much earlier in Mesopotamia and Egypt measurements of astronomical events had been made, and new metals and alloys developed largely for use in making weapons. However, it was Greek civilization, from the sixth century BC onwards, that made a number of contributions to our understanding of the world which have been an enduring cornerstone of Western civilization. Other parts of Greek science, especially the heritage of Aristotle (384–322 BC), were lost for hundreds of years, and when rediscovered in the West in the Middle Ages, provided one of the stimuli which fed the growth of modern science.

Greek scientists and philosophers were probably the first to suggest that the earth might be a sphere, and to estimate its circumference, as well as estimating the distance of the earth from the moon and the sun. They also developed the first atomic theory. Aristotle taught the importance of observation and his observation of the natural world led to important advances in the understanding of biology. Perhaps more important still Greek philosophers provided an enduring framework for the theoretical understanding of the structure of the world. Pythagoras of Samos and the community he founded (late sixth and seventh century BC) developed the concept of the world as an ordered place, and therefore as a place that could be understood and described using the tools of mathematics.

Other ancient civilizations understood some of the basic principles of science. It is common knowledge that the Chinese invented gunpowder, but their achievements went much further. Indian astronomers tabled the movements of stars and planets, and Arabs, as well as being the guardians of much of Greek culture when it was lost to Europe during the Dark Ages, were creative mathematicians and chemists (the names algebra and alkali point to our debt to Arab scientists).

In none of these places, however, did science 'take off' as it did in Western Europe in the sixteenth and seventeenth centuries. One of the great questions facing historians of science is why the West developed a self-sustaining science when none of the other civilizations achieved as much. Certainly part of the answer lies in the rediscovery of the Greek heritage. This, however, cannot be the whole story, otherwise we should have expected the Greeks themselves to have made the vital breakthrough. Part of the story lies in what the Arabs taught to the West; a small part may have arrived in Europe over the spice routes with gunpowder from China and India. Why, uniquely, did the synthesis find a receptive soil in the West, growing until it took on a powerful life of its own?

The comparative failure of Greek science has frequently been analysed, though often by historians anxious to press the claims of Christianity as necessary to the rise of science. The reasons suggested are nonetheless instructive. For the Greeks, science was never conceived as a separate branch of human endeavour. The more theoretical aspects of Greek science belonged with philosophy; the more practical with the artisans and labourers. The philosophers believed that the universe was *necessary*, that is to say that it must take the form which it does because of some higher principle lying behind it, or because all the component parts of the universe have a purpose towards which they are moving: the apple falls to earth because earth is its natural home to which it desires to return. To those who hold such views, philosophy, the systematic application of human reason, assumes a central place. It can deduce the form of the universe from these hidden ideals. The structure of the universe will be discovered by thought rather than by experiment.

Plato (427–347 BC) insisted that beyond this messy, changing world in which we live is an *ideal* world, governed by simple mathematical principles. The world we experience is a pale shadow of the ideal. To some extent, Aristotle – who had been Plato's pupil – argued against this, insisting that the objects of the everyday world did have an existence of their own. He therefore commended the observation of nature, and made detailed observations himself, which is one reason why the rediscovery of his work in the late Middle Ages was so important for science, but for Aristotle explanation was still always conceived in terms of teleology and purpose. Philosophy remains more important than science.

There are exceptions, but the general trend of the later followers of Aristotle was to picture stability and changelessness as leading to perfection. The same is true, to an even greater extent of Plato and his followers, the neo-Platonists, who were later to be particularly influential among the early Christian theologians. Movement and change were seen as unfortunate imperfections in the universe which must be explained, or explained away. It was only much later that philosophers began to realize the challenge of explaining change and motion in their own terms.

The great Greek philosophers may not have taken the pantheistic beliefs of their contemporaries very seriously, but they at least paid lip service to the general tendency to pantheism and the deification of nature. As much as they were anywhere, the gods were everywhere. Nature was personified as part of the system of divinity. Such a system is bound to discourage scientific experimentation. If the natural world was god or part of god, then it must be impious in the extreme to experiment upon the world.

If pure reason can discover the secrets of the universe, then philosophers are going to be valued more highly than craftsmen. If the world must necessarily take the form which it does, then sooner or later logic and pure reasoning will deduce why it takes this form rather than any other; there is little need for experimentation. The close alliance between experimental scientist and craftsman – often simply one and the same person – which may be one of the key factors in the rise of modern science was thus unlikely to develop in ancient Greece. Indeed it may be that the prejudice created there against the value of manual work was a significant factor in delaying the rise of science. We shall explore these points again in more detail in the next section.

We find little consensus when we come to evaluate the importance of Greek science to the rise of modern science in the sixteenth and seventeenth centuries. We should probably view the Greek heritage as the most important of a number of streams that fed into modern science. The rediscovery of the work of Aristotle via the Arabs was dramatic, and had important consequences for both science and theology. Despite some initial resistance, Aristotle's works quickly became an important part of a renewed orthodoxy which, in due course, Galileo's writing seemed to threaten. There were significant scientific achievements in the thirteenth and fourteenth centuries, such as the development and application of mathematical methods, and – consciously following Aristotle – a renewal of interest in detailed observation of the natural world.[8] Modern historians of science often stress the continuities between the science of the Middle Ages and that of Copernicus and those who followed him. Some writers place great emphasis on the importance of Christian teaching as a stimulus here, noting especially the doctrine of creation or, more controversially, the importance of the work of Aquinas in suggesting that the universe is rationally ordered but does not have a necessary form, and is therefore ripe for investigation.[9]

Any adequate theory will need to account for both the continuities and discontinuities between the late Mediaeval period and Renaissance science. That Copernicus did usher in a scientific revolution is not in dispute, but it may be that the revolution was at least in part caused by the ability of sixteenth-century scientists to build on the work of their immediate predecessors, the late Mediaeval schoolsmen, rather than automatically assuming that the most ancient authority must be the best. The story of modern science seems to be both that of a new beginning and of building upon a firm base.

Renaissance science and the importance of creation

Renaissance humanism spread through Europe in the fifteenth century. Andrew White and many Victorian historians thought that this rediscovery and re-evaluation of Classical values saved science from the stifling embrace of theology. An alternative view is to picture humanism as merely an interruption in the pattern of harmony between science and religion; Christian doctrines providing a continuity and a motivation which was essential to the rise of science. Hooykaas, for example, thinks that for many seventeenth-century scientists, to secularize science was to *christianize* it, by freeing it from the tyranny of the old philosophies.[10] It is unlikely that either extreme view can be sustained, but nonetheless a number of writers suggest that specifically Christian insights were important to the rise of science.

The Christian doctrine of creation makes the explicit claim that God has chosen to create the universe. It was made and is sustained by God. Belief in God's sovereignty and omnipotence usually leads to the claim that God *could* have made any number of different worlds, but in fact chose to make the universe in which we exist; the universe is not necessary but contingent. A *necessary* universe would be one whose form could be derived from underlying principles not dependent on the world, and hence whose form must be deduced rationally, rather than discovered experimentally. This is the universe imagined by the Greek philosophers. A *contingent* universe is one whose form depends on something (God) beyond itself and which is dependent upon God for its continuing existence, not in a necessary way but through God's deliberate choice. Because it is contingent, rational thought can deduce very little about the form this universe takes, or why it takes that form. Hence the importance of practical experiments in order to discover the form of a contingent universe.[11]

Pantheist theologies picture the universe as being godlike or even as literally being the body of god. They therefore suggest that it is impious, dangerous even, to interfere with, or probe, or experiment upon this godlike substance. By contrast, a doctrine of creation maintains that there is a definite distance between God and God's creation, so that physical experiments do not involve desecration of the divine. Christian doctrine in addition stresses God's continued sustenance of the created order and his care for it. The creation is valued by God (Genesis 1.31). It is therefore important for Christians to learn all that they can about God's beloved work of creation.[12] Some writers even see the Reformation as a return to sources in *two* ways: a return to the book of scripture *and* to the book of nature. After all, the psalmist exhorts us to 'taste and see that the Lord is good'![13]

In order for experiment to lead to significant understanding, it must be the case that the universe is a cosmos rather than a chaos. To claim that the universe is a cosmos is to claim that it is rational in its construction, and that the results generated by our experimentation will make sense.[14] It is possible that the Hebrew Bible's emphasis on God as a giver of laws may have contributed to the concept of scientific laws governing the natural world.

One final consequence of the doctrine of creation may also be of importance. Christian belief in creation has intimate links to the concept of a history that is not circular but progressive.[15] The Israelites' sense of God directing their recent history may have led to their curiosity about ancient history and the creation of the world in the first place. The belief in God's action in creation, which continues through redemption to a final consummation, means that Christianity can give a positive value to change and progress. Although theologians have often been slow to realize the fact, Christianity, in theory at least, can accept change much more easily than Greek philosophical thought. Christians have sometimes felt that to seek change is to interfere with the sovereign will of God, but more often an understanding of human stewardship of the world has combined with Christian concern for the neighbour to suggest that progress in technology and medicine, for example, can be seen as God given ways in which to share God's love with all humanity.[16]

Puritan, Protestant and Catholic scientists

Can we move from the very general case made above to discover specific instances of the positive contribution of Christian thought to science? Robert Merton writing in the 1930s was the first to suggest a link between the Puritan ethic and the rise of modern science.[17] According to Merton the Puritans saw the study of nature as almost an act of worship, revealing the glory of the creator. They were one of the first groups to acknowledge that routine and mundane work might be pleasing to God. Although not himself a Puritan, George Herbert makes the same point:

> A servant with this clause
>   Makes drudgery divine;
> Who sweeps a room, as for thy laws,
>   Makes that and the action fine.

Diligence in such things soon became a hallmark of Puritanism. For Merton 'the combination of *rationalism and empiricism* which is so pronounced in the Puritan ethic forms the essence of the spirit of modern science.'[18] Merton also noted that a high proportion of the early members of the Royal Society – the most important early scientific organization – were Puritans. In a similar way Reijer Hooykaas sought to construct more general

links between Protestantism and the rise of science: 'Metaphor-
ically speaking, whereas the bodily ingredients of science may
have been Greek, its vitamins and hormones were biblical.'[19]

From his perspective as a scientist and Catholic priest, Stanley
Jaki made the case for the importance of the Christian metaphysical tradition and natural theology. He stressed the importance
of the Catholic contribution, and believed that the Protestant
distrust of natural theology had far reaching and unfortunate
effects:

> The birth of science came only when the seeds of science were
> planted in a soil which Christian faith in God made receptive
> to natural theology and to the epistemology implied in it . . .
> The next two centuries saw the rise of philosophical move-
> ments, all hostile to natural theology. Whatever their lip service
> to science, they all posed a threat to it.[20]

These brief summaries should be enough to suggest the major
problem with such studies. Different authors, writing from different perspectives, reach very different conclusions, usually conclusions sympathetic to their own faith communities; they are
writing as apologists rather than historians. John Brooke makes
a more carefully neutral study, but is not unsympathetic. Science
and religion in early modern Europe were so closely intertwined
that it seems likely that each must have influenced the other,
although there is another possibility: 'The problem in a nutshell
is whether particular forms of scientific and religious commitment
might not separately depend on ulterior forces of social and economic change.'[21] The coincidence of the development of modern
science in *Christian* Europe has not yet been proved to be more
than that – a coincidence. We still await formal demonstration
of the causal connection between the Christianity and the science.

The significance of the doctrine of creation for the relationship
between science and religion has seemed important to a number
of commentators in the twentieth century, but it is difficult to be
sure that similar considerations were genuinely helpful to the
expansion of science from the thirteenth century onwards.
Modern writers may simply read their own concerns back into
the period.

It may also be wise to refrain from boasting about the importance of Christianity for the rise of science. A number of commentators from within the environmental movement have seen damaging links between Genesis 1.28: 'God blessed them, and God said to them, "Be fruitful and multiply, and fill the earth and subdue it; and have dominion over the fish of the sea and over the birds of the air and over every living thing that moves upon the earth," ' and modern exploitation of the natural world. At least some of the consequences of modern science provide little of which the church should be proud.[22]

Perhaps we must remain content with a more general point. The significant relationship may not be between science and Christianity, let alone particular forms of Christianity, however suggestive the coincidences between their interests. The primary significance may simply be that the great majority of scientists from the earliest times up to and including the Renaissance were driven by theological rather than scientific considerations. They investigated the universe out of a sense of religious duty, or in order to discover more about their gods.[23]

Moving the earth

Living in the twentieth century it is difficult for us to realize just how strange and unnatural the Copernican system must have seemed to people living in the sixteenth century. If science is simply 'organized common sense', to use T. H. Huxley's phrase, then it is hard to see how Copernicanism could ever have been accepted. The earth shows none of the characteristics of fast movement, and indeed presents to its inhabitants the very model of stability. Of course all around us upon the earth's surface we see the evidence of change: this is the sphere of impermanence and corruption, but the earth itself retains its fixed position. For a thousand years or more people had gained relief from their insecure lives by looking upward to the heavens, where nothing changed and serenity reigned. The astronomy of Aristotle and Ptolemy provided a model of a fixed but corruptible earth, with hell beneath it, encircled by the crystalline spheres of the heavens, which was obviously in full agreement with the observations of common sense. The fact that the crystalline spheres of Ptolemy were not quite so simple and perfect as at first believed was an unfortunate fact, but one that the mathematical astronomers could easily encompass with their ever more intricate pictures of spheres within spheres. The Ptolemaic model also provided theological reassurance in a very physical way. The universe modelled God's economy of salvation: humans fell into hell or rose to the heavens. As the seventeenth-century English Protestant schoolmaster Alexander Ross wrote, if the earth did move why had not people noticed before now? Stanley Jaki captures the apparent unreasonableness of the new model when he speaks memorably of Copernicus 'raping' the senses.[24]

When he first suggested his, literally, revolutionary solution to the intricate problem of the calculation of the orbits of stars and planets, Copernicus was well aware that he faced opposition from many different quarters. Initially he was reluctant to publish his work. Himself a canon of the Roman Catholic Church, he allowed a local bishop to persuade him to publish, and a Protestant pastor helped see the book through the press. The pastor, Andreas Osiander, caused much confusion by providing his own, anonymous, preface which suggested that the whole Copernican system was simply a refined *calculating* device and not to be taken literally. Copernicus himself took no part in the later controversies, dying only a few days after the publication of *De Revolutionibus Orbium Coelestium* (*On the revolutions of the Heavenly Spheres*) in 1543.

It is true that traditionally astronomy *had* been seen as simply a calculating device, as such providing a useful service to the church in calculating the dates of festivals. Copernicanism could thus be held, or rejected, in a radical way as a model of the real universe, or in a conservative way as a more or less useful calculating device.[25] To complicate matters, Copernicus was no great observational astronomer, and for many years no physical test was available to distinguish between the old and new systems. Indeed in 1588, Tycho Brahe, who was a very fine practical astronomer, proposed a third system where the planets orbit the sun, which in turn orbits the earth. Brahe's system, although later clearly shown to be wrong, marked an important move away from the old Ptolemaic models, as did his observations a few years earlier of a new star and a comet, both beyond the orbit of the moon, and so situated amongst the supposedly unchanging crystal spheres.

Later, Johannes Kepler (1571–1630) was able to demonstrate

that Brahe's observations actually did provide genuine observational evidence in favour of Copernicus, although the true orbit of the planets around the sun turned out not to be circular but ellipsoid, a further deviation from the circular simplicity of Aristotle and Ptolemy. When Galileo became the first person systematically to observe the heavens though his telescope, it was soon obvious to him that the sun and the planets were not unchangeable and perfect and that Copernicus' system, although contrary to common sense, was the best available to interpret the evidence from observations as to the real state of the sun and the planets. He published his results in his *Starry Messenger* (1610) and *Letters on Sunspots* (1613). Nonetheless, the evidence in favour of the new system did not become conclusive until much later.

In this section we have attempted to think ourselves back into the ways of thought of the contemporaries of Copernicus and Galileo. To them, the evidence for the stability of the earth seemed unquestionable, a simple common sense result of the observations of the senses which we ourselves share at that level. In the same way, when educated people looked up at the stars in the sixteenth century they saw the unchanging perfection of the spheres. This belief is more difficult for us to understand, for the simple fact is that the heavens *did change* and our ancestors did notice the changes. The supernova of 1054 leading to the creation of what we now call the *Crab Nebula* was a major event, and Chinese astronomers were meticulous in noting it and many other similar, if less dramatic, changes in the sky. Galileo's telescope simply multiplied the number of imperfections which could be seen by the naked eye. For Western scholars, however, belief in the unchangeability of the heavens was so deeply embedded that even the explosion of a supernova could not dent their faith – the heavenly spheres did *not* change, therefore any change must be taking place elsewhere despite appearances. Galileo's contemporaries were also well aware that the senses could be fooled, and so were not inclined to abandon well-tested general beliefs on the basis of a few (questionable) observations from a new device like the telescope. We shall see in chapter 5 that Thomas Kuhn makes use of many similar examples to raise hard questions about how science really works, and how firm is its reliance on observation.

To return to Galileo for the moment, the choice facing his

contemporaries was not a simple one. The new system of Galileo and Copernicus did have some experimental support, but Ptolemian astronomy had stood the test of time, and – with the necessary adjustments – it still worked. Was there enough evidence to support its overthrow, and the overthrow with it perhaps of a whole way of looking at the world?

Moving the church

How did the church react to all this? As we might expect by now, the militant Victorian Andrew White pictured total and organized opposition from both Catholic and Protestant churches. In fact many of the leading figures in the new astronomy were devout Christians, a number being priests and pastors. At first there seems to have been little *theological* opposition to the revolutionary ideas; indeed at first few seem to have realized how revolutionary they were, and there is evidence that both Catholic and Lutheran scholars often accepted the calculations, whilst rejecting the implied model which lay behind them.[26]

On the Protestant side, both Luther and Calvin seem casually to have dismissed the new teaching, but probably more because it contradicted common sense than for any deep theological reasons. Melanchthon, the first great systematizer of Luther's thought, did seek to defend Aristotelian teaching, but perhaps more out of a misguided educational conservatism than for any theological reasons.[27] The most plausible reading of history is that whilst there were isolated instances of attempts by the different Protestant authorities to suppress Copernican teaching, in Sweden as late as 1679,[28] these attempts were isolated and not concerted and they were largely in defence of Aristotelianism or simple common sense rather than because Copernicus contradicted scriptural teaching. Indeed Hooykaas has little trouble in showing that Calvin's doctrine of accommodation coped easily with the new astronomy. By *accommodation* Calvin meant that the inspiration of the scriptures by the Holy Spirit was such that the text presented the possibility and challenge of salvation in the plain language of the age, rather than in a scientifically correct way. In Calvin's words: 'the Spirit, as it were, stammers with us'. Only later, when the Bible began to be ransacked for proof texts against Rome, did the incompatibility of certain scriptural texts with the Copernican system come to be seen as a serious problem.[29]

Similarly, within Catholicism there was at first little organized resistance to the new astronomy; in the years following the Reformation other concerns were rather more pressing. As defensive measures were taken by the Catholic church against the new Protestants and their teaching, however, they led to a greater centralization of power in the Roman bureaucracy. This had the side effect that authority on scientific matters passed from individual scientists into the hands of the ecclesiastical bureaucrats. It was this change which caused Galileo's difficulties. One of the great points at issue between Protestant and Catholic churches was the Catholic insistence that the church must be the sole interpreter of scripture. Accordingly, by the beginning of the seventeenth century the Roman hierarchy had pronounced that Copernicanism was at variance with the church's understanding of the Bible. As the leading advocate of the movement of the earth, Galileo was well known to the authorities. Equally for his part, it seems likely that Galileo knew that potential trouble awaited him and so attempted to proceed with caution.[30]

The precise details of the argument between Galileo and Rome remain obscure. Two different records survive of his first formal brush with Roman authority in 1616: one, held by the authorities, suggests that Galileo was reminded of the official disapproval of the Copernican teachings, and agreed not to teach them himself. The other account, retained by Galileo, simply records that he was reminded of the official prohibition.

In 1632 he clearly attempted to avoid trouble by presenting the arguments in his book *Two Chief World Systems* in the form of a dialogue, so that he personally would not be too closely identified with the powerful advocacy of Copernican theory that the book contained. Unfortunately, Galileo made the tactical error of putting rather weak arguments in favour of a stationary earth, which had previously been used by the current pope, ironically a former friend and protector, into the mouth of the foolish character Simplicio. In addition, Galileo, as a lay amateur, was quite prepared to enter into controversy as to how the scriptures should be properly interpreted using, but probably not inventing, the much quoted dictum: 'The intention of the Holy Ghost is to teach us how one goes to heaven, not how heaven goes.' Despite this

quotation his argument in fact advocates a multi-layered interaction between scripture and science.

The complexities of the issues involved and Galileo's careful
attempts to protect his own position meant that by the time he
faced the Roman authorities again in 1633 he was viewed with
suspicion, as someone who had overstepped the mark, both in
science and theology. He was believed to have broken his earlier
commitment not to teach the new astronomy, and to have been
devious in his attempts to avoid censure. This time Galileo was
condemned and spent the rest of his life under house arrest. He
formally renounced Copernican teaching, and almost certainly
did *not* whisper 'but it *does* move' after the renunciation; by then
he was an old and broken man. Brooke captures Galileo's tragedy:

> Relatively few scientific works were placed on the index. The
> attempt to put a stop to the moving earth stands out because
> it proved so tragic an aberration – a personal tragedy for Gali-
> leo and, in the long run, a tragedy for the Church, which
> overreached itself in securing a territory that would prove
> impossible to hold.[31]

Copernicanism contradicted common sense and the age-old
traditions of both science and theology. It seemed incompatible
with the plain meaning of parts of the Bible, but neither Protestant
nor Catholic authorities found great difficulty in accommodating
that particular problem. The real difficulty for simple and learned
alike seems to have been the very novelty of the new astronomy.
Looking back we picture humanity as dethroned from the centre
of the universe, and made aware of our loneliness, for the new
system suggested a much greater size to the universe than had
previously been imagined. None of this, however, seems to have
troubled contemporary writers, some of whom indeed were exhil-
arated that in this new astronomical wisdom humanity had at
last surpassed the wisdom of the ancients. As the pious Kepler
demonstrated the reasonableness of the new system with his
detailed observations, so his contemporaries were elevated by the
idea that man was now thinking God's thoughts after him.[32]

A mechanical universe

The displacement of the earth from its fixed foundations did not simply turn scientific pictures of the world inside out: it also had serious consequences for the very nature of science and scientific explanation. In Aristotle's system position, status and purpose had gone together. The elements each had their proper place, so that fire naturally flew upwards, as stones fell down, both desiring to return to their natural home. Although Aristotle did not go this far, many of his later followers personified the earth and planets, giving each their own soul, and picturing an organic relationship between different parts of the universe, remnants of which can still be seen in the debased astrological theories of today, where it is assumed that the position of the planets will influence the character of individuals. The work of the sixteenth-century astronomers began to question the whole of this elaborate and interconnected structure. The magnitude of the change was slow to be appreciated, but by the end of the seventeenth century the usual form of scientific explanation had changed from organic metaphor to mathematically exact mechanical model.

At first sight it seems unlikely that a new philosophy to replace Aristotle would have its roots in French Catholicism, but that is precisely what happened. A thoroughgoing mechanist philosophy was propounded by René Descartes (1596–1650), a French Catholic layman, and developed and propagated by Martin Mersenne (1588–1648), a friar, and Pierre Gassendi (1592–1655), a priest. If previous philosophies had pictured the universe as organic, Descartes went to the opposite extreme. For him, matter was totally passive, having no properties of its own, and was thus dependent upon God for everything. It was shaped by the mathematical laws imposed on it by God, and, in Descartes' scheme these laws could be derived directly from our knowledge of God. So, bringing together two things which might seem strange companions to us, Descartes sought to safeguard God's rule over the universe by picturing it as totally mechanical. Brute matter was separated from the spiritual soul, leading to the so-called Cartesian dualism, which was so influential in later years. For Descartes even animals were simply machines. It was the possession of a soul which, by God's grace, elevated humanity above the whole mechanical world, animate or inanimate.

We cannot here enter into the argument as to whether Descartes' ideas were primarily philosophical or theological: the distinction may be more important to modern writers than to Descartes himself. We should note that *theological* (or philosophical) principles led Descartes to his mechanical universe and thence to the formulation of a detailed set of *scientific* conservation laws, which described the conservation of the amount of matter and the amount of motion in the universe. It is plain that Descartes' scientific theories were dependent upon his philosophical and theological concerns, leading to the criticism that his conception of the universe relies rather too heavily on philosophy and mathematics, and not enough on the experimental testing of his theories in the real world. Descartes' world is the world as it supposedly should be rather than as it is.[33]

Descartes' mechanical philosophy opened up a typically English middle way for Robert Boyle (1627–1691) and the other 'Christian Virtuosi', as they were named, who sought to avoid the extremes of both Puritans and High Churchmen in the aftermath of the Civil War. The mechanical philosophy provided an ordered picture of the universe, ruled by God through the mechanism of law, just as the sovereign ruled a well-ordered kingdom, and without any need for the potentially destabilizing direct intervention of God at every moment as claimed by the fanatics, who in the time of the Civil War had wrought such havoc in England. In Boyle's view the mechanical philosophy was intelligible and clear, replacing Nature (with a capital 'N') by Godgiven laws. Boyle's theology is usually labelled *voluntarist* because in it God is pictured as *choosing* to act in this particular way, allowing room for his general providence in creating and sustaining the universe, his particular providence to achieve certain ends, and, from time to time, his miraculous intervention. Each different mode of action was believed to demonstrate God's supremacy in equal measure.[34]

A mathematical universe

The great achievement of Isaac Newton (1642–1727) in his *Philosophiae Naturalis Principia Mathematicia* (*Mathematical Principles of Natural Philosophy*, 1687) was to formulate in a precise mathematical way the laws which Descartes and the English

Christian Virtuosi had sought to describe as the means through which God governed the universe. Newton realized that the law of gravitational attraction which was responsible for making the apple fall to earth was the same law responsible for keeping the moon or the planets in their orbits (whether or not there *was* a real apple remains uncertain!).[35] The formulation of the law required both great mathematical skill, and a clear appreciation of what constituted a scientific explanation according to the new world view.

Newton's work did not simply appear from nowhere, but genuinely depended on much that had gone before. Thus, although he was a scientific giant of the first order – and knew himself to be so – there is also more than a little truth in his modest repetition of the dictum that he had simply been a pygmy standing on the shoulders of giants. Without the preparatory work of others, Newton could not have achieved his synthesis. Newton's work marks the final break with the Aristotelian system in two ways: he demonstrated that the same laws applied in the heavens as on earth, ending the age-old separation between the two spheres, and he also provided a complete, or almost complete, mathematical description of those laws, thus removing the need for explanation in terms of purpose or aim.

The new mechanistic philosophy was developed, at least in part, in order to safeguard God's sovereignty over the universe and to describe how God exercised his control. As we have seen, it provided an extremely effective model through which modern science was able to develop its theories. But there was a paradox at the very heart of the philosophy. By setting out to show just how efficiently God governed the universe through natural laws, a dilemma soon became apparent. In order to demonstrate the total sovereignty of God, and God's efficiency as creator, it was in the interest of the theologian to seek to account for everything that happened in the universe *without reference to the particular action of God*. If an event could not be placed within the scheme of natural law, the mechanical philosophy suggested not so much God's miraculous intervention as his incompetence in the initial construction of the universe and its laws. As Leibniz objected, if God had to remedy the defects of his creation, this was surely to demean his craftsmanship.

Newton was well aware of such issues. For him God's

omnipresence more or less constituted space, and provided a strong reason as to why gravity could be taken to be a genuinely universal law. Newton's God was everywhere at all times, and so usually worked through natural causes, but sometimes more directly. It is well known that Newton could not make the law of gravitation account for all astronomical phenomena: in particular, it appeared to him that the motion of the planets around the sun must be gradually slowed by their motion through the aether. Hence, reasoned Newton, from time to time God must intervene, in a more direct way than through his constant provision of the law of gravity, in order to ensure the continued stability of the solar system. Perhaps God sent comets crashing into the planets in order to restore them. But like all direct theological involvement with scientific laws such speculations were vulnerable to later discoveries. If comets performed the function Newton suggested for them, then why should they in turn not simply be governed by the self-contained laws of nature? More seriously, when some years later Newton's fears about the gradual running down of the system were shown to be based on inaccurate data and calculations, the whole universe would seem more than ever self-contained. When Laplace exclaimed to Napoleon that 'he had no need of that hypothesis', he meant only to exclude theology from his day-to-day scientific calculations; but there were many others who were only too glad to remove all consideration of God from any possible connection with the physical world.

The first scientific revolution

Between the publication of Copernicus' *De Revolutionibus* and Newton's *Principia* a scientific revolution did take place. Both the universe that was described and the proper form of the scientific description of the universe changed beyond recognition, though as we have seen the change was gradual, taking over a hundred years, and the new science was in recognizable continuity with the old.[36] Three significant changes stand out:

1. The most obvious change was the displacement of the earth from its fixed, but lowly, position at the centre of the universe. We have traced some of the consequences of this change in the past few sections.

2. Although the image of God as clockmaker had appeared as

early as 1377 in the writing of Nicole Oresme,[37] it was only with the work of Descartes that a consistent mechanical philosophy was formulated, soon ousting the old organic pictures. Early historians, such as White, saw in the mechanical concepts a move away from supernatural and superstitious religious ideas. More recently historians such as Hooykaas have tended to comment positively on this 'de-deification' of nature, believing that the mechanical universe fitted better with biblical views than organic Naturalism. To remove the myth from nature, and substitute mechanism and law, is not so much to secularize as to christianize our concept of the universe.[38] A potential pause for thought, however, is provided by the suspicion that Cartesian mechanistic ideals have in fact licensed vast cruelty to the animal kingdom and a cavalier disregard for the environment in general, surely a perversion of humanity's Godgiven domination of the world. Mechanistic models have proved themselves not to be an unmixed blessing.[39]

3. Not only did Newton picture the universe according to a mathematical model; his achievement showed future generations what form genuine scientific theories must take. For more than two hundred years Newton provided the model for scientific explanation. Brooke describes this ideal:

> [T]he ability to create two worlds, to relate the real world to an idealized mathematical model, was one of the techniques that made modern science possible. The process of abstraction that was required came more easily in a mechanical than an organismic universe. And the more successful the method, the more it encouraged the view that the most fundamental elements of creation were precisely those amenable to mathematical analysis: the shape, arrangement, and motion of particles.[40]

Only in the 1920s with the development of a systematic theory of quantum mechanics would this view be challenged, and it remains true today that the most serious argument against quantum mechanics, deployed among others by Einstein himself, is that the new theory does not meet this tried and tested Newtonian criterion.

Beyond the myths

A brief summary may be helpful.

An absence of warfare. During the period of the scientific revolution many, probably most, scientists professed a religious motivation for their work. No doubt this was in part simply an expression of the conventional piety of the age, but it does stand to demonstrate that there was no sense that it might be incongruous for priest, pastor or pious layman to express their religion through works of science. The analogy of the two books, God understood through his writing in nature as well as through his writing in the scriptures, was in constant use, being employed extensively by Galileo among others. Occasionally scientists did fall foul of the religious authorities on account of their science, Galileo himself providing one of the very few examples. As we have seen, however, even the case of Galileo is not clear cut. Power politics, the apparent ridiculing of the pope, and Galileo's claim as a *layman* to interpret scripture, all contributed to his condemnation.

On other occasions it is later writers looking back who have seen a scientific martyr, when in fact the unorthodox believer, who happened to have practised science, was condemned for his religious beliefs rather than his science. Giordano Bruno, for example, burned by the inquisition in 1600, was certainly a martyr, but on account of his highly unorthodox religious beliefs – for him Christianity and the church had corrupted an earlier Egyptian religion – rather than on account of his science which was hardly mentioned at the trial. Religion provided the motivation for the early scientists, and, as we have seen in the case of Descartes, may even have influenced the form of the theories they produced.

A lack of proof. On the other hand, it is also true that precise causal links between the rise of modern science and Christianity remain elusive. The arguments of apologists such as Hooykaas and Jaki are suggestive, and modern science did in fact become established in sixteenth-century Europe rather than anywhere else. However, the various statistical attempts to prove a correlation between particular religious beliefs and the success of science remain inconclusive. It may well be, for instance, that some other factor lies behind both the rise of Puritanism and the rise of science. All that we can state with certainty is that the science of this period and the religion of its people were intimately intertwined. On particular occasions Catholicism may have held back, and Protestantism encouraged particular scientists and developments within science, but in general it is clear that both were at the very least not seriously antipathetic to the rise of science.

From handmaiden to partner. The relationship between science and religion certainly changed during this period. Whereas at the start of the period science was clearly subordinate to theology, by Newton's time the two were coming to be seen as more equal partners, not least because it seemed to be in the interests of theology that scientific theories attained a measure of independence. Theology, which had begun as 'queen of the sciences', was now simply one discipline amongst others. By the end of the seventeenth century the links between science and religion were becoming less obviously necessary, and in the eighteenth and nineteenth centuries it would become possible to speak of the complete autonomy of science. This has little to do with any hostility between science and religion and is only partly a measure of the increasing maturity of science; it is also a reflection of the increasing complexity and hence compartmentalization of society.

Chapter 3

Darwin's Century – Warfare and Harmony

Science versus Religion – the antithesis conjures two hypostatized entities of the later nineteenth century: Huxley St George slaying Samuel smoothest of dragons; a mysterious undefined ghost called Science against a mysterious indefinable ghost called Religion; until by 1900 schoolboys decided not to have faith because Science, whatever that was, disproved Religion, whatever that was.[1]

Owen Chadwick makes the point with his customary clarity and economy. The supposed dragon-slaying took place at the meeting of the British Association for the Advancement of Science in 1860, when Thomas Henry Huxley (1825–1895), 'Darwin's Bulldog' and Samuel Wilberforce (1805–1873), the Bishop of Oxford were among the speakers at an open meeting called to discuss the implications of Darwin's *On the Origin of Species by means of Natural Selection*, less than a year after its publication in November 1859.

The Oxford meeting lives in popular mythology, but the British Ass, as it was affectionately known, provides many other significant markers as to the state of relations between science and religion during the great changes of the nineteenth century. Founded in 1831 it was a society self-consciously dedicated to the advancement and popularization of scientific views, the meeting point between educated society and the men of science. It also sponsored popular meetings for workmen, and two of these meetings thirty years apart demonstrate how the intellectual climate of the age changed, in such a way as to affect even the ordinary working man.

In 1838 the Reverend Adam Sedgwick, Professor of Geology at Cambridge, stood on Tynemouth beach and addressed an immense crowd of more than 3000 'colliers and rabble (mixed with a sprinkling of their employers)', leading them 'from the scene around them to the wonders of the coal country below them, thence to the economy of a coal-field, then to their relations to the coal-owners and capitalists, then to the great principles of morality and happiness, and last to their relation to God, and their own future prospects.'[2] The clerical Professor of Geology at one of the old established universities made the connections between science, religion and political economy. All naturally belonged together, and it was as proper for a priest of the established church to demonstrate scientifically the bounty of God's creation and the God-given nature of society as it was for the 'colliers and rabble' to accept his teaching on the scientific necessity of the whole picture. As John Durant notes, 'Sedgwick spoke for a tradition in which pebbles, piety and politics were intimately intertwined.'[3]

Thirty years later, in 1868, Thomas Henry Huxley addressed a similar meeting in the Drill Hall at Norwich. His title was *On a Piece of Chalk* and he led an enthralled audience through many of the developing sciences as he described the occurrence of chalk in the familiar English countryside, its chemistry, and its origins in the mud of ancient seabeds as the remains of exotic and extinct creatures. Along the way he speculated on the aim of science as it seeks to explain the world around us. Do we invoke special creation or the operation of natural causes? 'Choose your hypothesis; I have chosen mine.' The seemingly modest attempt to understand more about a piece of chalk had led to an explanation of the natural world entirely in terms of natural causes. As Huxley concluded: 'A small beginning has led us to a great ending.'[4] The coiner of the word agnostic carefully and deliberately claimed that the explanation of the natural world lay within itself and could not be connected to the claims of religion. Like Sedgwick before him, Huxley's audience of working men were eager to accept the reasonableness of his case. 'A man got up and said "they had never heard anything like that in Norwich before". Never "did science seem so vast and mere creeds so little".'[5]

To understand what had changed in the thirty years between these two great popular lectures is to encompass many of the perennial debates, not simply between science and religion but also on the very nature of scientific explanation.

Natural theology

The opening illustration of William Paley's *Natural Theology* (1802) is so well known as to need only brief recapitulation. The author imagines walking across a heath and kicking a stone. How did the stone come to be there? Perhaps it had lain there for ever. But suppose a watch had been found, had that also simply always lain there? No,

> For this reason, and no other, viz., that, when we come to inspect the watch, we perceive (what we could not discover in the stone) that its several parts are framed and put together for a purpose . . .

How do we explain the world around us? What we see is a diversity of plants and animals each well adapted to live in the very different surroundings in which they find themselves. The variety of habitats and the way in which the plants and animals found in each are enabled to make use of this variety is surely remarkable. John Ray's camel is almost as well known as Paley's watch. How astonishing, wrote Ray in 1691 in *The Wisdom of God in the Works of Creation*, that the camel is found in precisely those desert places where its lack of thirst is particularly useful. This must be an effect of providence and design.[6]

The influence of natural theology is usually traced from the time of John Ray and Robert Boyle, whose 1691 will established the Boyle Lectures 'for proving the Christian religion against notorious infidels' through the high point of Paley's writings to the Bridgewater Treatises, again endowed by bequest, this time by the Earl of Bridgewater, whose 1829 will left the immense sum of £8000 in order to publish a work

> On the Power, Wisdom and Goodness of God, as manifested in the Creation; illustrating such work by all reasonable arguments, as for instance the variety and formation of God's

Creatures in the animal, vegetable, and mineral kingdoms; the effects of digestion [etc.] . . .[7]

Hindsight can lead us to doubt the effectiveness or validity of natural theology, and certainly some of the eight Bridgewater treatises were more valuable than others, whilst works such as *Water Theology* and *Insect Theology* suggest, at the very least, an overspecialization. The judgment of Richard Dawkins in *The Blind Watchmaker* (1986) may serve as a useful counterbalance. As the title of his book suggests, Dawkins has no time for the design argument. He begins, however, with a sympathetic appreciation of the work of Paley, commenting that he could not imagine being an atheist himself at any time before the publication of the *Origin of Species* in 1859. One of the Boyle lecturers wrote in 1713:

> [T]he works of God are so visible to all the world, and withal such manifest indications of the being and attributes of the infinite Creator, that they plainly argue the vileness and perverseness of the atheist, and leave him inexcusable.[8]

The popularity of natural theology during the two hundred years leading up to 1859 can be viewed separately from scientific and religious perspectives. *Scientifically* the design argument often seemed the most reasonable explanation. The state of the world, *why* things were as they were needed explanation. The simple response that God had made the plan, laid down the design or created each species to fit into its appointed place was perceived as a perfectly proper *scientific* answer. *Theologically*, at the time of the Enlightenment, the reliability of revelation and the traditional doctrines was coming under increasing challenge. Authority was now supposed to reside primarily in human reason applied critically, and not in any ancient texts. John Locke wrote in *The Reasonableness of Christianity* (1695) that 'revelation is natural reason enlarged'. As Russell suggests, the image here is of revelation simply magnifying things which are already known in other ways.[9] We learn all that we need to know about God from a study of the natural world, revelation provides clarification or even unnecessary detail; the stuff of petty doctrinal disputes rather than the essence of true faith.

Part of the reason for the persistence of natural theology was its adaptability. Both Christians and Deists could use its methods for their own ends. On the one hand, writing at the same time as Paley, Tom Paine in the *Age of Reason* could dismiss all theology as merely human opinion concerning God and then praise science as the study of the divine laws governing nature. On the other, a few years later, Sedgwick could use the fossil record, which seemed to demand a series of repeated and progressive acts of creation, to reject all static, mechanical and Deist pictures such as Paine's.[10]

Philosophical difficulties: Hume and Kant

It may seem strange that before Paley or Paine wrote their influential works, David Hume (1711–1776), the Scottish philosopher, had written his *Dialogues concerning Natural Religion* (published posthumously in 1779), which appear – to most modern philosophers at least – to demolish the very possibility of natural theology or the design argument. Hume makes two powerful points. Firstly, he claims that all talk of natural theology is circular. It is only *because* we believe in God as the creator of the world, that we see evidence of design as we look around us. Hume has a strong case here. For instance, it has been suggested that the persistence and popularity of natural theology in Great Britain was due in part to the comparatively equable climate – Britain experiences no earthquakes, no volcanoes, no famine – and a high standard of living. To quote Paley: 'it is a happy world, after all'. In less salubrious climes natural theology received a more sceptical hearing.[11]

Second, Hume asks, why do we assume that the complexity of the world and the well-adapted nature of its lifeforms to their habitats *requires* an explanation such as that provided by a creator? Immense assumptions are demanded by the leaps from a mechanism constructed by a human craftsman to the natural world and then to natural theology's assumption of a creator. In Hume's eyes, such assumptions can never be justified. We don't possess a series of worlds to observe or upon which to experiment. In the face of this lack of data we are quite mistaken to assume that the existence of the universe demands an explanation such as that provided by a creator.

Starting from rather different premises the German philosopher, Immanuel Kant (1726–1806), had reached an equally disturbing conclusion: natural theology could never prove the existence of God, certainly not the existence of the Christian God with all his moral attributes. Belief required faith, not scientific proof. The most that could be hoped for was that natural theology might provide a suggestive analogy. Consideration of the watchmaker and the watch may suggest how God might relate to the creation; they can never prove the relationship.

Why did the devastating analysis of Hume and Kant fail to stop the popularity of Paley's writings? Why did natural theology remain so popular for nearly a century after Hume and Kant until Darwin effectively put an end to it? Partly because Hume's scepticism cannot be limited to religion and theology. A thoroughgoing application of Hume's methods shows that science needs its unprovable assumptions as much as theology. But such considerations were not widely realized until long after Hume and Paley had written. More influential at the time was probably the feeling that neither Hume nor Kant, for all their philosophical astuteness, had succeeded in disposing of the question in a satisfactory way. The universe may not logically need a explanation and God may not logically provide one, but human beings will continue to seek answers. And until a more satisfying and comprehensive explanation became available, that provided by natural theology would do nicely both for theologians and scientists.[12]

Genesis and geology

From about 1790 to 1850 the new-born science of geology enjoyed great public prominence and played a leading part in the important contemporary debate as to the meaning of science for society. That it should have been so is not surprising as geology was the first of the descriptive sciences to emerge from 'the chrysalis of "natural history" '.[13] Copernicus had expanded space beyond the wildest imaginings of the human mind, and seemingly beyond the frame imagined by the biblical writings. Now in the eighteenth century the new interest in geology seemed to demand a similar expansion of time. In the seventeenth century the scholarly Archbishop James Ussher (1581–1656) had calculated the date of the creation of the world to an autumn day in 4004 BC.

He was well aware that the Old Testament genealogies and the other ancient authorities on which he relied were less than perfect, but this was the approximate age of the world according to a straightforward reading of the early books of the Bible.

From the close of the seventeenth century, if not before, people looked around themselves and wondered how the natural landscape had been formed, what accounted for the irregularities of the mountains, and – most intriguingly – what were fossils? Answers began to form. The *Neptunists*, following Abraham Werner, assumed that the shape of the earth was the result of the action of water. Periodic and enormous rises in the seabed laid down the rocks as we see them. It was easy for the Neptunists to make Noah's flood a historical event, perhaps the greatest of all geological events, with only minor changes still continuing. Calculations began to be made as to the amount of water necessary to cover even the highest mountains – for the biblical accounts suggested that no land was left uncovered, and the fossils of marine creatures are found high among the Alps. The calculations did not make sense: the quantity of water required was simply not available.

The *Vulcanists* suggested a different, more violent picture of the formation of the surface of the earth. Volcanic eruptions and earthquakes had disrupted the surface of the earth, and thrown the former seabed high into the mountains, which explained the position of the fossils. According to the Old Testament chronologies the Flood began on Sunday 7 December 2347 BC.[14] Had all this violent activity really taken place so recently, and if so, why were there so few hints of it in the biblical narratives?

Human exploration and inquisitiveness, together with ever more extensive mines and quarries, soon began to produce a steady stream of fossils. Examining them, it became clear that they must provide important clues as to the history of the earth. Despite ingenious alternative suggestions it was obvious to most observers that they were the relics of living creatures somehow converted to stone. Different fossils were associated with different layers (*strata*) of rock. Did this suggest that different animals and plants had lived in this same place at different historical times? More ominously, some of the fossils were of unknown animals, extinct species. How could this be accounted for? Surely the benevolent creator-God cared for all the creatures that he had created. Did the geological evidence mean that he discarded some and created others in their place? Did God change his mind?

Gradually the evidence for a long time span became overwhelming and the work of James Hutton (1726–1797) finally linked together the gradual action of water and the more violent effects of earthquake and volcano, both acting over a vast timescale to explain the state of the earth. The few thousand years of Moses rapidly expanded to many millions of years in the hands of Hutton and Charles Lyell (1797–1875). *Uniformitarianism*, especially as later developed by Lyell in successive editions of his *Principles of Geology* from 1830 onwards, soon became the geological orthodoxy, profoundly influencing Darwin, who read the book during his voyage on the *Beagle*.

What evidence there is suggests that the public had no great difficulty in accepting that the days of Genesis were not literal days but instead extended epochs, and perhaps little more in accepting that Noah's Flood was no universal inundation. Certainly the exponents of natural theology, when they had to, took it all in their stride. A suspicion remains, however, that something was changing. Charles Gillispie, whilst seeing no simple explanation, notes that a large segment of British opinion was unsettled:

> In retrospect it is apparent that, although on the surface the problems raised by Vulcanism, uniformitarianism, the *Vestiges*, and Darwinism were not the same, actually the pattern of reaction was a constant one throughout. Behind the discussion, therefore, was something more than always met the eye: the common tendency of all these theories to remove the hand of God from the course of events in the material world.[15]

The mention in the preceding quotation of Robert Chambers' *Vestiges of the Natural History of Creation* leads us to consider the development of evolutionary theories before Darwin, which Chambers did so much to popularize.

Evolution before Darwin

The latter part of the eighteenth century saw revolutions in natural history paralleled by rebellion in America and revolution in France. First in Britain and then elsewhere, agricultural and industrial 'Revolutions' brought about profound changes in the way everyone lived their daily lives. Is there a link between scientific theories of evolution and the more general revolutionary trends? Before we can hazard an opinion we must detail some of the important scientific and philosophical background.

Geology gave a history to the earth far longer and more complex than that of creation, Fall and Flood imagined by the biblical commentators. Throughout the eighteenth century naturalists, especially French writers influenced by the Enlightenment, turned their attention to classifying and understanding the natural world, and increasingly the solutions they offered began to imply a history of change and development for life upon the earth as well as for its rocks. One of the earliest to tackle the subject was Buffon, whose many-volumed *Histoire Naturelle* appeared between 1749 and 1785. He suggested that species varied through time, but only within strict limits. Buffon also made an early attempt, which drew much criticism, to harmonize the history of the world and its *epochs*, as he called them, with the days of creation recorded in Genesis. Jean-Baptist Lamarck (1744–1829) went further, and by stressing the long timescale available, developed a theory in which species naturally adapted themselves to their environment and passed on these favourable adaptations to their offspring. Many later, progressive versions of evolutionary theory take their name from Lamarck.

In 1796 Laplace published his detailed version of the nebular hypothesis, suggesting a mechanism by which the planets of the solar system might have evolved to their present state. By this time Curvier had already begun his work on fossils, which would conclusively demonstrate that species which had once flourished were now extinct. The new science of embryology, studying the development of the foetus in the womb, soon noted that it seemed to pass successively through a series of stages each of which had similarities with ever more complex creatures. The solar system, the earth, and life itself were each shown to have a history. It is true that drawing the emergent historical sciences together like this in a single paragraph is bound to be misleading; nonetheless everywhere old ideas of a static order were crumbling.

If the French provided a scientific background, then the Germans contributed to a changing philosophical atmosphere. Hegel's new philosophy promoted ideas of process and change where Western thought had previously been accustomed to static views of perfection. Some German scientists began to find the mechanical analogy, which had been seen as the ideal for all scientific explanation, restricting. They returned to organic models as better able to picture the growth and development of plants and animals. Again in Germany, romantic ideas of Nature, with a capital 'N', and conceived as some form of power in itself (more usually herself), began to be influential.[16]

The background to Darwin's work is thus rich and varied. The historian of science is presented with a series of genuine dilemmas in trying to describe the soil from which his work sprang. We can agree with John Brooke that 'There was no linear succession of scientific insights, inexorably culminating in Darwin's theory of natural selection.'[17] Certainly, scientifically it seems agreed that the mechanism which Darwin proposed and his understanding of the philosophical implications of natural selection were genuinely novel contributions. That much-overworked phrase 'Scientific revolution' truly applies to Darwin's work, perhaps more so than to any other single piece of science.[18]

By contrast, Adrian Desmond, who is also Darwin's biographer, has brilliantly evoked a hitherto hidden scientific underworld, composed of the dissidents and heretics from Edinburgh and the new London medical schools whose radical politics hungrily fed upon the evolutionary speculations of Lamarck. It was just this view of evolution and the history of the world which was popularized by Chambers in his book *Vestiges of the Natural History of Creation*. The 'Vestiges' of the title referred to the fossil record and the story which it might tell of the earth's history. Desmond's hypothesis is that the evolutionary science of the London dissecting rooms took the shape it did because of the politics of these scientists and their lowly position in society. Evolution implied change, and Lamarckian evolution implied that creatures could change and improve themselves.[19]

This optimistic and hopeful creed could become the basis of a truly revolutionary doctrine; it certainly had a long appeal to later liberals and progressives, and even to twentieth-century Marxist governments, when it found a new champion in the work of T. D. Lysenko, whose neo-Lamarckianism became the official doctrine of Russian biology in Stalin's day, much to the dismay of less ideologically driven scientists. The Russian biologists' discomfort arose from the fact that unfortunately for the radicals this version of evolution proved difficult to sustain scientifically, and was certainly scorned by Darwin. The search for indisputable and direct scientific connections between the *Origin* and previous work is thus unrewarding. Instead, as has often been remarked, evolution 'was in the air'.[20]

'Each according to his kind': classifying the species

By the start of the nineteenth century the great voyages of discovery to new worlds had begun to give way to the detailed naval surveys that were so necessary to protect the interests of any great maritime trading power. Alongside the surveyors travelled the official artists, the collectors and the enthusiastic naturalists. When – if – they returned from their long voyages, the natural historians back in Europe were brought face to face for the first time with the immense riches of the flora and fauna of the world. What did such variety mean? If they were to make scientific sense of this cornucopia then it must all be classified. In Sweden, Linnaeus (1707–1778), often called the second Adam so assiduous was he in naming new specimens, had earlier begun to bring order into an unruly world. Linnaeus brought his Enlightenment sense of order to bear on the natural world. It would soon be said that men covered the earth from one pole to another interrogating nature in his name.[21]

What did Linnaeus' classification of all life into families and species mean? Those that seemed to have similar structures were gathered together into groups, according to sophisticated, but still more-or-less everyday principles. Members of one species did not interbreed with members of another, and the offspring of one species always belonged to the same species as its parents, each reproducing according to its kind, as seemed to be implied in Genesis.

In truth, the identification of Linnaeus' families and species with the Authorized Version's translation of Genesis 1.11: each type of living thing 'yielding fruit after his kind', was a great imaginative leap, which would hardly have been possible without the legacy of Plato and especially Aristotle, to confirm the commonsense conviction that species were fixed. And, if fixed, then presumably – following a fundamental Christian conviction – each and all created by God, and thus given distinctive function and purpose by his creative *fiat*. Modern versions of Genesis tend to avoid the problem by translating the words to mean that each plant carries its own (particular) kind of seed.

This heady mixture of biblical principles intermixed with classical philosophy was given another twist in that such a fixed, unchanging and perfect scheme was soon understood to encompass not only the natural world but human society as well. What God had created, the established church protected. At the end of the eighteenth century revolutionary chaos in France only served to strengthen the English understanding that to tamper with any part of the divinely given status quo was to risk disaster. The individual creation of species became an article of faith, faith in the established order of society as much as in Christianity, but then the two were hardly to be distinguished at the time.

Darwin's voyage

Given the importance of the work of Charles Darwin (1809–1882), both scientifically and culturally, it is not surprising that there is a large and active interest in the man and his achievements. The following discussion is greatly indebted to the work of Adrian Desmond and James Moore and especially their biography of Darwin.[22]

Charles Darwin had as grandfathers two of the giants of the eighteenth century, both in their different ways typically successful products of the early industrial revolution. Dr Erasmus Darwin is today remembered, if at all, for championing an early Lamarckian version of evolution – of which his grandson disapproved; it contained too few facts. His other grandfather was Josiah Wedgwood, of the pottery dynasty, and the fortunes of the two families remained closely intertwined: In due course Charles married his cousin, Emma Wedgwood. Charles' father was a wealthy medical practitioner in Shropshire. Old Erasmus Darwin had been a notorious freethinker, and the Wedgwoods had Unitarian leanings, though with increased wealth came respectability and a return to the responsibilities of the Anglican church. Thus Charles Darwin had a stake in the landed establishment of his time and its religion, but his family's history also bequeathed him a radical and sceptical streak and distanced him from total identification with the conventional wisdom of his age.

Like so many who later went on to revolutionize their chosen disciplines, Charles' education was undistinguished. Following the family tradition he began his medical studies at Edinburgh, only to discover that he had could not suffer the primitive surgical techniques of the time. He transferred to Cambridge to study for ordination, but his interest in natural history, begun in Edinburgh, soon came to the fore, against his father's wishes. Although established and wealthy, Charles' father still believed he needed a profession, and in the 1820s there was no such occupation as scientist. Nonetheless, good connections and no shortage of money meant that he was offered the prospect of a two-year voyage surveying the coasts of South America, as gentleman companion to the captain of a survey ship, *HMS Beagle*. In the event the voyage lasted five years, from 1831 to 1836, during which time Darwin had the opportunity to observe the geology and natural history not only of South America, but also of the Pacific Islands and Australia. Captain FitzRoy, who proved not to be an easy travelling companion, gave Charles some scientific duties, but he was largely left to make what he could of his task.

Popular myth pictures Darwin visiting the islands of the Galapagos, off the Pacific coast of South America, finding there different animal and bird species on each island, and spending the next few years puzzling over an explanation before he arrived at the hypothesis of evolution. In fact, the Galapagos finches, which were to become so important later, so little impressed him at the time that he failed to label his specimens with their island of origin and was later forced to seek recollections from other members of the *Beagle*'s crew to help him reconstruct their distribution.[23] However, in visiting South America and the islands, Darwin was faced with a whole variety of biological problems for which he began to seek explanations.

Variety was the key word. Why were there so many different types of animals and plants? The detailed questions began to form on the voyage; the first perceptions of an explanation only later. Why were the animals on different sides of the Andes mountains so different, when the climate of the two regions separated only by inaccessible mountains seemed so similar? Why did the habitat of very similar, but separate, species overlap on the South American pampas – surely two separate creations by God were not necessary? What about the South American fossil record, with its now extinct species and families seeming to exist alongside fossils of animals very similar to those still living. Why had some species and families died out while some continued to live?

From transmutation to natural selection

Later, back in London, and working with other specialists on the specimens he had brought back, the questions began to come into focus. Why were so many similar species found, each specific to a particular island. Why were they all so similar to each other, and yet clearly distinct species? In the case of the Galapagos, why were they so similar to the animals of South America, whose coast lay reasonably nearby, but very different from the populations of other Pacific island groups? Would it not be more reasonable to expect all islands dwellers to be more alike than their continental neighbours? And why were animals found on some islands of a group and not on others which seemed equally hospitable: did chance play a part in the distribution of species?

Darwin agonized for twenty years about whether and how to publish his theory. During this time, he kept a series of notebooks, and wrote rough sketches of the theory which he showed to a few favoured friends, from this material and his letters it has proved possible to reconstruct in some detail the progress of Darwin's thoughts.

Darwin's reading during the voyage of the *Beagle* had included Charles Lyell's *Principles of Geology*. Lyell explicitly set out to explain the form of the earth as he observed it using only geological forces which he could also observe operating. Darwin, who was a serious geologist himself, becoming secretary of the Geological Society soon after he returned to Britain, took this principle to heart. True scientific explanation would be in terms of presently operating causes; in other words it would be lawlike.

The first notebooks show how soon after his return Darwin

was experimenting with the possibilities of evolution, or *transmutation*, as it was usually called in the 1830s. The very phrase *the transmutation of species* was disturbing. It implied the disturbance of a fixed order. By mid-1837, within a few months of the end of the voyage of the *Beagle*, Darwin was convinced of transmutation. Recent biographers suggest that perhaps his encounter with the 'primitive' humans of Tierra del Fuego meant that he was less worried than Lyell and his establishment friends about the effects of transmutation on human society. So far as Darwin was concerned 'ape ancestry' could not be more degrading than the spectacle of primitive human society which he had witnessed in South America. Darwin already knew that some humans were primitive; for him the question was how to explain the civilized society of other humans. Although the casual reader of the *Origin* would never guess the fact, Darwin included humanity in his evolutionary schemes from the very first.[24]

As Desmond and Moore make clear, it is remarkable how much is contained in Darwin's first transmutation notebook. There are the familiar tree pictures, relating living species to extinct ones known through their fossils. There is a discussion of the key role of the environment: species either adapt to changes in the environment or become extinct. Darwin also muses that these chance changes make it absurd to speak of one animal being 'higher' than another.[25] At this stage Darwin thought that he could see what had happened as the islands off South America were populated by migrants from the continent, which slowly developed into separate species once isolated on their own islands. However, he had progressed no further than Lamarck in suggesting how this might happen. Perhaps animals simply learnt to become better adapted to their surroundings, and were able to pass on their gains to their offspring. Perhaps there was a physical secretion of the brain, allowing instincts to pass from generation to generation.

A year later in August 1838, Darwin read Malthus' *Essay on the Principle of Population*. The essay had first been published forty years before in 1798. Malthus painted a stark picture. Human population tends to increase much faster than any possible increase in available food supplies; Malthus assumed that each generation of parents produce four children on average, so that unchecked the population would double in each generation, whereas the food supply would increase much more slowly, by arithmetic (2,4,6,8 . . .) as opposed to geometric progression (2,4,16,64 . . .).

Malthus' mathematics have sometimes been questioned, but to Darwin it now seemed obvious that, whatever the niceties of the mathematics, *all* living creatures tended to produce more offspring than are needed for a stable population to survive. The population may increase for a time but eventually it will exhaust the food supply, unless disease or natural disaster take their toll first. Slowly Darwin realized that this struggle for survival could mould a species from its previous form until the individuals that remained were better adapted to their environment, that is to say, more likely to survive and breed. Again by stages, Darwin realized that the change was not from a species perfectly adapted to the old environment to one perfectly adapted to the new. Instead the change was from one compromise species, whose form limited what chance variations were possible, to a new species whose form was determined not according to upward progress or some plan of perfection, but simply according to which chance variations happened to be adapted to survive the harsh conditions of the Malthusian struggle for survival.

From his intimate knowledge of the work of the stock breeder and pigeon fancier, Darwin was beginning to understand how *artificial selection* worked – the breeders chose individuals that showed particular features and bred them until the features became more and more marked. Perhaps nature worked in a strikingly similar fashion, except that now no one – not even God – *chose* which individuals survived. Over long periods of time chance, helped by Malthus' hard struggle, produced the observed results. This was *Natural Selection*. By 1842 Darwin had written out a sketch of his theory, and from now on little essential would be changed. Desmond and Moore briefly summarize the theory: Darwin began with the farmers and their varieties and moved to natural variation:

Then he piled on the arguments for 'descent' in general. The old fossils became common ancestors of diverse modern groups. He explained island colonization and diversification. Classification became as simple and natural as a gentleman's genealogy. So much was explicable: the rudimentary organs

– remnants of once-functioning parts; and the unity of plan, where wings, hands, and flippers reflected a common inheritance.[26]

Darwin's achievement

On the Origin of Species by means of Natural Selection was finally published in 1859. Darwin had spent twenty years worrying over his theory, and was finally pushed into publication by the coincidence of Alfred Russel Wallace's quite independent discovery of the essentials of natural selection.

What was Darwin's achievement? In the *Origin* he brought together a series of general insights, none of which were his discovery, and suggested that, *together* – this was his contribution – they might serve to explain great categories of previous puzzling facts. Part of the concluding chapter of the *Origin* illustrates Darwin's argument:

Nothing can at first appear more difficult to believe than that the more complex organs and instincts should have been perfected, not by means superior to, though analogous with, human reason, but by the accumulation of innumerable slight variations, each good for the individual possessor. Nevertheless, this difficulty, though appearing to our imagination insuperably great, cannot be considered real if we admit the following propositions, namely, – that gradations in the perfection of any organ or instinct, which we may consider, either do now exist or could have existed, each good of its kind, – that all organs and instincts are, in ever so slight a degree, variable, – and lastly, that there is a struggle for existence leading to the preservation of each profitable deviation of structure or instinct. The truth of these propositions cannot, I think, be disputed.

Darwin *was* a good conventional scientist. He could observe, collect and experiment with the best, but – and the fact that the *Origin* is one of the few scientific works that has remained in print in its own right is significant here – he was also something else. He could not win his readers' agreement through the formal logic of his case. Instead, he sought to persuade them of the reasonableness and simplicity of what he was proposing. If it is true Thomas Huxley's supposed reaction on first reading the *Origin*: 'How extremely stupid not to have thought of that!' is exactly the response Darwin was hoping to produce in his readers.

Darwin's method broke the rules of conventional science. Since Francis Bacon, and especially since Newton, it had been assumed that the central work of science was the collection of facts, and the production of hypotheses or rules simply from those observed facts. The hypotheses would then suggest fresh experiments, whose factual results would help refine or replace the original hypotheses. Science began with the specific and experimental before moving to the general. Darwin reversed the usual procedure. He suggested general rules, and then described how nature could be interpreted to demonstrate that the rules were indeed obeyed. As has often been pointed out, Darwin's hypotheses could never be proved because detailed experimental tests could never be devised. The hypotheses were too grand: the whole of nature could not be brought on to the laboratory bench. Equally a laboratory timescale could only demonstrate modifications *within* species: the famous case of the peppered moth which survived when industrial pollution rendered its camouflage useless by evolving to a new, more discreet colour only demonstrates that rapid changes can occur within a species. However suggestive this might be, there are no laboratory demonstrations of the evolution of new species.

On the other hand, all was not as clear cut as it seemed to Darwin's opponents. Back in the eighteenth century David Hume's sceptical philosophy had demonstrated that the absolute proofs which Baconian induction seemed to supply were in fact an illusion.[27] Secondly, it was quite unreasonable to expect Darwin to supply experimental proof of his theory. If science was to be confined to those areas for which experimental proof could be provided, then it could only be of use in extremely limited areas of the world around us. Darwin's lack of proof was not a consequence of the inadequacy of his theory so much as a consequence of the subject matter which he sought to explain. One of the marks of true innovation in science is that it extends the methods of science as well as explaining new subject matter. This Darwin succeeded in doing. Finally, Darwin was not alone in his challenge to the established canons of the philosophy of science. To use the technical vocabulary, the methods of Baconian *induction* were beginning to seem inadequate by the mid-nineteenth century – not just in biology but also, for example, in the explanation of the behaviour of gases by means of the new statistical kinetic theory. Darwin's *hypothetico-deductive* method would come to be seen as a valuable addition to the armoury of science, rather than to be criticized as resulting from the inadequacy of a poor scientist, as was a common jibe at the time.[28]

A powerful general theory

Within a few years of the publication of the *Origin*, it was obvious that Darwin had provided his fellow scientists with a powerful explanatory tool, which is not to imply that, presented with the theory of natural selection, they at once accepted Darwin's suggestions as self-evidently true. As we shall see, scientists as much as theologians had reservations about Darwin's proposed mechanism. Accepting the details or not, however, scientists could not fail to look at the natural world in a new way and to begin to find answers to some intractable old questions. If each species had not been specially created for its own habitat, but had been modified to make use of it, then this explained a host of biological oddities. Take, for instance, a nineteenth-century favourite, the case of the upland goose. Why did this curious creature have webbed feet, which seemed so out of place in its natural habitat far from any expanses of open water? Initial migration of other geese from their old, watery, habitat, followed by evolution which was limited by the form of the original goose, suggested a possible answer. The lack of perfect adaption, which told against special creation, was a strong point in favour of evolution.

Darwin himself sometimes introduced a theological consideration into his argument: the chance nature of natural selection was less obnoxious to him than the assumption that God had specially created, for instance, the ichneumon wasps, whose young were hatched within and fed upon the bodies of living caterpillars.

The geographical distribution of species across the world, so arbitrary in terms of special creation, now made elegant sense. As animals and plants spread by migration, they were suitably modified, not from scratch, but developing from their forebears, hence the unexpected resemblances between different species. Island species, once they had migrated, developed separately, which explained the richness of the Galapagos species. And, purely by chance, some islands were populated by migration; some were not. The strange shape of the schemes of classification of animals and plants now made sense as part of this picture of modification from pre-existing forms, and much of the fossil record could now be placed within the same scheme as representing the forebears of living creatures, or dead-ends in the evolutionary scheme. Perhaps most powerfully of all, vestigial organs, such as the human appendix, were the evolutionary remnants of organs that had once served a useful purpose.

The great strength of Darwin was in the scope of the explanations which he provided. Huxley's 'How extremely stupid not to have thought of that!' is the reaction of someone seeing the world for the first time in a new way. From the very beginning, and this can be observed even in Darwin's own treatment of his theory, the details were considered far less important than the fundamental conception. Darwin himself saw natural selection as the principal but not the only means of evolution. In successive editions of the *Origin* he allowed more and more weight to be given to other means of evolution and less to natural selection. Modern science judges that his first suggestion of the supreme importance of natural selection was the correct one, but this is to make use of hindsight. For Darwin it was not that simple. The assumptions which he was forced to make about variation and inheritance were dubious.

Darwin's scientific difficulties

Darwin faced particular problems because he did not make use of Gregor Mendel's work on genetics, with its concept of genes and the indivisibility of the basic building blocks of inheritance. Before Mendel's work became widely known it was very difficult for scientists who favoured evolutionary explanations to understand how favourable characteristics, even if by chance they should appear, could avoid being diluted among the population in general which did not possess the new variation. At the time, Darwin resorted to dubious special pleading, for instance, following Lamarck and suggesting that the environment helped to produce useful variations which could then be inherited. With the help of Mendel's work it came to be realized that variations could be small but not *infinitely* small − they were literally like building blocks, and were present or not but could not be subdivided. Thus favourable variations could be transmitted from generation to generation even when initially possessed by only a small minority of a population. But Gregor Mendel was an obscure Austrian monk, and although he demonstrated his ideas much earlier (a key paper was published in 1866), the wider scientific world did not appreciate his work until the beginning of the twentieth century. Ironically, Darwin possessed at least one book describing Mendel's theories, but he either never read it, or never appreciated its significance.

Thus Darwin did not know the origin of his variations, and indeed the structure of the cell and especially of the nucleus was only being established during the nineteenth century. Some of the early writers on evolution took the opportunity to emphasize the possibility of God's direction at this level of the process, and even committed Darwinians rarely choose to emphasize the chance nature of the variations.

Everyone acknowledged that natural selection needed a long timescale in which to operate. The best guess was hundreds of millions of years. Was the earth that old? The physicists thought not. William Thomson (Lord Kelvin) produced detailed calculations based on the cooling of the earth's core which allowed only fifty million years or so. Physics seemed to place a large stumbling block in the path of biology, and the difficulty would not be overcome until the importance of radioactive decay, and the heat it produces, was discovered, early in the twentieth century. Taking into account the effect of radioactive processes the probable age of the earth was extended to several billions of years.

These scientific difficulties, together with the philosophical problems which we have already mentioned − none of the leading philosophers of science of Darwin's time could accept his theory − were formidable. And yet the theory stood. In *The Post-Darwinian Controversies*, James Moore writes:

> [D]espite his cogency of argument, Darwin experienced real difficulties in maintaining his theory, even in the face of those

who could accept the idea of descent with modification. The reason was that both the phenomena of natural selection and its presuppositions, as he conceived them, were vulnerable to attack. For twelve years Darwin adjusted his theory to compensate for these conceptual weaknesses. In the end the theory stood, but neither so elegantly not so impressively as before.[29]

Clearly Darwinism did not solve all the problems of biological origins. Instead, its strength lay in its ability to highlight problems which suggested fruitful new lines of research: scientists could worry away at an anomaly until it succumbed. At the same time, Darwin's fundamental hypothesis was not fatally damaged by any individual difficulty. The reason that Darwin's basic insight remains the cornerstone of modern biology is to be found here. Darwinism was a powerful resource, fruitfully used by scientists to extend their new ways of seeing the world into one new area after another.

Thus Darwin's success has an element of the paradoxical about it. Natural selection was little understood, and much distrusted, not without some scientific justification. The scientific problems would only be resolved years later. Despite this, however, the idea of evolution had taken hold; science had extended its writ into another new area; and people thought they understood something of the origins of the natural world, even if they were more reluctant to apply evolution to their own origins. Finally, Herbert Spencer, and the other evolutionary philosophers of the nineteenth century, gained a quite spurious credibility for their theories by virtue of their association in the public mind with Darwin.

Responding to Darwin

Any simple picture of scientists and Christians dividing into opposing armed camps over the issue of evolution was finally laid to rest by James Moore's comprehensive study *The Post-Darwinian Controversies*. We have seen above the complexity of the intellectual situation at the time. A few scientists, Thomas Huxley prominent amongst them, were concerned to attack the vested interests of the church – and were prepared to use any appropriate weapon in the struggle.[30] Many other scientists and philosophers of science were legitimately worried about the scientific basis of Darwin's work. The great majority of scientists, like the great majority of the population, were at least nominally Christians. Their response to Darwin was due to a whole variety of factors, and certainly not simply to the strength of their religious commitment. Many theologians and Anglican clerics were also amateur, and in some cases extremely competent, naturalists, Charles Kingsley (1819–1875) being the best known. The response of the clerical naturalists to Darwin also seems not to have been determined primarily by their religious convictions.

From the start there were those who did have genuine religious difficulties with Darwin's theory. When theologians attacked Darwin, however, they usually did so on the grounds of his science or philosophy of science rather than by initiating a direct theological assault. On the other hand, in the popular press, then as now, there was little space for subtlety. Darwin's work was 'The Ape Theory' and the *Origin* and Genesis were often crudely contrasted: 'Scientific men are not at liberty to ignore the statements of Scripture.' There was, however, no general or organized opposition until much later.

A detailed description of the early responses to Darwin by theologians remains controversial. It seems likely that some strands of conservative opinion were adamantly opposed to Darwin from the start. We have suggested that the concept of the unchangeability of species results from a philosophical interpretation rather than a direct reading of the Bible, but it was inevitable that many conservatives would identify fixity with God's revelation and thus see Darwin as denying the truth of God's word.

At an opposite extreme, much liberal Christian opinion could easily identify with the optimistic creed of progressive evolutionism. For many liberals, God guided the development of life upwards towards the crowning achievement of humanity. This world view has little in common with the complexities of the biblical story of fall and redemption, and equally little in common with Darwinian evolution, with its description of change by means of chance variation and harsh struggle. Darwin himself gave a hostage to fortune when he allowed Alfred Wallace, the joint discoverer of natural selection, to persuade him to adopt Herbert Spencer's phrase 'The Survival of the Fittest'. For Spencer and the liberals, the phrase implied an inevitable onward

progress towards perfection (perhaps through war and the elimination of the unfit; but that was the price of progress and was
inevitable, and therefore right). For anyone who understood
Darwin's natural selection, the 'survival of the fittest' simply
meant that the fittest were those who survived: the phrase is
meaningless, and has caused endless unnecessary misunderstandings.

In the nineteenth century, of course, few people understood
Darwin and natural selection. It was more general concepts of
evolution which were widely discussed, and, by the end of the
century, accepted by educated opinion. It is not surprising that
religious people and theologians were no exception to this. Many
rejected any form of evolution; many did not. Frederick Temple,
who was to go on to be Archbishop of Canterbury, embraced a
version of evolution as early as 1860, when he preached at the
famous British Association meeting at Oxford. But Temple's
evolution was progressive and guided evolution, with little room
for the chances of natural selection. Henry Drummond, an evangelical revivalist in his preaching, was another who accepted
evolution. In *Natural Law in the Spiritual World* (1883) and *The
Ascent of Man* (1894), he pictured science and religion as one,
combining the progressive evolution of body and soul. Drummond's conservative evangelical friends, who included D. L.
Moody, were largely unconvinced. Charles Kingsley, by contrast,
was a liberal theologically, but well understood the implications
of Darwin's theory. For Kingsley, 'an interfering God' had been
replaced by 'a living, immanent, ever-working God'. [31]

A small but influential number of Christian theologians were
able to understand fully the implications of Darwin's work and
to accept it alongside their orthodox Christian theology. The
American Calvinists Asa Gray and G. F. Wright are the best
known. They were both scientists, a botanist and a geologist,
who were also well-equipped to understand the theological implications of natural selection. In Britain, the Anglo-Catholic Aubrey
Moore (1843–1890) wrote extensively on evolution, seeing in
Darwin's theory the opportunity for the church to return to a
more complete doctrine of God. The Christian God was not the
divine visitor, appearing from time to time to perform the work
of special creation by making another species. By tying themselves to such beliefs, Christians 'have come to acquiesce in a

sort of unconscious Deism'. Darwin helps us to see that this is neither good science nor good theology. Science has pushed the Deist's god further and further away,

> and at the moment when it seemed as if He would be thrust out altogether, Darwinism appeared, and, under the guise of a foe, did the work of a friend. It has conferred upon philosophy and religion an inestimable benefit, by showing us that we must choose between two alternatives. Either God is everywhere present in nature, or He is nowhere. He cannot be here, and not there.[32]

Evolution and the progress of society

The situation in the nineteenth century was complicated by two other factors, which had little to do with the science involved.

Firstly, as we have seen, the fixity of species was associated not only with the truth of the Bible, but also with the stability of society. If there was an inevitable upward progress, then the radicals agitating for change had a strong case, and those who claimed that their rule over society was not only benevolent and paternal, but also sanctioned by God, a weaker case than they had thought. Sociologists of science have even suggested that Darwin choose Malthusian evolution rather than Lamarckian, at a time when there was little scientific evidence for the mechanism of natural selection, because its doctrine of the struggle for survival fitted much more comfortably with his Whig capitalist heritage (and inheritance) than Lamarck's inevitable progress. Even so, as we have seen, Darwin hesitated long before publishing his work:

> I am almost convinced (quite contrary to the opinion I started with) that species are not (it is almost like confessing a murder) immutable. (Letter to Hooker, Jan 1844).[33]

Sedgwick's well-known review of Chambers' *Vestiges of the Natural History of Creation*, published in the same year, illustrates the point: If the book is true, he thundered, then 'religion is a lie, human law is a means of folly, and a base injustice; morality is moonshine'.[34]

Secondly, Darwin published his work at the time when scientists were pushing strongly to establish science as a profession. Until then science had been the realm of the gentleman eccentric, or the clerical naturalist. Now it was to be a proper, salaried profession. The amateurs must be removed, and those who knew what was best for science must control the levers of power. Thomas Huxley and many of his generation had seen the church exercise its control of higher education, and they disliked the results. Patronage if it was to be exercised would be controlled by them, and positions awarded on merit to professionals like themselves. A group of the leading radical scientists formed the secretive X Club, and plotted the future course of science.

Huxley's most recent biographer pictures a crusade, a 'jihad' is his phrase, with the clerical naturalists, whose loyalties were believed to be divided, as the chief casualties. This is the context for another of the famous or infamous remarks on the relation of science and religion. One of Thomas Huxley's reviews of the *Origin* stated his view of the stark opposition of science and old fashioned theology:

[T]he cosmogony of the semi-barbarous Hebrew [is] . . . the incubus of the philosopher . . . Extinguished theologians lie about the cradle of every science as the strangled snakes beside that of Hercules.[35]

This was all good populist nonsense, setting the scene not for total warfare between science and religion but for the series of skirmishes which, looking back, have formed the popular myth of the relationship between science and religion.

Enduring questions

Some of the complexities of this chapter must now be drawn together, as far as is possible. In those first responses to Darwin, and indeed in the continuing Christian response since, what genuine theological issues come to the fore?

The authority of the Bible   We cannot avoid the familiar question of the status of the Bible. This was not a new issue. The generations prior to Darwin had faced very similar questions, over the relation of Genesis and geology, but whilst there were real difficulties the storm experienced then soon died down. Nor was the issue first raised by the geologists. Instead we are transported right back to the church's response to Galileo. For anyone with a keen sense of history the episode of Galileo served as an instructive warning. Conventional ways of reading the Bible might be at variance with the results of new sciences. Mature reflection on the church's problem with Galileo suggested to most thoughtful minds that in such a struggle the conventional reading would probably be forced to defer to the scientific perception.

The debate over geology had already sharpened the questions. How should the Bible be read? How could readers disentangle the philosophical and cultural presuppositions which they brought with them to their reading from the word of God in the text? Thus, how could confusion be avoided between the religious truths of the Bible and newly-discovered truths of science? In a postmodern age these seem particularly contemporary questions, but they are all to be found in the educated response to the results of the geologists. Darwin raised no new questions, but – for some Christians at any rate – the sophisticated answers which were available did not seem to do justice to the problem. The reasons for this are probably to be found in another issue Darwin raised, that of the status of humanity. Over Galileo, or even geology, the doctrines involved could be dismissed as peripheral. The issue of our own origins addressed a central doctrine of Christianity.

The origins of humankind   Was humanity made in the image of God or not? Was the human being the result of God's express will, as the reading of Genesis seemed to suggest, or an odd accident (as Darwin might be taken to imply), or the pinnacle of the evolutionary process, as the liberal evolutionists maintained? Even Darwin's fellow discoverer of natural selection, Alfred Wallace, found it hard to believe that a construction so complex as the human brain had arisen by chance. By contrast Darwin, from the very beginning of his thinking about evolution, understood that he was endeavouring to explain human life and society, and not simply animal origins.

As we have seen, most people found this difficult to accept. Surely human society must have meaning, function and purpose beyond the chance workings of natural selection? A natural human desire for meaning here becomes confused with Christian belief. The Bible and the whole structure of Christian theology give an almost supreme importance to human life. There were few theologians who could accept the whole of Darwin's vision and build a theology consonant with it, although as we have noted, there were those such as Aubrey Moore who eagerly rose to the challenge. For most people, Darwin seemed to present a stark choice between the meaninglessness of chance origins, and the care of a loving God.

The purpose of nature The position of humanity was the issue which everyone noticed. In the broader view, however, the place of men and women may perhaps be understood as a particular case of a more general consequence of Darwin's work. This was the elimination of purpose from nature. Darwin had been trained in a view of natural science which accepted the harmony of theology and nature. 'From nature up to nature's God' to use the popular phrase. Special creation was merely one aspect of natural theology. By the time Darwin began to work, natural theology was beginning to seem too blunt a tool. Lyell's programme of using only the tools immediately to hand was carrying the day. The task of science was to disentangle itself from religious speculation and to seek to explain the world in terms of presently operating causes. Speculation about origins, purposes and ultimate meanings should be excluded. As John Brooke remarks on Darwin's attempts to explain the life of the Galapagos islands: 'This was simply too tantalizing a puzzle to solve by invoking the will of God.'[36]

The irony of Darwin's intimate knowledge of Paley was not lost on his contemporaries. John Tyndall, one of Huxley's fellow members in the X Club, was President of the British Association in 1874 and his Presidential Address (the notorious 'Belfast Address') was seen at the time as something of a high point in the clash between science and religion. As Tyndall joyfully pointed out: 'It is the mind thus stored with the choicest materials of the teleologist that rejects teleology, seeking to refer these wonders to natural causes.'[37]

The separation of science and religion The whole long British tradition of natural theology assumed one domain of knowledge with easy and harmonious relations between the two books of Reason and Revelation. By contrast, Tyndall and Huxley also assumed a single domain, but one whose content was dictated by science. In Tyndall's words: 'Science claims the entire domain of cosmological theory.'[38]

In practice, historians suggest, the effect of Darwin's work, together with other nineteenth-century changes, was to create two domains of knowledge where previously there had been one. Not in any simple way, or as the result of any one change, science and theology had finally become separate disciplines.

Natural selection is not atheistic in itself, but its effects are secularizing: 'any theory of origins that is capable of sustaining an indefinitely large number of different philosophical and religious interpretations is profoundly secularizing in its effects'.[39] James Moore is correct to deny the universality of warfare between science and religion, but one of the long-term effects to which Darwin's work contributed was the fragmentation of the world, or of human descriptions of the world, where once a single form of explanation had sufficed.

From pebbles to chalk: the British Association

We have travelled full circle. We can now understand something of how the change occurred between the meeting of the British Association in 1838 with Sedgwick's pious synthesis of pebbles, politics and piety on the beach at Tynemouth and the similar meeting in Norwich in 1868, when Huxley refused to countenance origins and purposes beyond the piece of chalk in his hand. The way in which people understood the world had changed. Biology and geology would no longer allow theological explanations, at least at the level of practical science. Science could no longer be used to justify either the theology or the politics of society. The men of science, with their newly-coined name, scientists, had emancipated themselves, and put the parsons to flight – from the British Association, and large areas of professional society. Finally, and almost most remarkably of all, ordinary working men had noticed the change, and now cheered Huxley as they had once listened obediently to Sedgwick.

In this chapter we have considered some of the great landmarks in the growing Victorian fascination with the power of science: the British Association meetings at Newcastle in 1838, Norwich in 1868, and John Tyndall's Presidential Address at Belfast in 1874. We must finish as we began with the meeting at Oxford in 1860. Huxley St George slew Samuel smoothest of dragons. Or did he? At the start of this book we met Canon William Tristram, the first scientist to make use of Darwin's theory of natural selection when he sought to account for the variation in the form of the beaks of different species of Saharan larks. A textbook example of a progressive cleric we might think, until we remember that he was reconverted away from the concept of natural selection by Bishop Wilberforce's speech at the Oxford meeting.[40]

Wilberforce himself thought that he had won the argument and floored Huxley, whilst Joseph Hooker, friend of Darwin and Huxley, considered that Huxley had given a poor performance, and that he, Hooker, had saved the day. Ironically, because within a few years the proceedings of the BA were reported at quite extraordinary length in the popular press, the great confrontation went almost unreported at the time, except by those who took part including Wilberforce, who proudly published his own version of the meeting – not the action of a defeated man. These partisan accounts were rewritten over the years to serve their authors particular purposes.

Samuel Wilberforce possessed one of the best brains on the bench of bishops, and his attack upon natural selection, although mixed with a general condemnation of all liberalism, was not a blind and bigoted attack on all of Darwin's work. Wilberforce drew on the advice of eminent, if conservative, naturalists, especially Richard Owen. Owen, the foremost authority of the time, was very much opposed to Darwin's theory. With the benefit of hindsight it is easy to forget the powerful scientific arguments ranged against Darwin which we have reviewed in this chapter. Even Huxley was only a recent convert to the truth of the evolutionary hypothesis, having himself attacked earlier versions of evolution.

As an aside Wilberforce did ask Huxley – who was not among the invited speakers – a question as to whether the apes were on his grandfather's or grandmother's side. The crowd demanded a response, and Huxley's reply was no doubt along the lines that he would prefer to have an ape for a grandfather than 'a man highly endowed by nature and possessed of great means of influence and yet who employs these faculties and that influence for the mere purpose of introducing ridicule into a grave scientific discussion'. But that, of course, is Huxley's version of his words, which some reports suggest simply were not heard above the general hubbub. Most recent accounts stress that it is now impossible to reconstruct what in fact happened at the meeting; perceptions of the event differed so widely that it makes no sense to talk of a victor.[41]

What actually happened at Oxford in 1860 was not really important. The affair would soon be seen as the champion of Christianity being routed by the champion of Scientific Naturalism. Which lets us see the real significance of the episode. It is a myth. Within a very few years the public perception was that there had been a battle over Darwin and that science had won: 'Darwin's *Origin of Species* had come into the theological world like a plough into an ant-hill.' The victory of science was pictured in the vanquishing of Wilberforce by Huxley. The episode set the tone, became a paradigm, for the later relations of science and religion. Never mind that it may never have happened; it seemed to exemplify the truth.[42]

Chapter 4

What is Science? – The Philosophy of Science

Our review of the history of the relationship between science and religion has shown how difficult it is to define what we mean by 'science'. In this chapter we shall see if philosophy can help, and consider what implications the study of the philosophy of science has for any possible relation between science and religion.

What is science?

It is often claimed that science is different from all other human activities, and with some justification. Few of us imagine that we can improve the words of the Gospels, or rewrite Shakespeare to advantage. And yet in its own sphere science has usually claimed to do just that. Newton was the greatest scientist of his age, still revered as an exemplar of how to do science, and yet every undergraduate physicist knows more and better science than Newton. Newton himself understood this when he modestly remarked that he had simply been a pygmy standing on the shoulders of giants.

The spectacular practical success of science has led many people to believe that science grows and develops and increases its knowledge about the world in a quite different way from other human endeavours. It is sometimes said that the whole modern world view is founded on this understanding of the uniqueness of science. In the next chapter we shall see how this view of science faces a major challenge from some sociologists. This challenge must be taken seriously, but it is very recent and still highly controversial. For most of the last few hundred years science has been seen as both straightforward and reliable in its quest for knowledge; how different – it is often remarked – from religion and other superstitions.

Can we formulate any rules that will help us to understand what science is and how it works? Some writers are confident that we can easily find answers to questions such as: Is Creationism science? Or Scientology? Is Freudian analysis scientific? When Marx talked of *scientific* materialism, what did he mean?

In this chapter we will consider the work of philosophers of science to see if they can help us to define the nature of science. In the next chapter we turn to the sociologists and their very distinctive perspective. That discussion will bring us face to face with the postmodern claim that 'Science' – old, imperialistic, absolutist science – is dead, and that humanity is now moving into new ways of understanding the world.

The importance of understanding what science is

Why are grandiose claims made for the status of science? What it is that is different about science? Why does it grow? How does it build upon its past? Is there a scientific method which if properly applied will guarantee success? Or are there a number of related ways of doing science? Can we recognize this scientific method? Does it depend on the subject matter being studied? Or can it be applied to all forms of human striving after the truth? Certainly many of the great scientists of the nineteenth century thought that humanity was on the verge of a new era when society, politics and our understanding of ourselves would be revolutionized by the elimination of what they often called 'theology' and its replacement with 'scientific' methods. At the end of the twentieth century we have learnt that Marxism and Freudianism don't necessarily deliver the progress which we routinely expect from other sciences. Again we must ask the question why? What is special about science? And can we learn to distinguish real science from pseudoscience?

It is with questions such as these that we shall be concerned in this chapter. The philosophy of science is a complicated subject with its own technical language and concerns. It is important to cast more than a glancing eye over its domain for a number of reasons.

- We shall see how difficult it is to describe precisely what scientists do, or what science is. Even this supposedly most rational of human activities is difficult to justify in terms which are either totally logical or entirely rational. This discovery may give some confidence to those who wish to assert the importance of religion and theology, not only in the private sphere of personal belief, but also in the public world of argument and dialogue.

- We shall also discover that science does not possess any guaranteed methods by which it can interrogate the natural world in order to prove what is true. It is both the limitation and the glory of science that it is one human activity among others. This might reassure those who are concerned at the tendency to defer to the knowledge of the scientific expert, especially when experts claim to be able to make pronouncements beyond their own areas of particular expertise; a scientific education does not provide a shortcut to infallibility.

- Nonetheless my hope is that once we have explored in some detail just how science does work then we shall be left with an enhanced respect for the work of scientists and a qualified but secure confidence in the achievements of science.

The beginnings of modern science: the method of induction

Francis Bacon (1561–1626) was one of the first people to express the idea that science is the progressive accumulation of knowledge about the material world.[1] Certainly his name will always be linked to what is now known as the *method of induction*. According to Bacon and his followers – John Stuart Mill in the nineteenth century was a particularly influential exponent of these ideas – science consists of the collection of facts or data and the subsequent organization of the data into significant categories. Once a sufficient amount of data has been collected, the scientist can draw provisional conclusions from the tables of facts which have been drawn up, and can test the generalizations produced against new facts. The original hypothesis will be either confirmed or need to be refined. Thus science gradually expands to take account of newly-observed data. The classification of the living world into kingdoms, families and orders according to the principles of Linnaeus is a classic example of the application of the method.

Bacon's description of science was attractive and simple to understand. It gave a reason for the success of science, which was that science was not hindered by any outside presuppositions – the scientist came fresh and unencumbered to his subject. Who scientists were, what beliefs they held, or where they worked were irrelevant; all was laid aside at the door of the laboratory. Bacon talks of 'idols' which control and distort our minds and from which we must be free if we are to understand the world.

Scientists today still talk of letting the facts speak for themselves, but Bacon realized that the enterprise was not quite as straightforward as this. Progress in science is achieved when certain things are recognized as similar and compared. Imagine that we decide to learn more about the sea. We will probably quite quickly establish the differences between plants and 'creatures'. Then by looking closely at our categories we may decide that there are differences between say, jellyfish and fish with backbones. The distinction between the fish and the sea mammals will probably take longer to establish, but it is clear that meticulous observation and careful thought about those observations can advance science by a great deal. It does not provide a guarantee of total or immediate success, as the involved debates in the early meetings of the Royal Society – the most prestigious of all British scientific institutions – on the behaviour of sea monsters demonstrate.[2]

Practical problems with induction

The method of induction requires that we categorize everything we observe, but how are we to decide which things are alike? Surely whales are more similar to sharks than to voles, and yet modern science has decided with impressive unanimity that in fact the opposite is the case. For modern scientists the common characteristics of mammals are more suggestive than those of large sea creatures. Bacon asked the scientist to categorize the natural world as it is observed, but the categories which prove to be interesting to science are rarely those which lie on the surface. The scientist must bring judgment and experience to the work of classification. More seriously, the way we look at the world can never be entirely neutral. How do we decide which facts we shall record, which are relevant, and which are important?

An example may help to suggest the complex way in which scientists work. The original discovery of radioactivity, at the end of the nineteenth century, was not the result of careful observation but pure chance. By accident the French physicist Becquerel happened to put a photographic plate in a drawer which already contained a lump of pitchblende. Only when he discovered that the plate had been ruined did he eventually search for the cause. What could possibly mimic the action of light when the plate had been careful sealed? By a mixture of careful observation and the trial and rejection of possible hypotheses, Becquerel and other scientists began to derive an explanation of radioactivity.

The key to the discovery was *not* the chance placing of the photographic plate in the drawer but the combination of that chance with the chance that it was discovered by someone who realized that what had happened was significant. Most photographers, and no doubt many scientists, would have thrown the plate away with a shrug. Equally, once he had realized what had happened, Becquerel's role as a scientist was not then merely to observe what happened when the chance – which had by now become an experiment – was repeated, but instead to work hard to eliminate all other factors except the relevant observations of the plate and the uranium compound.

How can we decide what is relevant? Colour plays a very important part in our everyday observation of the world, and yet for most scientists colour is an irrelevant property when trying to describe the natural categories of the physical world. Even the trained scientist will not always find it easy to know what is relevant and what not. The theory of evolution by natural selection gained great support from the observation that isolated islands within a group often contain many different species of similar plants and animals. And yet, as we have seen, Charles Darwin did not even label his Galapagos' specimens with their island of origin, so that when the significance of the differences between them became apparent to him years later, he was forced to try to reconstruct their island of origin. All subsequent scientists, of course, taught by Darwin how to categorize the world, have understood the importance of such things, and hence made more specific observations.

We might say that practically Bacon does give some pointers to some of the important features of science, but that his method does not describe how scientists in fact work, nor does it describe how they should work. The all-powerful computer, with its ability to swamp scientists in every discipline with mounds of data, has only served to reinforce an old truth. The judgment of the scientist, exercised in choosing between observations, and in understanding which facts are significant, cannot be excluded from the scientific method.

Philosophical problems with induction

The method of induction does not provide a complete picture of the practice of scientists, and for the philosopher induction poses even more serious problems. The discussion of these is usually associated with the work of David Hume (1711–1776), the sceptical Scottish philosopher.

The scientifically powerful part of the inductive method occurs after the observations have been categorized or tabulated, when the scientist makes generalizations from the observations. Because scientists have observed gases to expand as the temperature increases, they draw the general conclusion that all gases always expand as their temperature increases. Why, asks the sceptic, do you suppose this will happen? What can possibly give you confidence that you can predict the future? This has happened countless times in the past, we might reply, and nothing has changed, therefore, of course it will happen in the future. Yes, says the sceptic, my watch has always told the correct time in the past, but now that its battery has run out it will not do so in the future.

The usefulness of the principle of induction in science relies on our common-sense intuition that, everything else being equal, what has always happened will always continue to happen. It is a good common-sense principle on which to base our daily lives but, as philosophers since Hume have continued to point out, we cannot offer any proof for it. There is no way that we can generalize from a finite number of observations about the past to prove a general statement about what will always be the case.

It is important to note that it would have been disastrous for the progress of science if scientists had ceased to use induction because of Hume's objections. Hume raised a philosophical difficulty, which in spite of two hundred years attention by philosophers still remains. Scientists, knowing the day-to-day value of induction, continue to make use of the method, and science continues to develop. There is, however, no longer any philosophical justification for what they do; they simply persevere because the method continues to yield results.

We began this chapter by asking what was special about science, and what helped it to grow. The first answer offered was that the use of Baconian induction provided a neutral and assured method which separated science from all other human activities. The philosophical problems caused by induction, however, mean that this apparent advantage is removed. Scientists will continue to rely on their observations, and continue to generalize from them, but philosophers have failed to answer Hume's attack. We rely on the method of induction not because we can prove its superiority but because it has usually proved reliable in the past. In doing this the scientist must exercise informed judgment, and cannot rely on absolute proof.

Popper and deduction

One response of philosophers to the problems raised by Hume was to attempt to describe the uniqueness of science in terms of *deduction* rather than induction. The precariousness of induction can be compared to the logical certainty of deduction. In a deductive argument, the conclusion follows automatically from the premises:

A: All scientists are mad
B: This person is a scientist
Therefore
C: This person is mad

Deductive arguments become interesting when a logical application of the method leads to interesting and unexpected conclusions. Given the problems with induction, can science be described in deductive terms?

In the single most important text in the study of the philosophy of science, *The Logic of Scientific Discovery* (written in 1934, but not published in English until 1959), Karl Popper (1909–1994) attempts to describe the whole scientific exercise in deductive terms. For him, science is concerned with producing reasonable hypotheses which can be refined and tested against other parts of science and, crucially, which can be tested against the practical applications and experiments of science. A hypothesis makes a prediction. Does the experiment confirm the prediction?

> If this decision is positive, that is, if the singular conclusions turn out to be acceptable, or *verified*, then the theory has, for the time being, passed its test: we have found no reason to discard it. But if the decision is negative, or in other words, if the conclusions have been *falsified*, then their falsification also falsifies the theory from which they were logically deduced.[3]

A well-known illustration of Popper's method of falsification is the hypothesis that *All swans are white*. Continued observation confirms the hypothesis; it is verified time and again as we observe the swans on the rivers around us. All is well until the first explorers visit Australia and bring back a picture of a black swan. Only one observation is enough to falsify our hypothesis.

The great attraction of Popper's scheme is that he deals with what is certain. He rescues science from the problem of induction. He also suggests a reason for a strict demarcation between science and the pseudosciences. Why is science better than witchcraft or astrology? After all, all theories are merely unrefuted conjectures. We can have no more conclusive, positive proof of the General Theory of Relativity than of the influence of the stars on my character. The difference, according to Popper, is that true science is falsifiable. The specific predictions of science can always be tested and disproved; superstition yields only vague generalizations.

Popper's strength is also his weakness. All he can describe are the failures of science. He can tell us why theories are (or should be) abandoned; he cannot describe the positive content of science in any detail. He has avoided the problem of induction, but at the cost of forbidding us to possess full confidence in the positive content of science; all we can be certain about are its failures.

We began by seeking to explain the reasons for the growth of science, and Popper has instead lead us to the situation where only *negative* results can be relied upon as scientific. According to his theory, the whole edifice of the *positive* results of science is simply waiting to be falsified. Popper allows us a firm logical base for the necessary critical activities of scientists – after Popper's work we can justify the rejection of failed theories, but even the greatest of the philosophers of science, and Popper deserves the title, cannot provide us with a logical justification for the positive achievements of science.

The scientific community

There have been attempts, notably that of Imre Lakatos (1922–1974) to build upon Popper's insights whilst saving the content of science from the full rigours of falsification.[4] Popper was aware that *in practice* scientists did not always abandon their theories at the first hint of a negative result, and also that the whole community of scientists had a role to play in the business of science. Lakatos and others developed these insights in various ways. Instead of theories simply being falsified and falling by the wayside in a rather profligate manner, Lakatos suggests that good scientific practice should demand that 'falsified' theories are only rejected when they can be replaced by more adequate theories. Science is no longer a purely logical enterprise built with only those building blocks which can be absolutely relied upon; instead it has become the practical exercise of choice between alternatives.

In fact Lakatos goes further and replaces talk of theories with that of *research programmes*. Groups or communities of scientists operate with complex networks of theories. *Core theories* are those which are at the centre of a community's shared system of understanding. For Lakatos these are very general theories which the community believes to have stood the test of time. Because they are general theories, there are no easy or direct ways in which they can be tested. A core theory needs to be connected to the outside world by a series of *auxiliary hypotheses*. It is these auxiliary hypotheses which are subject to test and experiment. They can be falsified, but falsification of an auxiliary hypothesis only implies that it will be modified, not that the core theory should be abandoned.

Early atomic theory provides an example. If atoms are built up of simple building blocks then the atomic weight of each element should be in a simple ratio with the atomic weight of other elements. Some early experiments confirmed this hypothesis. In many cases, however, the measured atomic weights of elements often did not fit this simple pattern. The fact that this was not the case did not lead to the immediate abandonment of the theory, but to a series of suggested new hypotheses to account for the awkward facts. The idea of atomic theory was too powerful, and its usefulness too great, to allow it to be abandoned because of one inconvenient set of experimental results. The issue was only resolved many years later when it was realized that an element may be composed of different isotopes with identical chemical properties but different atomic weights. What the early experiments had measured was this mixture, which is why the expected ratios were not seen. If the theory had been given up too early, the final breakthrough to an understanding of isotopes might have been greatly delayed.

Lakatos claims that his hierarchy of auxiliary hypotheses and core theory allows him to remain true to Popper's philosophy, whilst at the same time explaining the actual reluctance of scientists to change their well-established theories.

Lakatos tried to model his philosophy of science on the actual practice of scientists, and claimed that in practice rival theories could exist alongside each other. To describe this situation he developed his idea of competing research programmes. Research programmes can be *progressive* when the theories which underlie them are generating testable predictions ahead of experimental verification, *stagnating* when the programme succeeds in explaining the results of experiment only by making *ad hoc* additions to its surrounding framework of auxiliary hypotheses, or *degenerating* when there exists a fully-fledged alternative research programme which can explain the same range of facts in a fashion that is scientifically more acceptable.

A scientific programme for theology?

Theologians have recently become interested in the application of Lakatos' ideas to theology. In *Theology in the Age of Scientific Reasoning*, Nancey Murphy hopes to demonstrate that theology is a science because at least some ways of doing theology conform to Lakatos' description of a research programme.[5] Unfortunately this raises a number of problems. In the scientific field, it has not proved easy to apply the details of Lakatos' method to particular cases – who would want to claim to advocate a degenerating research programme? As applied to theology, all that Murphy can demonstrate are some similarities between the way loose-knit groups of theologians operate with shared ideas, some more deeply held than others, and Lakatos' communities of scientists who share research programmes. This hardly seems enough to be able to go on to claim that therefore theology is indeed a science.

Behind the detail lies the important realization that science is performed by communities with shared ideals, in which scientists who have considerable investment not simply in science, but in one particular way of doing science, work together. The very complexity of modern science means that it will rarely be possible to imagine a crucial experiment which will disprove the fundamental theory upon which a community has based its life in science. To admit this is not to accept that science and astrology are after all equally valid, for any scientific community, according to Lakatos, will continually test and modify its auxiliary hypotheses. Real criticism and growth is possible as these hypotheses are genuinely tested against the real world of experiment and observation. These auxiliary hypotheses can be modified by the community with comparative easy without endangering the core theories.

It is also possible to envisage the very rare circumstances when the core theories themselves come to be challenged, at first outside the community, but later also by those who have invested so much in them. In the next chapter we shall discover that sociologists of science draw very different conclusions to those of Lakatos when they consider the creative role of the scientific community.

The scientific communities which we have described here can

be pictured as *communities of faith*. They are held together not simply by the chance of working on similar problems, or using the same laboratories, but by the stronger bonds of ideals and choices, shared within the group, but not necessarily by other scientists. It was the work of Thomas Kuhn which first drew widespread attention to such models of the way in which science is undertaken.

Scientific revolutions

Imre Lakatos' concept of scientific research programmes was in part a response to the work of Thomas Kuhn (1922–1996). Kuhn claimed to provide an alternative version of the philosophy of science, one that began not with abstract logical problems, but with a description of the actual practice of scientists. Straddling the boundary between history, philosophy and sociology, Kuhn's writing is much less technical than much modern philosophy; one reason why it has been widely read and discussed. Unusually, Kuhn has been read by many scientists. Some have given his work a warm welcome: here, almost for the first time, was a philosophy of science which they could recognize and understand. Others have felt that Kuhn undermined the central principles of science. It is not surprising then that Kuhn's work is the single most important foundation of the work of the sociologists which we shall consider in the next chapter, and it often quoted as one of the roots of postmodernism.

In *The Structure of Scientific Revolutions*,[6] Kuhn asks his readers to remember how scientists learn science in the classroom. They listen to accounts of important experiments from the past, sometimes repeating them for themselves and work through the mathematics of basic theories. Like all students they encounter what their teachers think is important, and in the process become familiar with tried and tested methods.

Students of science never experience the failed experiments or the frustration of chasing after false leads that lie behind the successful formulations presented to them. The sheer amount of knowledge contained within most developed sciences means that it would be impossible for students to learn for themselves by trial and error. They must accept what is given on the authority of the teacher and the scientific community. Thus, says Kuhn, we induct new scientists into the community, from the start expecting them to accept what is given less because they have grasped its truth for themselves than because they accept the authority of the community.

Kuhn took great care to describe the way science is performed. Usually scientists work within a community with shared methods, aims and ideals. The picture is almost one of a mediaeval guild of craftsmen passing on their shared knowledge to apprentices and working within fixed traditions. The whole ethos of the community, its way of doing things, Kuhn suggests, is involved in the continuation of science, as well as the repetition of formal proofs. It is perhaps easiest to locate his much-discussed concept of the *paradigm* here. Kuhn's critics note that he uses the word in many different ways: to stand for the entire constellation of beliefs, values, and techniques held by a community, as a deeply held fundamental theory, or as a classic experiment which may demonstrate either the reasonableness of the theory or provide an example of good scientific practice, to give only a few of his meanings.[7] Despite the ambiguity, Kuhn is pointing us to important truths about the way in which knowledge is shared and transmitted within communities.

Kuhn contrasts how scientists work in periods of *normal science*, as described above, with *scientific revolutions*. The most controversial suggestion which he makes is that from time to time the shared understanding of the community, its paradigm, in one or more of the senses listed above, comes under threat. Unlike Popper, Kuhn suggests that scientists can happily accept a number of challenges to their basic theories. They can simply modify the theory with *ad hoc* additions or discount the importance of the contrary results. None of this challenges the basic paradigm of the community, and Kuhn suggests that it is helpful to science that it does not. The growth of science is partly accounted for by the fact that most scientists most of the time do not worry about the correctness of their overall theories but simply work away at clarifying the details. Too much concentration on the fundamental basis of the theories of science would paralyse the community and prevent progress.

Paradigms and paradigm shifts

In times of scientific revolution, however, the difficulties may accumulate so that it becomes impossible to ignore them. At the same time an alternative paradigm, seeking to explain the difficulties, and advocated by a different group of scientists – a new community – may become available, and there may come a time when the bulk of the scientific community changes from one paradigm to another. Kuhn calls this *paradigm shift*. How are such decisions made?

It is here that we begin to realize how controversial Kuhn's description of science is. Kuhn's first readers took away the radical message that there can be no rational choice between competing paradigms, because the paradigm we embrace influences everything. In a much quoted passage Kuhn describes the work of astronomers before and after Copernicus. Before Copernicus the heavens were considered immutable. Stars and planets moved, but in perfect orbits and without suffering change or decay. Once Copernicus had painted a different picture which embraced the possibility of change in the heavens, astronomers – looking through the same instruments which they had always used – soon saw the evidence of sunspots and other changes. Indeed, as Kuhn tellingly notes, Chinese astronomers, unencumbered by a belief in the immutable heavens, had seen these effects centuries before, and without the aid of telescopes:

> The very ease and rapidity with which astronomers saw new things when looking at old objects with old instruments may make us wish to say that, after Copernicus, astronomers lived in a different world.[8]

Scientists holding different paradigms live in different worlds. According to Kuhn, different paradigms are *incommensurable*, which means that we cannot compare theories if they gain their fundamental meanings within different paradigms. The different communities of scientists talk different languages, value different sorts of experiment, and therefore live in different worlds.

Before the work of Einstein, scientists assumed that light and radio waves travelled through an aether in a similar way to waves travelling through water or any liquid. The aether seemed to provide a useful bridge between the work of Newton and the electro-magnetic theory of Clerk Maxwell. Hence, a large number of nineteenth-century experiments set out to discover the aether and to describe its properties. Einstein's theories, however, suggested a new way of looking at the physical universe, with no place for an aether. In future there would be little point in conducting experiments to discover the aether.

If major scientific changes happen in this way, then there is no rational way for scientists to choose between different theories. Within a paradigm, science is conducted in a fairly rational way, although Kuhn lays emphasis on the shared traditions and learnt techniques of a community. When paradigms change scientists seem to have no rational means of making decisions. In his later work Kuhn softened the concept of incommensurability and allowed that they were ways in which partial comparisons at least could be made between science before and after such changes.

One astute critic has remarked that Kuhn knew some history but not enough.[9] He was right to take us back to the real practice of real scientists, and to describe the revolutionary nature of scientific change, but he forgot that all revolutions can be described in terms of both radical change and continuity. History teaches us that the revolutionary is often anticipated, and that the old often survives.

Living with paradigms

Since he wrote, Kuhn's concept of the paradigm has taken on a life of its own. The term paradigm shift has become almost as common as the quantum leap in popular discussion, and almost as empty of meaning. As we have seen, Kuhn himself must take some of the blame for this, as he used the concept with so many different meanings in his original work. Theologians in particular have welcomed the concept of communities held together by shared paradigms, describing any change of belief as a paradigm shift.[10] The definition of the community in terms of its shared beliefs – which are not translatable, and certainly not to be evaluated against other sets of beliefs – has great resonances for postmodern definitions of society and science.

Has the paradigm of the paradigm outlived its usefulness? Kuhn himself points to two meanings of the term as being especially significant.[11] The first is the overarching system of beliefs, values and techniques of the community. Remaining within the original scientific context, it is useful to remind ourselves that scientists operate with a complex set of values, not all of them scientific, not all easily falsifiable in the way that Popper imagined. On this model a paradigm shift is not any minor change in a belief system, but a major upheaval so great that the whole value system of the community is upset. In religious terms we might speak of the Reformation, or the original founding of the Christian faith from within Judaism. Only the most profound changes should be labelled as paradigm shifts. But notice that even in these cases there is some continuity with what went before.

The second useful meaning of the concept is that of a good example, a key experiment which shows how science should be performed at its best. We shall see in the next section of this chapter, and in the following chapter, that real experiments tend to be both theoretically and practically messy – the interpretation of what they mean usually involves the exercise of skilled judgment. Nonetheless the experiment as paradigm is an important feature of science and the education of scientists. Michelson and Morley's long series of experiments trying to detect the aether drift which later became important in the establishment of the Theory of Relativity, or the experiment of Cronin and Fitch which demonstrated the non-conservation of parity (the so-called 'left-handedness' of the universe) are often quoted examples. In religious terms we might talk of the death of Christ on the cross, or of the parable of the prodigal son, as being central, paradigmatic, to the meaning of Christianity.[12]

The importance of the scientist

A common thread has run through much of our discussion thus far. It is the claim that when a scientist comes to formulate a theory, or to choose between different possible theories to explain the data, there are no laws of logic or philosophy which can be used with certainty to inform the choice which has to be made. Scientists regularly use induction, but it remains philosophically suspect. In trying to replace it, Popper can only provide unquestioned rules to identify what is false. Even for Popper the positive work of science has to rely on the consensus of scientists to determine what is reasonable. Lakatos and Kuhn, in their different ways, highlight the role the community has to play in making such choices.

It is possible to develop an informal set of 'rules' which should govern theory choice, and indeed as part of his attempt to modify the harshness of his original thesis, Kuhn himself produced such a list.[13] Some of these rules are obvious. Theories must be *accurate*, the consequences of a theory must be in agreement with experimental results. Theories must be *consistent*, both internally and with other accepted theories. Other rules are more difficult to judge. Kuhn suggests that theories should have *broad scope*, that is that they should have a significance which extends beyond a set of limited observations. Kuhn also lists the popular criterion of *simplicity*, and the equally useful attribute of *fruitfulness*, that is, a theory's ability to generate unexpected predictions and consequences. But how can we decide what constitutes simplicity or fruitfulness? How are we to judge sensibly between simplicity and accuracy? One of Kuhn's most telling points in *The Structure of Scientific Revolutions* is that there is often a tension between a simple, new theory and an accurate and comprehensive older theory, which succeeds only by virtue of many complex additional hypotheses.[14]

Does the application of such less than infallible rules means that science cannot be wholly rational? This has been the subject of much speculation by both philosophers and, as we shall see in the next chapter, sociologists. Some philosophers have attempted to demonstrate that a set of informal rules can be used in a strictly rational way, but it is preferable to emphasize the insight of Michael Polanyi (1890–1976), a chemist turned philosopher. Polanyi wrote before the current debate had begun, at a time when most of the academic community would have held up science as the only undoubtedly objective model for all knowledge. He had to fight hard to justify his insistence that our knowledge could be both objective and personal. Polanyi writes of the need for commitment, skill and judgment in science, and of the personal participation of the scientist:

I have shown that into every act of knowing there enters a passionate contribution of the person knowing what is being known, and that this coefficient is no mere imperfection but a vital component of his knowledge.[15]

Forty years after Polanyi wrote, many of his insights, which once seemed so controversial, are now taken for granted. We must acknowledge his claim that the fact that there is an *art* to knowing does not imply that our accumulation of knowledge is not at the same time rational. Indeed the fact that the achievements of science *require* a skilful human input might make the scientific endeavour seem all the more remarkable.

Looking and understanding

To make a very broad generalization, we have so far been examining what scientists *do*. We have seen how difficult it is for philosophers and those who study science to reach agreement. These difficulties will multiply even more as the focus of our attention now turns to attempt to answer the question of what science itself *is*.

How do the theories of science relate to what I do when I open my eyes and look around me at the world? When I open my eyes I see, observe, certain things around me. For obvious reasons we can label these everyday things as *observables*. The theories of science will attempt to tell me why these observable things are the way they are, and do what they do. Often this is only possible, or is very much easier, if our theories describe other things – which we cannot see – *unobservables*, in order to help us understand the behaviour of things in the everyday world. Science tells me, for example, that the water in this glass, which I observe, is in fact composed of atoms of oxygen and hydrogen which have combined to form water molecules. It insists that this other, unknown, liquid can only be water if it is also composed of similar molecules.

But in what sense do those atoms and molecules, which I do not see, exist? In the 1840s the atomic hypothesis was simply an interesting idea that might help to picture what happened in complex chemical reactions and aid chemists in their bookkeeping. By 1900 it was still possible to argue that atoms were only a useful calculating devise, but most scientists took their reality for granted. At about this time physicists began to explain atoms in terms of other, smaller components. Within a few years, quantum theory demonstrated that almost all the old pictures of atoms were totally misconceived. And yet, few people today doubt the existence of 'atoms'. Indeed, high-powered microscopes now allow us to 'see' atoms, or at least, to see images on a screen which are interpreted via a complex set of theories to be representations of actual atoms.

There are two main ways in which to describe the relation of science and its theories to the world: realism and empiricism. *Empiricism* is the name given to a loosely defined set of views linked by the claim that our knowledge of the world is firmly fixed in our observation of the world. For empiricists, science gains its objectivity because it begins from observations which can be described in language independent of any theoretical assumptions. It is possible to describe what we see in an unambiguous and simple way. Equally, empiricism claims to be agnostic about what it is that scientific theories describe; that they work is all that matters. Thus empiricism is sometimes known as non-realism, because it claims to be indifferent to any reality that scientific theories may (or may not) picture. Empiricism is also linked to *constructivism*: empiricist theories are understood to construct reality rather than to discover it.

By contrast, *realism* claims that the power of science derives from the fact that it is attempting to describe reality. Scientific theories are more or less accurate representations of how things really are. We shall see later that there are many versions of the realist position, and *naive realism* – which understands scientific theories as direct and straightforward descriptions of reality – has few, if any, adherents today. *Critical realism*, however, remains popular both among practising scientists and, especially, with many of those who accept that there is a positive relation between science and religion: both disciplines, perhaps, seek in their own ways to describe a common reality. Although such a picture can seem persuasive, we must be careful not to accept it uncritically. It could be that critical realists bring to their understanding of science unconscious assumptions about what constitutes an explanation of the world. Critical realism may be simply wishful thinking. Thus it will be important to discuss the strengths of empiricism sympathetically before looking in detail at realism.

The importance of observation

Empiricism has been extremely popular among philosophers of science and those scientists who make the effort to try to understand what science is doing. The priority given to observation seems to allow a neutral way to decide between competing claims. This minimizes the need for the scientist to bring subjective skills such as the exercise of judgment into the rational world of science. As we shall see, empiricism has come under sustained attack since the 1950s, but still remains a popular and powerful position.

For our purposes, *positivism* can be described as a more theoretically developed version of empiricism. Ironically in view of the fact that the name was specifically chosen by Auguste Comte (1798–1857) for its 'positive' associations, it has now fallen out of favour, and many of those whose views would naturally seem to merit the label positivist prefer to call themselves empiricists of one variety or another! It is not too fanciful to trace a line of descent from Hume through Comte via the logical positivists of the Vienna Circle, who flourished between the two world wars, and with whom Popper was associated, to contemporary advocates.[16]

Positivism and empiricism overlap greatly. Many of the features described in the next paragraph would apply to both theories. If there are any significant differences, it may be that positivists would hold *more* strongly to *more* of the propositions, whereas empiricists would tend to agree with the overall position but might well dispute some of the individual points.

Empiricists and positivists begin by giving a high value to the role of observation in science. Looking for a fixed point they settle on the trustworthiness of what we see, and the simplicity of interpreting what these things mean. We shall notice later that, in fact, observation and what we observe are far from simple or uncontroversial. For the moment, however, let us accept the starting point offered. To take a straightforward view of observation means that we can apply Popper's tests of verification and falsification. Scientific theories are scientific because they can be compared with one another by reference to neutral, observed, data. Hence the importance of the claim that a sharp distinction can be made between observations and observation language, on the one hand, and theoretical statements, on the other. Scientists are able to make rational choices between alternative theories by allowing the data to speak for itself. To return to a previous example, I can see the difference between a white swan and a black one, and I can understand the significance of the sighting of a black swan.

The great importance given by empiricists to observation corresponds to the low value given to all theoretical statements. For them, the real business of science is in describing and comparing observations, and, above all, in making predictions. Theories are only important in so far as they help this process. To understand is an impossible dream, but to predict is a powerful reality.

Positivists, and many empiricists, would go further and follow Hume in denying that a description of real causation is central to the scientific endeavour. Hume asks what we really mean when we say that one event is caused by another. According to him we fool ourselves if we think that we understand the relationship between events. All that scientists can possibly mean when they assert that one thing causes another is that the two are always observed close together, and that so far as is possible pure chance has been excluded. As always, it will be insisted that science describes what is observed in the world; it does not seek to explain through the mechanism of causation. So van Fraassen, a 'constructive empiricist', dismisses causes as 'flights of fancy'.[17]

This hostility to the need for explanation, and the sustained opposition of empiricists to the reality of theoretical entities is, of course, linked to their understanding that the real business of science is at the level of straightforwardly observing 'ordinary' things in the everyday world. For most realists, by contrast, causation, and the ability to describe its mechanism, remain central to the scientific enterprise.

It should by now be obvious that empiricists and especially positivists will be hostile to anything that could be labelled as metaphysics. This includes not simply the well-known dismissal of all religious metaphysics by the logical positivists and their followers as literal non-sense, but also a general hostility to the possibility of any principles underlying science which cannot be directly related to observable facts. Hence the so-called principles of uniformity or simplicity will be rejected out of hand. They poison the clear atmosphere of pure observation.

Instrumentalism

Instrumentalism is the name given to the thoroughgoing application of such ideas to the theories of science. Instrumentalists
claim that the theories of science are useful instruments to aid
our calculations but nothing more. This view of science is not
new. In chapter 2 we saw how Andreas Osiander added a preface
to Copernicus' work claiming that the new astronomy was simply
a refined calculating device and should not be taken literally. In
publicly recanting his theories under pressure from the church,
Galileo was forced to take a similar stance.

Other empiricists regard theories as less artificial and limited
than this, but would certainly deny that we can ever prove that
our theories are literal statements of the truth about the world.
The title of Nancy Cartwright's book, *How the Laws of Physics
Lie*[18] is self-explanatory. For Cartwright scientific laws don't
really apply to the universe, all they describe are the perfect
models which we imagine underlie the observed world. They give
results which are roughly correct, and usually accurate enough to
do little harm. But the real world – if we could ever know it –
is much more untidy than our artificial laws suggest.

Are theories convenient models or something more? The fact
that theories sometimes generate genuinely novel predictions suggests that they at least model some structures of the universe other
than those which we observe. Consider Maxwell's celebrated
equations which govern the properties of electricity and magnetism. In four elegant equations the nineteenth-century Scottish
physicist James Clerk Maxwell brought together many of the
observed features of static electricity and magnetism. In doing
so he demonstrated the intimate connection between the two,
which had been suspected before but not fully demonstrated. His
equations are one of the supreme achievements of science.

Thus far Maxwell's equations might be considered as a useful
model, concisely combining observational data from a number
of fields. But the equations contained a surprise. One of them
predicted the existence of a form of radiation as yet unsuspected
by experimentalists. Once the equations had predicted the new
phenomenon, scientists began to look for it, and within a few
years Heinrich Hertz had demonstrated the existence of radio
waves. The simple explanation is that in explaining how elec-

tricity and magnetism were connected, Maxwell's equations in fact described a deeper, unseen, reality, and in the course of describing this, he also unwittingly described some of its properties which had not yet been observed.

Theory and observation

Empiricism is built on the foundation that there is a firm distinction between theory and observation. We should remain agnostic about theory, and be suspicious of the real existence of anything which we cannot observe. The observations of science, the things we see – *observables* – are secure and real. Is this distinction between theory and observation really built on firm ground? The ironic way in which today we use phrases such as 'seeing is believing' or 'the camera cannot lie' suggests that at a popular level we understand perfectly well the complexity involved in turning the reception of light waves by our eyes into the conscious understanding implied when we 'see' something. The optical illusions of Escher's etchings or even the simple duck-rabbit drawing are well enough known to remind us of the difficulties involved in making even the most straightforward observation.

When the scientist looks through a microscope or telescope the difficulties are magnified with the image. Scientists need complex theories of how instruments work before they can rely on what they think they see. Indeed, when Galileo began using the telescope to observe the heavens, one of his first tasks was to persuade the scientific community that he was indeed observing the heavens and not simply recording some interesting oddities generated inside the telescope. The chain of interpretation from the faint pattern of tracks in a modern bubble chamber to the theory of sub-atomic particles is far longer and more complex.[19]

Some of these points are trivial, and we can usually obtain the agreement of scientists about how to relate what we think we see to the real world. But sometimes not. We have already seen how Western scientists only began to notice sunspots and comets among the planets once their theories allowed that the heavens could indeed change. Few people would today argue for the absolute divide between theory and observation. The way in which we observe the world is inextricably linked to the theories which we already hold about the world.

Realism

How important is the distinction between theory and observation? The fact that theoretical factors always influence our observations does not tell us anything about our ability to penetrate beyond the things we observe into the murky world of unobservables. We cannot directly see atoms, and even if powerful scanning electron microscopes can deliver fuzzy pictures of what their operators assure us are indeed individual atoms, this says very little about the truth of basic atomic theory. To take the issue further, and demand to see an electro-magnetic field, would simply be to make clear that we have failed to understand the nature of physical theory.

Empiricists will accept this position as a statement of theoretical limitation on the scope of science. Theories, and the theoretical entities which they describe are useful 'instruments', they simplify our calculations and help us to generate predictions; nothing more. Realists claim that it is possible to bridge the gap between observables and unobservables. They claim that the whole scientific enterprise, its success and growth, can give us confidence that our theories provide more or less reliable descriptions of the unobservable world underlying what we see.

The issue of realism in science may be similar to the question of fundamentalism or the 'literal' interpretation of the Bible in theology. For most of the time in which the Bible has been valued questions of how it was true were simply not asked. Only when the modern world began to present challenges to traditional authorities did it become important or even possible to frame questions about the truth of the Bible. In a similar way, perhaps, early scientists used their insights about the world without asking detailed questions about what a theory represented or why it worked.

It is easy to give a naive statement of scientific realism:

> [T]he picture which science gives us of the world is a true one faithful in its details, and the entities postulated in science really exist: the advances of science are discoveries, not inventions.[20]

Our intuitive instincts must, however, be modified a little to take account of the fact that science is constantly changing and has yet to reach its goals. Nonetheless this intuitive definition does point in the right direction. For the realist science is a story about what really *is*, so that scientific activity is an enterprise of discovery not invention.

Problems for realism

As we noted earlier, realism remains a very popular philosophy, at least in part, because it ventures an overarching explanation for science and the theories of science. This empiricism categorically refuses to attempt. Realism provides reassurance that what we are attempting does have meaning. Given its optimistic appeal, why is realism not universally accepted?

One of the most unsettling insights of the philosophy of science uses a rather frightening name to conceal a simple but important truth. *The pessimistic meta-induction* as it is grandly called, starts by recalling that all theories so far propounded in the history of science have been wrong. They all looked persuasive when they were set out; often they replaced another theory because they explained more than the old theory, or explained the same facts in a more elegant way. If they were genuinely scientific theories, they had their usefulness and often made predictions about the behaviour of some part of the natural world that were later confirmed. But they were wrong.

They were wrong because they were all later replaced by better theories, which made more powerful predictions. These later theories were in their turn eventually replaced. The history of science is littered with the corpses of dead theories. And if something has always happened in the past, we have every reason to suppose that the same will be true of our current theories (by the use of induction, hence the name; *meta*-induction because what is being described is an hypothesis *beyond* our everyday experience). This is simply to restate the insight which we used at the beginning of this chapter: every undergraduate physicist knows more and better physics than Newton himself.

Empiricists have often used this insight to insist that we can have no confidence in the truth of the theoretical frameworks which describe the world, and certainly no confidence in the 'metaphysical' truth which realists claim lie behind the theories and give them unity and coherence. Philosophers have no difficulty in showing that a theory that is only a little bit wrong is, philosophically speaking, just as false as one that is totally misguided. This is not dissimilar to the old problem of the slow watch. My watch is a minute slow, therefore it never tells the correct time. Your watch has stopped; it will be precisely correct twice in each 24 hours. This theory is approximate, it certainly contains errors and it will be replaced (when a better theory is available). Strictly speaking, therefore, it is false, *but it is also useful*.

Such a dilemma poses no problem for the instrumentalist, who does not waste time over the question of truth. These considerations, the instrumentalist might remark, only go to show how right I was to deny that science had a mission to explain, and modestly to restrict the aim of science to prediction.

Apart from becoming scientific fundamentalists, and arbitrarily declaring that our present theories are correct, there is no escape from this pessimistic conclusion. If we look at the development of theories, however, we shall see a pattern which is more interesting than that first suggested because more varied. We shall confirm our initial impression that all theories are sooner or later replaced, but on closer inspection it becomes obvious that theories in some areas of science are replaced much more frequently than those in other areas.[21]

The basic outlines of atomic theory, or the theory of infectious diseases, have stood the test of time. However, even well-established theories do change; they need to be modified by new observations. The realist has an instinctive explanation for this. Science progresses by moving nearer to the truth. In the early stages of studying new subjects, scientists may cast around for wildly different theories in order to understand even the basic outlines of the phenomena. Later broad explanations will be established which only need small modifications. Occasionally it turns out that the overall theory is misconceived and it is replaced.

The situation in cosmology over the last fifty years may provide an illustration. Observations made in the 1930s suggested that the galaxies were all moving away from each other at great speed. This needed an explanation where previously scientists had simply assumed that the universe had always been in the same condition. Various theories were proclaimed, including the steady state creation theory and the Big Bang. More detailed observations seemed to rule out the steady state theory and confirm the Big Bang. When recent experiments suggested that individual stars seemed older than the whole universe, raising serious questions for the Big Bang theory, the response of the cosmologists was not to abandon the theory but instead to look for suitable modifications to explain the discrepancy. What would have meant the abandonment of the theory even thirty years ago now simply means hard work and recalculation for the scientists. A realist would not see this as an example of the irrationality of scientists in continuing to hold to a discredited theory for sociological reasons. It would be claimed instead as an example of the general tendency of science gradually to draw closer to the truth.

Unfortunately, philosophers find it hard to distinguish between what is false and what is almost true (old comments about being a little bit pregnant spring to mind). Once Newton's theory was replaced, most scientists instinctively understood that their theories could not claim to be absolutely true, and yet many could not simply follow the instrumentalist position that theories were no more than useful tools. Recently philosophers of science who wish to retain some version of realism have developed concepts such as *verisimilitude* and *approximate truth* in order to describe the scientific enterprise more accurately. The absolute distinction of 'If not true, then false' is abandoned for the comparative 'Closer to the truth than . . .' To make such definitions philosophically watertight is exceedingly difficult, but they do provide for many people a definition of science which is intuitively more satisfying than that of the instrumentalist.[22]

The best explanation

Another approach open to realists is the so-called *inference to the best explanation*. What does a scientist do when faced with a problem? First, get to know the evidence, then turn it over in the mind and tentatively think of a number of possible explanations. How well do any of these explanations fit the evidence, are there any tests to discriminate between one hypothesis and another?

My computer screen went blank during the writing of this chapter. What caused the problem? A fault in the machine? The plug working loose from its socket? An overload causing the circuit breaker to trip? This is the usual explanation in my house, which is full of too many working kettles, fires and washing machines. Or was there an interruption in the main supply? This is possible but has been very rare in recent times. A certain amount of confirmation is available, because the circuit breaker leaves the lights unaffected and I notice that they have also failed. On this occasion it seems as if the unlikely explanation provides the best fit with the facts. A few moments later a neighbour rings to enquire if our electricity has also failed. The inference is confirmed.

Many philosophers have little confidence in the concept of inference to the best explanation. They point out that it has always been the stock in trade of detective story writers. The words of Sherlock Holmes ring in our ears: 'How often have I said to you that when you have eliminated the impossible, whatever remains, *however improbable*, must be the truth?' But is science really a detective story? In a story a certain number of facts, pieces of evidence, must be explained, and the master detective will arrive at a theory which must be true because it explains them all. Real life suggests that we can rarely know with certainty which pieces of evidence are relevant, nor can we rely on the satisfying confession, which so often follows the exposition of the detective's theory, to prove the case.[23]

Inference to the best explanation assumes a closed world, with a limited number of relevant facts and an equally limited number of possible explanations, one of which must be true. Only under such conditions can we rely upon its conclusions. The real world of real science is usually open to an infinite number of 'facts' about which we can construct an infinite number of theories. All we can be sure about our 'solution' to the problem is that it is the best that is so far available.

Van Fraassen uses the analogy of natural selection to show how little inference to the best explanation can prove. The scientific jungle, he suggests, is, like nature, 'red in tooth and claw'.[24] Theories will survive until ones better adapted to their particular niche appear when the less able will be killed off in the hostile environment. The analogy is not perfect, but it does suggest that just as Darwin's original theory proved a more powerful scientific tool than Paley's argument from design, in the same way better theories *naturally* prosper without the need to invoke the metaphysical assumptions of the inference to the best explanation.

The critical realist will accept much of the above argument. Real science in the real world is certainly not simply a matter of solving puzzles, but nonetheless scientists do use inference. Michael Banner persuasively describes Darwin's own work as a wonderful example of inference to the best explanation.[25] Darwin works by piling fact upon fact, until the rearranged picture that he has painted seems far more persuasive – to most scientists at any rate – than a scientific theory of special creation. As Darwin himself remarks, the whole book is one long argument, by which he seeks to persuade his readers, rather than the demonstration of a proof.

This is the key to the difference between critical realists and their opponents. For those who oppose inference to the best explanation, whether instrumentalists or creationists – strange bedfellows, but for once united here! – the aim is proof. For the critical realist, the aim is explanatory power. Inference to the best explanation *proves* nothing, but coupled with a critical realism it helps to *justify* the amazing explanatory power of science.

More than one explanation

A similar argument is provided by the fact that all theories are *underdetermined*. For any set of 'facts' that we wish to explain there will always be a number of different, and equally valid, possible explanations. Think of the proportion of an iceberg under water: the behaviour of the fraction that we see is dependent on the unseen bulk of ice. Or of the unconscious mind: in ways that we often find hard to predict, the unconscious mind profoundly affects, or even determines, the actions of the conscious subject.

Scientifically, it is always possible to envisage other theories that will explain the same facts as our chosen theory. A scientist will naturally have chosen a simple and economic theory, but this may be the one situation where reality is in fact more complex. Whatever the individual circumstances, in any situation, the philosopher can prove that the scientifically accepted theory is not the only one that fits the facts.

As we have seen, the occasional overthrow of preferred theories in the history of science shows that even long-established theories have no guarantee of truthfulness, but the philosophical point is quite general. No theory can ever be proved to be the only possible theory. An empiricist would find this to be a powerful argument against realism. If theories describe the real state of the real world, how can they ever be replaced? The critical realist will defend the position by reminding us that it was never claimed that the theories were true, simply that, all other things being equal, they were likely to be approximations to the truth. Again the distinction must be drawn between what can be proved to be true and what is a reasonable explanation. The first half of a remark of Einstein's is well known; the second part deserves equal attention: 'Subtle is the Lord, but he is not malicious.'

Realists will not be dismayed by the lack of watertight proof, or by the objection that different sorts of explanation seem to be appropriate in different circumstances. Indeed, sometimes it seems that no rational explanation is possible: quantum mechanics has always worried philosophers in this respect. Instead, realists will tend to reiterate the fundamental question: Why does science work? If, for a moment we accept the instrumentalist's description of theories as simply tools for generating predictions, we will still wish to ask why the tools are so powerful. The classic empiricist answer that they work because they work does not seem intellectually satisfying, or perhaps we should say that those who are satisfied by such explanations become instrumentalists, those who are not become realists! Most realists will suggest that theories are such powerful tools precisely because the realist account is true and that theories are gradually converging, not without false starts and the occasional error, upon an approximate description of the real state of the real world. Realists often go on to claim that realism is the only philosophy that doesn't make the success of science a miracle.[26]

Representing and intervening

We have tried above to justify realism in an abstract way. Ian Hacking in *Representing and Intervening* suggests a much more practical approach. For Hacking, we know something is real when we use it. So, following his example, the electron gains a particular reality not when we perform experiments to demonstrate its existence or describe its properties. Experiments can always be mistaken and their results can derive from a combination of unsuspected causes. Instead, we demonstrate the reality of the electron when, without thinking, we use electrons in our experiments upon other things.

> Experimental work provides the strongest evidence for scientific realism. This is not because we test hypotheses about entities. It is because entities that in principle cannot be 'observed' are regularly manipulated to produce a new phenomena and to investigate other aspects of nature. They are tools, instruments not for thinking but for doing ... The vast majority of experimental physicists are realists about some theoretical entities, namely the ones they *use* ... [E]ngineering, not theorizing, is the best proof of scientific realism about entities.[27]

Workmen take for granted the trustworthiness of their tools. Hacking appeals to our instinctive belief that to touch and feel is the proof of reality. 'Unless I see the mark of the nails in his hands, and put my finger in the mark of the nails, and my hand in his side, I will not believe' (John 20.25).

The reality of realism

It must be emphasized that the realism defended here is not a simple realism. Our theories do not describe the real world. Neither the models nor the mathematics are actually supposed to be final descriptions of the world. The history of science with its continual replacement of theories demonstrates that we must sit loosely to any particular theory. Nonetheless *critical realism* claims that the ideas of verisimilitude and approximate truth, however difficult to formulate, are the correct way forward. Scientists can have confidence that their theories are, on the whole, coming ever closer to a description of the state of the real world.

To believe in scientific realism may be somewhat similar to believing in the authority of the Bible. Almost all Christians believe in the authority of the Bible, but there is no consensus as to how that authority operates (via direct dictation, or the work of the Holy Spirit, or human reflection on divine action, for example) or what, exactly, it represents (absolute law, persuasive power or incomparable example?). We have already seen a difference between those who would tend to emphasize the reality of *theories*, a position perhaps particularly popular among philosophers of science, and those who would tend to emphasize the reality of *things*, a position claimed to be popular among experimental scientists, who it is suggested *know* the reality of the things they work with. But the distinctions do not end there. Mary Hesse points out that physicists working on particle theories tend to see the reality of their work in the mathematics. She claims that they do not doubt the reality of what they are working with, but rarely attempt to refer the maths to any traditional model. Hence, she wishes to call herself a *substantial realist* rather than a *structural realist*. Hesse's realism cannot be tied to the reality of *either* theories or entities. There have even been suggestions that all forms of *rational realism* miss the point because they are too analytic. It is claimed that even science relies on symbol and narrative – hence we should use the terms *symbolic*, *mythic* or *meta-narrative realism*![28] Given such complexity we must rest content with the assertion that the realist is one who demands that science is in the business of providing explanations as well as generating predictions.

The study of the philosophy of science has led us to reassert the value of a qualified, but genuine, realism. This tentative conclusion must now be tested against the questions of the sociologists, whom we will encounter in the next chapter, before we come to draw any firm conclusions.

Chapter 5

Making Science – Sociology and the Claims of 'Truth'

When we outlined the history of the relationship between science and religion we saw a complex picture emerge where no single metaphor can describe the relationship adequately. The nearest we can come to a simple picture may be that of science as growing up: from the very fragile beginnings of early modern science, nurtured at least in part by a Christian culture, through the difficulties of adolescence – including teenage rebellions – to a more mature adulthood. Science all the time growing in strength and in confidence, as techniques gradually expanded to explore different parts of the natural world. At the same time religion, or theology, undergoing the painful readjustment familiar to any parent as dependency is replaced by a new equality. Indeed it might often seem as if the newly adult sciences no longer need the support of their formerly strong, but now ageing and weakening partner, theology.

By the end of the nineteenth century, science – or the various different sciences – seemed to be powerful enough to attempt to arbitrate across the whole sphere of human experience. Henceforth, science would determine what was true and what false.

To Thomas Huxley and his followers such a situation was both necessary and natural. Science would sweep away vested interests and simply rely on the evidence to determine what was true and what false. And on the basis of true belief, a better world would be constructed:

> I say, on the strength of what is happening today, on a careful study of the evolution of conduct and fine sentiment during

the last hundred years, that the future, which is so dark for religion holds out to us the promise of that reign of justice and charity of which prophets have dreamed despairingly for more than two thousand years.[1]

That was written by an ex-monk, Joseph McCabe, who had become disillusioned with the church and joined the rationalist cause. He was surely unlucky to have published his optimistic creed of human progress in 1914. Even before the First World War, however, it was clear to most interested parties that solutions to the problems of the world would not all be discovered by science, and universally applied like a new set of scientific theories. The methods of science could not simply be expanded across all fields of human interest and culture, casually displacing the attempts of philosophy and religion to understand the human condition. Science was not simply Huxley's 'trained and organized common sense'; it was both more limited and more complex than that.

Once we begin to understand that science has its own methods and structures – which are not, as Huxley and his colleagues claimed, self-evident and universal – then we may also begin to wonder if science itself can be studied as a human construction like other parts of culture. Already, back in the 1880s, Samuel Butler had labelled scientists as the new high priests, and pictured scientific theories as expedient conventions, just like those of morality or religion.[2]

When we looked at the history of science questions were raised about why science began its explosive growth in early modern Europe; about the role of the church; and why theories were formulated at the time they were. In considering evolution we noticed Darwin's roots and sources, and the many influences upon him, some of which had little to do with science. Such issues are not important if 'science' simply emerges from its setting with its theories complete: unquestioned and universal truths. But if 'truth' is not simply what science knows, then we will need to examine these questions in more detail.

Our introduction to the philosophy of science has suggested that this is indeed the case and that science is not in any simple way the unique method of acquiring truth about the world that it is sometimes claimed to be.

Religious people and theologians are used to historians and sociologists asking similar questions about the form of their beliefs, but it can come as a shock to find sociologists categorizing science in the same way as religion. Are both 'belief systems' which their followers choose to adopt, science succeeding Christianity as the dominant belief of the West?

Before we begin to explore these issues a warning may be necessary. I have tried to allow the sociologists of science speak in their own terms. They have significant things to say, and their arguments can stand for themselves. However, as we shall see at the end of the chapter, I do not believe that the sociologists have yet succeeded in establishing their case so persuasively as they themselves believe. But we should not turn too quickly to their weaknesses without giving their case a proper hearing.

Constructing reality: sociology and postmodernism

David Bloor is one of the founders of what is known as the 'Strong Programme' of the sociology of science. In his influential book, *Knowledge and Social Imagery*, he ends a response to his many critics by retelling a story from the history of theology. In the same way that Ferdinand Baur and the Tübingen school tried to explain the doctrines of the church in terms of everyday political and social causes, Bloor claims, so the Strong Programme of sociology tries to understand science. And in just the same way as Baur was attacked in the nineteenth century, so the sociologists are attacked for disloyalty to the most cherished dogmas of our time.[3]

This chapter may seem to take us on a strange journey. The Strong Programme's critics have called it 'irrelevant' and a 'failure', 'preposterous', 'obscurantist' and 'recycling classical textbook mistakes'. In America a major debate known as the 'Science Wars' rages around similar issues.[4] The parallel with theology which Bloor draws should alert us to the importance of the issues we are discussing. This chapter describes a battle for the soul of science, and for that reason alone the story has a place here. In retelling the story of Baur, David Bloor claims the Tübingen theologian as his ancestor in the study of how society comes to acquire its knowledge of anything, and laments that ultimately Baur's influence was crushed under the weight of bigotry and reaction. He devoutly hopes that his fate will not be the same!

The claim made by Bloor and many contemporary sociologists is that both theology and science are the same sort of disciplines. They are not alternative, or competing, ways of describing the world which is how they have usually been understood until now. Instead we should see them as different ways of *constructing* the world in which we live. Some readers may recognize this language as being part of the great *postmodernist* project which seems to touch all aspects of contemporary intellectual life. The final reason for dealing with the subject matter of this chapter in a book such as this is that the new sociology of science forms one of the forerunners of the whole postmodern programme.

Sooner or later all human searches for knowledge must face up to their relation to the truth. In the nineteenth century what the postmodernists call the 'myths' or *narratives* of science seemed self-evidently true. In his helpful book, *A Primer on Postmodernism*, Stanley Grenz identifies two key 'scientific myths'.[5] The first is the myth of liberty. Scientific culture assumes that everyone has a right to knowledge, and that they are only denied access to knowledge by priest or tyrant, both of whom have understood the lesson that knowledge is power. Grenz's second scientific myth is that of knowledge itself. This myth leads us to believe that science will always and inevitably lead the growth and evolution of knowledge.

The success of science meant that in the nineteenth century theology was forced to defend itself in terms considered acceptable in the light of the scientific myths. Hence the work of Baur and many others to attempt to found a scientific theology. The very success of science meant that there was no demand for science to face up to its own relation to the truth until much later. Science was not understood as a myth, but as access to the truth which freed humanity from all myths. Only in the last third of the twentieth century has science been forced to stop and face these same hard questions about itself.

Studying science

It is easy to think that science provides an straightforward explanation for the state of the world, which is self-evident and needs no justification. For many years sociologists used the methods of science, gradually extending their study to all human activities. Eventually the question had to be posed, as to whether science itself was different, or if it too should be subjected to sociological examination.

Looking at the history of science, it is obvious that the growth and success of science did not simply happen. Let us take two examples. When we considered the early history of science, we discussed the claim that one important reason for the rise of science as we know it in the West was Christianity's role in providing a fertile soil in which scientific ideas could be nurtured and developed. A serious claim can be made that science grew in mediaeval Western Europe, rather than Ancient Greece or China or India, because the context of Europe from the thirteenth century onwards provided the stimulus necessary in order to allow the connection and development of ideas, which may have been present in other places, but were never built upon.

We have already looked briefly at our second example. Robert Merton was a pioneer of the sociology of science.[6] Merton considered the explosive growth of science in the seventeenth century and asked why what we now call the Scientific Revolution was concentrated on England, and at that time. He examined the membership of the Royal Society and other early scientific groupings, and claimed that far more Puritans were scientists than should be expected given their number in the total population. He went on to suggest that the religious values of the Puritans influenced the way they conducted their science, and thus help to account for their success. From this very limited study Merton derived his so-called norms of science: universalism, communality, disinterestedness and organized scepticism. He claimed that these were Puritan values which had been carried over into the new science and had proved to be precisely the values necessary for the scientific community to maximize the likelihood of achieving its goals.

These examples suggest that if we are to understand science fully, then we will need to look outside science for at least some explanations. Merton's work in particular leads to the idea that in order to understand what it is, for example, that attracts the attention of scientists at one time rather than another, or why science advances faster in one country, or among one particular social grouping, than in other places, then we will need to look at the society in which science is set.

To take another example from Merton, he argues that because England was expanding its overseas possessions and its foreign trade in the seventeenth century, then a great importance was necessarily put on accurate navigation. As Dava Sobel has recently shown, vast sums of money were offered in prizes and great ingenuity shown in seeking to solve the problems associated with navigation. The accurate mapping of the stars and the ability to know the precise time at any point on a voyage were matters not simply of scientific curiosity, but also of great economic and even political importance.[7]

Society has always played a large part in determining which branches of science to study, and within those disciplines which problems to attack. The temper of the age will help to determine how many intelligent people are interested in science – perhaps in seventeenth-century England with the universities closed to dissenters, the intellectual elite of an important and self-confident part of the population found satisfaction in science and technology rather than more traditional learned pursuits.

These factors which affect the development of science clearly arise from outside science itself. It is important to realize, however, that neither of these influences is claimed to affect the content of science. Once society has helped to determine what is to be studied, and how important it is to produce an answer to a particular problem, the shape of the scientific answer is assumed to arise from the work of the scientists alone. We must now ask if this assumption, one of the cornerstones of the traditional picture of science, can possibly be true.

The scientific community

It was probably inevitable that it was in the 1960s that the status of science began seriously to be questioned. In a decade when all sources of authority were threatened, and when it was axiomatic that the new was superior to the old, and the young to their elders, sociologists were hardly likely to lag behind the dominant social trends.

Did science really have an authority that was unique? Why was it special? Could there be a justification for treating one part of intellectual life in a very different way from all others?

At the same time, more academic objections were beginning

to surface. Philosophers had begun to show that there were alternatives to a realist philosophy of science. As we saw in the last chapter, it was possible to describe science in a way which did not depend on the direct connection between science and an objective, real world. The concept of postmodernism was only named in the late 1970s, but here, as we hinted earlier, is one of its most important roots. Science, the epitome of modern rationality, might not after all be built on entirely rational foundations.

In 1962 Thomas Kuhn published *The Structure of Scientific Revolutions*. As we have seen, this book questioned all the previously accepted assumptions about science and its theories. In a narrow sense, by stressing the importance of the scientific community, Kuhn was inviting sociologists to take a close look at science itself. At the most fundamental level, by showing that scientific theories were *in some sense* the construction of the scientific community (and not simply logical inferences or deductions from the facts), Kuhn further invited the sociologists not simply to explain the community, but also to examine the theories of science themselves. Kuhn later modified the degree to which he thought that theories were manufactured by the scientific community, but by then the impetus had already been given to a wholly new sociology of science. One very important feature of Kuhn's study was that the practical and theoretical implications were woven together in a manner that was immediately accessible – although in rather different ways – to both working scientists and sociologists.

Does the study of science need to take account of philosophy? After Kuhn, some sociologists thought that there was a more direct route to understand science:

All the traditional conflicts of epistemology, between realism and instrumentalism, rationalism and empiricism, deductivism, and many more, find expression in endless modifications and combinations, as competing accounts of science. And each such account implies a different foundation for the credibility and authority of science.

This difficulty, however, is illusory. Nearly all of these accounts of science are very heavily idealized, and represent the various utopias of our philosophers and epistemologists rather than what actually goes on in those places which we customarily call laboratories.[8]

What is needed, so this claims runs, are practical, down-to-earth descriptions of what really happens in laboratories. From these descriptions, a new picture of science will emerge, which is very different from the traditional understanding.

Through the laboratory door

It is not very revolutionary to claim that a laboratory is a social community like any other. Scientists perform experiments whilst working in larger or smaller groups, with a more or less obvious hierarchy. Depending on the science involved, they will use more or less expensive equipment. Since about 1970, sociologists have increasingly ventured through the laboratory door. Once inside, they have not simply investigated how the structures of the institution work. Following the opening provided by Kuhn, they have also begun to question the age-old distinction between science and the rest of life. It will be helpful to describe some of their findings before we return to think more deeply about their presuppositions.

Making choices

In 1714 Parliament offered a prize of £20,000 to whoever could come up with the solution to the problem of the accurate determination of longitude at sea, which was necessary for accurate and safe navigation. A Board of Longitude was set up with a mixture of scientific and political members to judge when the money should be awarded. As Dava Sobel has shown, the final awarding of the prize was preceded by years of infighting and politicking between different factions. John Harrison's successful demonstration of the timekeeping method only led to the grudging award of prize money years later.[9]

Today the grants and rewards of science are awarded by Research Councils and large Foundations, but, human nature not having changed greatly in the last two hundred years, the hidden processes remain similar.

A classic piece of research on the awarding of grants by the National Science Foundation in America shows how the very complex mechanism set up to ensure that proposals are fairly examined by competent judges in fact produces results that depend on the chance of which referee happened to be sent which proposal. The distribution of awards is not quite random, most of the best proposals are funded and most of the worst rejected (the study has to rely on the general consensus of scientists as to 'best' and 'worst'). For the larger group of proposals in the middle, however, there is little consistency about the process. Decision making here is like wine-tasting, writes the author of the study, or even choosing the winner in a beauty contest. Given the amount of paperwork that the process generates, tossing a coin would be both quicker and cheaper for everyone involved![10]

As we move out of the realm of scientific politics into real science there are still decisions to be made. Modern apparatus is almost always very complex. How is the scientist to decide when the necessary testing of the equipment can finish, and the gathering of real results begin? Usually the answer will be that the apparatus has been properly set up once it has started to produce the results we expect. But this, of course, is in danger of becoming a circular argument. There are safeguards: it is customary to make benchmark measurements on calibrated samples. Against this, those very odd readings which were obtained when the experiment was first switched on and have now been discarded may having been telling us of some unsuspected new discovery, or perhaps the normal readings which we are producing now that the apparatus is functioning 'properly' are simply being generated because we have fiddled with the equipment until it gives us what we want to find.

Science in practice: the proof of relativity

In their book, *The Golem – what everyone should know about science*, the sociologists Harry Collins and Trevor Pinch discuss a number of scientific experiments with the aim of explaining to a general readership what really happens in science. One of the most interesting parts of the book is their description of Eddington's 'proof' of the theory of relativity.[11]

Eddington's experiment is one of the classic experiments of the twentieth century. It involved the measurement of the movement of the apparent position of stars near the sun due to the bending of light by the sun's gravitational field. Einstein's theory of relativity suggested that the light would appear to bend. It is not usually realized that the old Newtonian theory also predicted the bending of light, but by only about half the amount that Einstein expected. Arthur Eddington set out to test this apparently simple difference between old and new theories, but at the time of his experiment (1918 when the experiment was performed, and a year later when the results were announced) no one understood the implications of the general Theory of Relativity well enough to make a definitive prediction.

The measurements themselves were difficult to perform, as they could only be made by observing stars very close to the sun during a total eclipse. Total eclipses of the sun are few and far between, and when they happen only cover a small part of the earth's surface. The impatience of scientists was such that they could not wait for an eclipse to occur above an established telescope, which would have been properly calibrated. Instead telescopes were moved to Brazil and to an island off the coast of Africa where rough and ready corrections had to be made to compensate for the expected errors. All this meant that it was difficult to make the necessary corrections for the movement of the earth, and also difficult to take the necessary reference photographs at night to match the pictures taken during the eclipse, so that the apparent movement could be measured. Even to observe the stars there must be a clear sky. As it turned out, clouds stopped a full set of photographs being taken of the eclipse.

A total of twenty-eight photographic plates were obtained by Eddington, only one series of eight being of good quality. The remainder were a series of eighteen poor plates from Brazil, and two very poor plates from Africa. These two pictures were the only ones that Eddington himself obtained; all the others came from his colleagues in Brazil. Eddington's two poor plates gave about the correct answer if Einstein's theory was correct, and if the calculations which Einstein had used were also correct. On the other hand they were very poor in quality, and Eddington seems to have used a complicated method to obtain his answer which depended in part on *assuming* that Einstein was correct, the very thing which he had set out to prove. The good set of prints from Brazil gave about the correct figure, although the result was numerically a little large. The long series of eighteen poor plates gave a answer which supported Newton's theory rather than Einstein's. Eddington, however, decided that a 'systematic error' must have occurred in preparing these photographs and so discarded these results.

Collins and Pinch describe Eddington's experiment in detail because, they claim, their book sets out to describe 'how science really works and ... how much authority to grant to experts'. They claim to help readers to understand how scientists must exercise judgment at each step of their experimental work. What may, at the time of the experiment itself, have been a finely balanced decision, soon comes to be understood – in the mind of the public, and even of the scientists involved – as a decisive proof. The authors suggest that 'science needs heroic moments of proof to maintain its heroic image'.[12]

The approach taken in *The Golem* is characteristic of the new sociologists of science. Their assumptions have recently come under strong counter attack in the columns of *Nature*, the world's leading scientific journal. Two physicists writing there ask why Collins and Pinch choose only to tell part of the story? Why don't they continue beyond Eddington's original experiment to include the many later – and much more precise – confirmations of relativity? It may be that, at best, the sociologists are only describing a very small part of the scientific process, that moment when the evidence is quite finely balanced between the old and new theories. But, say the physicists, science moves on and better evidence, tipping the balance decisively one way or the other, soon becomes available.[13]

Despite this reasonable criticism, we should not ignore the importance of making choices: in deciding which experiment to perform (or, in deciding which to fund); in deciding which results are relevant; in deciding what it is that we see; and in deciding what the results of an experiment mean. This list is not exhaustive, for example, every time an experiment is written up for a journal, the writers must decide how to present the untidy world of the laboratory in the formal prose of scientific language. Sociologists have described the process as a 'perversion' and 'fiction'.[14] It is simply another place where real choices are made. Finally the journal must decide whether or not to publish the paper. The rigorous system of refereeing of scientific papers means that several people will be involved in the decision, but it cannot guarantee objectivity, only conformity to certain agreed norms.

Learning the skills

We have described Eddington's experiment in detail, but that was an exotic project. What happens day by day in the ordinary laboratory? It will be helpful to give one example, again reported by Harry Collins. In 1970 a group in Canada reported building the first high-powered laser of a particular kind. Once the research was published many other groups set out to copy the original laser. Collins made contact with most of the scientists involved, and was very closely involved with one group which began its work at his own university.[15]

At first glance it might seem that a scientific paper published in one of the journals is like a cooking recipe: it will only be necessary to follow the written instructions and a perfect result will be guaranteed. In fact, none of the groups trying to build the laser produced a working model from the published papers alone. Successful groups needed personal contact and discussion with those who had already succeeded:

> In sum, the flow of knowledge was such that, first, it travelled only where there was personal contact with an accomplished practitioner; second, its passage was invisible so that scientists did not know whether they had the relevant expertize to build a laser until they tried it; and, third, it was so capricious that similar relationships between teacher and learner might or might not result in the transfer of knowledge. These characteristics of the flow of knowledge make sense if a crucial component in laser building ability is 'tacit knowledge'.[16]

Collins suggests that scientific knowledge is transmitted not so much through formal published papers as by the acquisition of *tacit knowledge*. A scientist is like a craftsperson in that much of what is known cannot be written down, but is essential for the continuation of science. This is not a novel thought, but Collins develops his reasoning in some detail through a series of propositions: '[1] Transfer of skill-like knowledge is capricious ... [2] Skill-like knowledge travels best (or only) through accomplished practitioners ... [3] Experimental ability has the character of a skill that can be acquired and developed with practice. Like a skill, it cannot be fully explicated or absolutely established ...

[4] Experimental ability is invisible in its passage and in those who possess it . . . [5] Proper working of the apparatus, parts of the apparatus *and the experimenter* are defined by the ability to take part in producing the proper experimental outcome. Other indicators cannot be found.'[17]

Eventually, by trial and error, Collins' colleagues built a working laser. However, when the team leader moved to a new laboratory, Collins again observed, and indeed actively helped, as he attempted to build a second laser. This time, even though the same person was building a second laser, there were several days of hard work before what should have been a working machine in fact sprang into life. There is nothing unusual in this, any scientist reading the account of the building of the second laser would probably be inclined to think that it started to work much quicker than could have reasonably been expected. However, Collins' point is important: much vital scientific knowledge is not conveyed by the written word through formal papers but passes unseen, and often unrealized by those involved, from expert to apprentice, and even the expert often only discovers by trial and error what is important.

Collins has another proposition about this kind of knowledge transfer in science. He suggests that ignoring this reality, and simply assuming that science is completely described by formal communications such as published papers and equations is catastrophic (his word) for our understanding of science because it gives an entirely erroneous picture to those outside who must rely on scientists' own descriptions.[18]

Repeating experiments

An important assumption underlying the way we understand science is that its results are 'proved' because experiments written up in the scientific journals can easily be repeated by other scientists in different laboratories. Science is unique, runs this claim, because the success of an experiment does not depend on an individual genius, or a particular way of doing things, but is instead open and universal. Traditional definitions of science, as 'trained and organized common sense', for example, rely heavily on such ideas. In the nineteenth century it was common to award disciplines the accolade of being scientific if they were seen to conform in this way: hence, scientific history or even scientific theology (the sort practised by Baur). We have seen that this is not quite the straightforward claim that it pretends to be, but it can also be challenged in a more fundamental way. How often are the experiments reported in the journals actually repeated?

Not very often, according to the sociologists. Occasionally a particular experiment catches the imagination of the scientific community or even the public. In that case laboratories may try to repeat the original findings. The first high-powered lasers described above, or the attempt to produce 'cold fusion' had dozens of imitators. But most experiments are never repeated. A commonly reported remark is that success in repeating an experiment will bring someone else the Nobel prize, and failure only the frustration of wasted time and the endless checking of apparatus for mistakes. Why bother to repeat what someone else has already done? It appears that what usually happens is that an experiment is repeated with subtle (or not so subtle) changes; the new group will attempt to improve upon the original work.

From a theoretical perspective this can lead to problems. To repeat *exactly* what someone has already done is not particularly interesting, and may anyway simply repeat any mistakes made in the original experiment. If a new group builds and uses the same apparatus as has been used before, they may well produce the same results, but perhaps all they are doing is systematically observing some oddity of the apparatus rather than of nature itself. On the other hand if the new experiment is very different from the original and does not work for some reason, then it may always be claimed that it is too different to produce the looked-for result.

This is a similar problem to that encountered in the last section. 'Mere replication' is trivial and uninteresting; genuine novelty may not reproduce the original experiment closely enough to be convincing. We can tighten the screw further: sometimes even falsification, which Popper taught scientists to think of as the decisive, unquestionable test, can be doubted. Perhaps the second experimenter who failed to achieve the expected result was not skilled enough or dedicated enough, or perhaps the apparatus was not working properly. But how can we be sure that the apparatus is working properly unless we find a positive result, but perhaps a positive result cannot be found because the first experimenter has made a mistake ... Harry Collins has christened this, and similar problems, the *Experimenter's Regress*.[19] According to him scientists can always argue their way out of unwanted situations, and there is never an objective answer to stop the regress circling backwards.

A less pessimistic view of the situation is that at every point scientists are forced to exercise judgment and to negotiate with their fellow scientists as to the significance of any particular result. Some experiments *will* be repeated, and the skill of the scientists involved will be to judge what minor modifications enhance or detract from the strength of the repetition. In a little known but superbly designed experiment at the end of the nineteenth century Oliver Lodge built a huge (and dangerous) apparatus involving spinning metal flywheels simply to confirm the negative result of Michaelson and Morley's experiment on the aether. We might note, however, that Lodge's experiment is now forgotten.[20]

Those less impressed by the theoretical problems unearthed by the sociologists will also point out that much of science involves the daily repetition of what were once controversial experiments, but are now so much taken for granted that they are no longer noticed. This situation is similar to that which Ian Hacking describes concerning the reality of unobservable entities, such as the electron, which we noted in the previous chapter.

Although sometimes framed in extreme language, which is therefore difficult to defend, what sociologists like Collins help us to understand is that there are no fixed rules telling us when it is important to repeat an experiment, or what constitutes an experimental confirmation, that can always be applied to any situation. Many scientists and philosophers assume that science possesses a comprehensive set of rules which determine everything. In fact, science is more complicated than that. The consensus which does genuinely emerge around significant experiments is the result of negotiation as well as demonstration.

Making practical judgments

At first sight, it might have seemed as if the philosophical problems of science could be resolved simply by turning to the facts, to the raw data of experiment which form the bedrock of science.

But, as should be becoming clear by now, scientists bring their ordinary humanity into their laboratories, they make good and bad choices just like everyone else. They also bring a set of philosophical and other presuppositions which they use continually in their work – telepathy does not occur, therefore all parapsychological experiments are flawed; Professor X is a good experimental scientist therefore his results can probably be trusted, unlike Professor Y.

At every turn we are forced to concede that Popper's view of science as uniquely and simply obeying logical rules and submitting its whole substance meekly to the test of falsification is at best an impossible ideal, and at worst seriously misleading. In a significant study, Michael Mulkay asked a group of scientists what they thought of Popper's philosophy of science. Most knew of his work, which is in itself remarkable as working scientists often treat philosophy with suspicion. It may be Popper's attempt to provide a clear distinction between science and non-science that they find attractive. Mulkay discovered, however, that scientists tended simply to pay lip service to Popper's values, or to assume that they represented the best in normal scientific practice. Mulkay's conclusion is that meaning of even a straightforward term such as 'falsification' depends on judgment and context. All rules need judgment when applied to specific situations. A philosophical description is only useful after the science has been completed, when it will be used to justify the published results. Continuing scientific work which has not yet been completed is too specific for the generalized rules of philosophy to apply.[21]

Our provisional conclusion at the end of this section, which has sought to look through the laboratory door, is that real science is much more nearly described by Michael Polanyi's picture of skilled knowledge than by Popper's austere philosophy of falsification. What Polanyi did not perhaps fully appreciate is that when we acknowledge that scientists must bring their humanity into the laboratory, we cannot simply praise the need for the skilled exercise of judgment. We also allow into the laboratory a host of all too human factors which the old ideals of science had sought to keep at bay.

Science as it really is?

It will be useful to summarize the sometimes disturbing – sometimes outlandish – claims of the radical sociologists of science in a series of questions:

Are the philosophers wrong?

In the same way that anyone else might carry with them a card indicating allergies, or particular medical needs, the physicist Murray Gell-Mann is reported to carry with him at all times a doctor's prescription forbidding him to argue with philosophers on the grounds that it could be dangerous for his health.[22] Philosophers are an easy target both for scientists and sociologists. In establishing a new discipline the sociologists of science have tended to write in black and white terms, which can be easily dismissed by their critics, but their criticism of the traditional philosophy of science does raise difficult underlying questions.

The first part of this chapter has aired the sociologists' claim that many of the traditional assumptions about the way science is performed are simply wrong. Experimental decisions are not governed by fixed rules, but are instead the products of the exercise of skill, and of complex negotiations between scientists. An important debate rages as to whether and how published experiments are either confirmed or falsified by repetition. Even when apparent falsification occurs judgment must often be used to decide whether or not the original results really have been falsified. The pure objectivity of science is replaced by involved scientists and their skill, judgment and negotiating ability. Such qualities are inevitably formed differently in particular individuals, in part by the specific contexts in which they live. They cannot simply be learnt at will during scientific training.

Public construction and private chaos?

For all the disagreements between them, traditional philosophies of science assume a more or less smooth progress from the real world, or at least from the facts, or the experimental data, to the published results and theories of science. Part of the business of sociology, however, is to put the process that takes place in the laboratory under the microscope. Looking at the details of the actual process of science forces us to face hard questions. How does the smooth and seemingly effortless presentation of a scientific paper arise from the chaos of a laboratory? This leads directly to our next question.

Do scientists 'discover' the world or 'make' it?

A favourite description of science among the sociologists is that it is a *social construction*. Scientists are involved in the business of *Changing Order*, to borrow the title of an influential text.[23] For the moment let us make this claim in its strongest form.

Experiments generate confusing and contradictory results. The scientist decides which to 'see' and which to ignore. This process of decision goes far beyond the relatively uncontroversial recognition that all facts are theory-laden, and firmly asserts that facts are recognized as significant (*created*) by the scientist, whose vision has been shaped not only by scientific training as a competent craftsperson, but also by the politics and reward systems of science, and by the broader outlook of the whole of society.

A society is not simply more or less hospitable to the growth of science, it *makes* a science in its own image. Hence science is a social construction. Scientists, unconsciously, but at the behest of society, create or change the way in which the world is ordered. The natural order is not discovered but imposed upon an unformed chaos. One of the standard introductory textbooks on sociology discusses the sociology of science in a chapter with the title: 'Knowledge, Belief and Religion'.[24] For the author all knowledge, scientific or religious, has the same status.

Are theories in competition?

Support for this radical position can be found in the philosophical discovery, which we noted in the last chapter, that all theories are *underdetermined*. We saw there that any particular set of 'facts' can always be explained by more than one theory. This is a perfectly general philosophical conclusion, which does not depend on the theory involved. It receives obvious support, however, from episodes such as the replacement of Newtonian physics by the Theory of Relativity. The many instances which Thomas

Kuhn discusses in *The Structure of Scientific Revolutions* do seem to provide historical examples of underdetermination. One of Kuhn's fundamental claims is that the scientific community exchanges one paradigm for another partly at least on non-scientific grounds.[25] If there is no foolproof way for philosophy to lay down rules to tell the scientist how to judge between theories, then it is obvious that the judgments involved must make use of non-scientific factors.

Is science a special case?

Robert Merton's generation of sociologists still stood in some awe of science. They used the methods of science in their work as they considered the effects of social influences on science, and were naturally reluctant to be seen to question the authority of their own tools. They were clear that these social influences were only at the edges of the scientific process. The speed with which science developed, and the particular problems studied were proper subjects for sociologists. The central core of science, its *cognitive content*, was left untroubled by their work.

Inexorably, the attention of sociology moved towards the cognitive 'centre'. Our examination of the laboratory showed that decisions made there must involve the social context both of the laboratory itself, and of the scientist as a member of a wider society. These extra-scientific influences are often described as *micro-level social influences*. Whether or not even larger, ideological influences determine the content of science is more difficult to determine.

The so-called *Strong Programme* of the sociology of science claims to detect ideological influences in the way theories are formed. Does the Uncertainty principle, for example, derive from the insecurity of the Weimar republic; would the content of modern physics be very different if Heisenberg had not lived through that period?[26] It is abundantly clear that Darwin was helped to formulate his theory by the progressive, evolutionary temper of Victorian England, but was the content of the theory *determined* by the need of that society to believe in competition and 'the survival of the fittest' rather than a more co-operative model, which might have fitted the 'facts' equally well?[27]

David Bloor developed his *Principle of Symmetry* as an uncompromising statement of the Strong Programme. Those who are investigating the process of the development of science must learn to give equal treatment to ideas which later come to be seen as true and those which come to be seen as false. The aim of the sociologist should be to explain *why* something is eventually accepted as 'true' strictly in terms of known social processes. Thus the sociologist must accept that all possible answers are potentially acceptable or 'symmetric'. The sociologist can never appeal to the natural world as being the final arbiter, or as providing an explanation for the content of science. It is hardly surprising that this claim has been persistently attacked by critics.

There is a genuine problem at issue here. Bloor's claim is that the study of the development of science must proceed like all good modern history, and ask questions in terms of the knowledge available at the time under consideration; his critics accept that *history* must be written in this way, but claim that science can be justified by the use of hindsight to provide definitive proof concerning accurate or misguided theories. Bloor looks for social factors to explain the growth and success of science; his critics claim that science succeeds because it describes, with increasing accuracy, the real world.[28]

Can the sociology of science be scientific?

By questioning the 'scientific' basis of science, are the sociologists sawing off the branch on which they are sitting? Or, is their method the only way in which to understand knowledge in today's world? We can do no more here than to note both the contradictory nature of the exercise, and its intimate connection with postmodernism. Michael Mulkay, in a serious attempt to be humorous about the implications of such a programme, catches the complex issues involved:

> [A] paradox of the sociology of Science is that its scientific conclusions are formed within the cultural confines of Science, but the culture of Science requires that Science be understood from a detached, external perspective. It follows, therefore, that if sociologists are to understand Science scientifically, they must adopt a *non*-scientific perspective. The final twist, of course, is that Science either denies entirely the legitimacy

of such external forms of knowledge or treats them as inferior.[29]

People who consciously choose to adopt a relativist position are not sawing away carelessly at the branch on which they are sitting, they are merely acknowledging the fact that their own position is as culturally dependent as that of the next person. The relativist claim is that the rationalist's absolute position can be demolished piece by piece, until the rationalist is forced to retreat into *belief* in the virtue of rationalism, which cannot be proved *rationally*. A well-known defence of the relativist case ends by drawing a picture of the relativist observing the rationalist performing rites at the shrine of rationalism, and speculating on the cultural reasons for the persistence of that particular (*irrational*) belief![30]

The postmodernist or relativist does not suggest that there is a solution to this problem. There is indeed no set of implicit shared values or assumptions which the defenders of rationality can turn to as absolute, or can defend rationally. In the end, for the relativist, it all comes down to preference. We prefer the values and beliefs of our own group against those of others.

What about the physical world?

By now it may seem as if the sociologists have completely reversed the traditional picture of science. Instead of being unique, science is in fact subject to external influences in the same way as all human activities. The scientific picture is simply part of the reality we construct. This is, of course, one of the postmodern articles of faith:

> From the perspective of deconstruction, there is nothing upon which we can ground an argument for evolutionary biology as opposed to fundamentalist creationism, since both are discourses, with their blindnesses and their insights, and neither one can be said to be more or less accurate than the other, there being no pathway open from the text to the world.[31]

Traditionally, the business of science *has been* to construct pathways from the world to the text. We have seen that such a progress is complex, but is it impossible? There are large philosophical issues at stake here. Before we address these directly, however, it is necessary to ask what to a postmodernist will appear to be a hopelessly old-fashioned question: Does the physical world influence the content of science, or is the whole edifice entirely a human construction? In the next section we will investigate the claim that we can still believe in the rationality of science. What is necessary is to hold in balance on the one side all the complexities that we now understand are involved in the fabrication of scientific understanding, and on the other the claim that science is also formed by contact with a 'real' world beyond our social constructions.

Making science

Given the popularity of the postmodernist analysis of our condition, and its obvious links with the new sociology of science, it would be easy to assume that the final word has been spoken. It is indeed important to note just how much has been gained from the radical studies conducted since 1970. It is now almost uncontroversial to emphasize the importance of external influences on science.

To accept this much is not to denigrate science, but instead to understand its achievements more thoroughly. The Principle of Symmetry has proved a useful tool for historians and sociologists, who may no longer simply assume that the truth will be successful, but have instead to describe *how* scientists arrive at successful theories. Similarly, the assertion of the relativists that rationality and realism may not logically be proved can be seen less as a threatening statement to be disputed, than as a liberating truth. A belief in rationality and realism is indeed just that: a *belief*, but as I shall hope to demonstrate it may be the most reasonable belief for scientists and philosophers alike to hold.

In *Making Science*, the American sociologist, Stephen Cole, surveys the situation. He notes the success of what he calls constructive sociologists (that is, those who believe in the social construction of knowledge), and shows that many of his own studies support their position. Cole conducted the survey we considered earlier which demonstrated the large role of chance or luck in the awarding of scientific research grants. In another study he has shown that there is wide disagreement between scientists about the meaning of their work, just as wide in fact as that between the notoriously argumentative social scientists themselves.

Accepting this, Cole asks, how we can account for the large measure of consensus that is the supreme achievement of the natural sciences? Why, for instance, was Crick and Watson's famous paper on the double helix as the structure for DNA almost immediately accepted as true by the entire scientific community? Sociological factors ought to have suggested that the community reject it: Crick and Watson were relativity young and unknown, they had no particular authority within the community, and other more prestigious researchers (including at least one Nobel prize winner) were working on alternative solutions to the problem. Applying the Principle of Symmetry, the other groups ought to have rejected the double helix in order to advance their own ideas, or in deference to the scientific authorities. In fact, Crick and Watson's paper was quickly accepted into the scientific canon. Cole suggests that those who understand science as simply another social construction must seek to explain cases such as this.

When the traditional philosophies of positivism or realism were dominant, scientific consensus did not need an explanation. According to these philosophies, scientists agree because they are describing in a straightforward manner observations made, or the state of the real world. But if science is simply a social construction, then the constructivists must explain *consensus*. Surely the *interests* of scientists, which play so large a part in the new sociological descriptions, naturally pull scientists apart. How do they ever reach agreement, and – a particularly hard question – how it is that they sometimes reach it so quickly?

Cole pictures science as consisting of a *core* and a *frontier*. This model is similar to that of Kuhn and Lakatos, but different in detail. Core knowledge is what the scientific community understands to be true. Core theories do change from time to time, but at any one time are treated as correct. They also usually contain some ambiguities, which allow for new programmes of research to flourish. It is here especially that the creativity and development of science are generated.

The frontier contains *claims* to truth, but little consensus between scientists as to which truth claims are in fact to be understood as correct. At the frontier social influences will be important, but even here they should not be overestimated. When scientists consider the possible solutions to a given problem, 'evidence from the empirical world' and 'logical procedures' have an important role in ruling out most of the conceivable solutions. At the frontier, however, evidence and logic alone are usually unable to distinguish between the remaining possible solutions as proposed by competing groups of scientists.[32] We saw earlier that critics of *The Golem*, and other radical analyses of scientific experiments, made a similar point.

The core of science is very different. It is small but crucially important as it represents the consensus of the scientific community as to the best approximation to truth that can be achieved at the present time. The new sociologists are right to emphasize the chaotic nature of frontier science (Cole's choice of the word 'frontier' is an apt one), but they are wrong to generalize from the laboratory to the central core of science.

It is true that, as knowledge passes from the frontier to the core, non-scientific factors continue to be at work. Eminent members of the scientific community, for example, have a role as gatekeepers and evaluators in deciding which work is exemplary and which unimportant. At every stage subjective decisions are involved, but Cole is insistent that the most important influences on the content of core science are empirical evidence and explanatory theories.

'Science wars'

We have made one or two passing references in the course of this chapter to the response of scientists to the work of the radical sociologists. Most working scientists in so far as they are aware of the debate no doubt ignore the sociologists and continue, untroubled, in their daily work. In the United States especially, however, there has been a sustained counter-attack by scientists against what tends to be labelled in that country *Science Studies*. The so-called 'Science Wars' have received national attention.

Popular attention was caught in 1996 when a physicist, Alan Sokal, sent an article to *Social Trends*, a journal which specialized in discussions of social constructivism and postmodernism.

Sokal's article 'Transgressing the Boundaries: Toward a Transformative Hermeneutics of Quantum Gravity' claimed to use contemporary developments in science, such as the theory of quantum gravity, to demonstrate that 'physical "reality", no less than social "reality", is at bottom a social and linguistic construct'.[33] The article came complete with over a hundred footnotes and a bibliography running to several hundred citations. It was a hoax. Disconnected sentences are cleverly strung together with all the seemingly impressive references, and mean precisely nothing.

By hoaxing one journal all that Sokal has proved, as he himself was the first to point out, is that that particular journal has a rather careless system of vetting articles. But, according to Sokal, there is a more general point to be made: 'sloppy thinking and glib relativism . . . have become prevalent in many parts of science studies'.[34]

We can begin to construct an outline of the response of orthodox science to the sociology of scientific knowledge.[35] According to critical scientists, sociology only treats the earliest phases of discovery; it ought not, therefore, to make sweeping generalizations from these. It could usefully, however, examine in detail cases of unexpected prediction. These seem strongly to support the case that science is more than a social construction.

The sociology of scientific knowledge gives great attention to two areas: the lack of agreed philosophical ground rules in science, and the fact that science shares much more in common with other areas of experience than was previously thought. Both of these claims contain some truth. Scientists might respond, however, that sociologists ought to give more attention to the 'end-product' of science: science has developed both an impressive body of theories to describe the structure of the world, and – in technology – a vast number of different ways of interacting with the world. Each time any of these are used, claim many scientists, the social construction of science is disproved. Scientific knowledge is *robust*: it is much less susceptible to the whims of fashion than most other forms of knowledge.

The importance of experiment

It may be useful to make a clear distinction between two similar claims that are made about scientific theories. The argument of this chapter and the previous chapter supports the assertion that scientific theories are *underdetermined*: Our observation of the world does not unambiguously prove the absolute status of any scientific theory. There will always be other theories that fit the evidence. On the other hand, theories are not *undetermined*. A few theories do fit the evidence; countless more do not. All possible theories do not have equal value.

We have seen that experiments are complicated, and often do not provide definitive answers about the constitution of the world. It is illegitimate, however, to use that insight, cautionary as it is, to jump to the conclusion that experiments can tell us nothing, or that the scientist simply *invents* experimental results. Some things are possible and some impossible, as we have seen.

In the last few years, partly under the impetus of the attack from sociology, there has been a renewed interest in the status of scientific experiments. In his two important books, *The Neglect of Experiment* and *Experiment, Right or Wrong*,[36] Allan Franklin contends that the theories of science are, on occasion, crucially affected by experiment and that experiment can indeed convince the scientific community. We have seen that the role of experiment is by no means simple, but Franklin succeeds in demonstrating that the theories of the scientific community are certainly not independent of experimental results:

> [E]xperiment has a philosophically legitimate role in the choice between competing theories and in confirmation of theories or hypotheses and ... there are good reasons for believing in experimental results.[37]

At the conclusion of the last chapter we noticed a similar point when Ian Hacking talked of the reality of theoretical entities only being proved when scientists took them for granted and 'used' them in experiments designed for totally different purposes. A professor of physics with whom I discussed these issues commented, 'Collectively we can agree about the results. What other discipline has that?'

A tentative conclusion – explaining the real world

For all the helpful insights generated by sociology, the realist will finally return to the arguments of the previous section. Science *works*, not simply through its success in providing comprehensive and comprehensible explanations for the natural world, but also in changing and manipulating that world. Science is *not* simply about changing order, it is about changing the world. As Michael Banner concludes:

> [T]he success of science would remain a mystery, a coincidence, or a miracle, unless we can answer the question which we feel compelled to ask: 'Why do these theories and these methods enable us to cope with the world?' The answer is that the theories enable us to cope because they are true or approximately true.[38]

I suggested at the start of the previous chapter that the attempt to answer such seemingly simple questions as what it is that scientists do, or what science itself is, would prove to be an exceedingly complex enterprise. If these chapters have a value, it is not in a brief summary of conclusions, but in following the sometimes tortuous trail which we have pursued.

We have seen that the assertion that science is somehow different from all other human endeavours is difficult to sustain. Science does not operate with an absolute standard of proof, unavailable to other activities, which allows it a privileged position. Instead the success of science has been due to the sustained application of the classic human values of intelligence and judgment.

This does not, however, mean that there are not differences between those activities which we call 'sciences' and other human disciplines. Popper's insistence on falsification has been challenged both by the philosophers and the sociologists, but it retains a certain force. Despite all the objections, I believe that true sciences do indeed have a particular relation to their subject matter, which is the natural world in all its diversity. The principle of falsification does not allow us to make positive statements about the substance of the world, but it may still constitute a powerful tool against the pseudo-sciences. At key junctures, and with suitable qualification, are their theories open to falsification in the way that the theories of ordinary science can be tested?

We have seen that falsification is by no means the whole story, but the possibility of its use at even only a handful of key moments ought to remind us that science is not simply a self-contained human construction but exists in relation to the substance of the world.

In the previous chapter we rejected the claim of empiricism, that what we see is not only more accessible but also more real than everything else. Instead, we have accepted the realist claim that the distinction between observation and theory is less than absolute and that the business of science properly involves much more than the observed world.

In the present chapter, we have also rejected the claims of Kuhn's more extreme followers that the influence of the community is so great that the whole of science is finally determined by the community rather than by the external world. Non-scientific influences have been and remain important for the shape of science, but they do not override the links between the conjectures of science and the world which science seeks to describe. Postmodernism is immensely attractive in many ways in its rejection of the 'totalitarianism' of rationality in favour of the pluralism of different beliefs, but in its present state of development it does not seem to do justice to the claims of science to be influenced by a real, objective world.

The bridges built by experiment between the theories of science and the world are rather more precarious than the simple crossings of our everyday life. The claim of the realist which I have defended here is that they exist, and that science does indeed claim to describe *in some way* a real world, and that, in some measure, it succeeds. At their most thoughtful, scientists claim that by experiment, and through the skilled use of knowledge and judgment, they do not simply generate predictions, but seek to understand the world. This modest claim can be justified.

To make such an assertion, however, is to claim that science is indeed a rational activity. The accumulated results of the rational exploration of the world with a succession of ever more subtle scientific tools – the *theories* and *methods* of science as well as the actual physical apparatus – have given great support to the claim that ultimately the universe is comprehensible.

That science shows the universe to be comprehensible might, of course, be no more than an interesting curiosity, which is essentially the suggestion of the weak anthropic principle. The theist, on the other hand, will always be tempted to claim that the fact that the universe can be understood, and not simply as a human construction, lends support to the claim that it is comprehensible because God has made it: it is properly described as a creation. The cosmos is rational, it is claimed, because it is the creation of a rational being.[39]

Chapter 6

Scientific Views of the World

Study of the philosophy, and especially the sociology of science, can easily lead to disillusionment. After all the criticism and qualification does anything remain of the old ideal of science? Can we any longer believe that science aims to teach us more about the world in which we live, and helps us to live here in a better way?

This chapter will paint a broad brush picture of the achievements of science as they appeared at the close of the twentieth century. It will also make some suggestions as to how scientific views of the world may be compared with Christian views of God and God's action in the world.

What everyone should know about science

I cannot summarize the whole achievement of science in a few pages. What follows here is a personal picture of science. Many books attempt a general overview of one area of science, or occasionally of the whole field. As the subject changes almost monthly readers will be well advised to browse through the popular science shelves in a good bookshop rather than stick to any title suggested here. None of these books is perfect, but usually reading several will correct the bias and enthusiasm of each author. Full details of the books mentioned in this section are given in the first note.[1]

It is important, however, not to forget the insights from the sociology of science which we met in the previous chapter. We saw there that even scientists writing purely scientific papers are bound to be influenced by non-scientific factors. When someone writes a popular book on science these interests are likely to play a large part in the outcome. My perspective as a Christian theologian openly dominates and shapes this book. It is always useful to enquire what it is that motivates the writers we are reading. A book that will help any reader to cultivate a sceptical outlook is Harry Collins and Trevor Pinch's *The Golem – what everyone should know about science*. Collins and Pinch describe the real tensions of scientific life, and suggest why we should not always take science and the pronouncements of scientists at face value. The role of the scientist as infallible 'expert' in our society can be an unhealthy one. Of course, every sensible reader will remember that Collins and Pinch themselves are committed to the thoroughgoing application of sociology to science and are not therefore disinterested themselves.

Of those writing from the Christian perspective at an introductory level, John Wright's *Designer Universe* and John Houghton's *The Search for God* are comprehensive and reliable. At a more advanced level Arthur Peacocke has written both a general survey, *Creation and the World of Science* (comprehensive, although now twenty years old), and a more thematic treatment, *Theology for a Scientific Age*. The first part of *Theology for a Scientific Age* gives the reader a survey of what Peacocke regards as the essentials of scientific thinking for any well equipped theologian.

One of the few attempts to survey the whole of the scientific enterprise in an accessible form is that of Robert Hazen and James Trefil entitled *Science Matters*. The authors were appalled by the lack of even basic scientific knowledge on the part of American college graduates and set out to correct it. The book covers an ambitiously large range of sciences and so cannot go into any depth, but it is helpful and reliable.

Once we begin to consider individual sciences the range of available writing becomes vast. In physics Paul Davies (P. C. W. Davies) always writes with openness to the religious implications of science. Together with John Gribbin he has written *The Matter Myth* which provides a wide-ranging summary of modern physics. Russell Stannard, who has written extensively on science and religion, has also published a series of children's books, which can be shared by adults to provide good introductions to the complexities of modern physics. Stannard's *The Time and Space of Uncle Albert* has rightly become a classic introduction to relativity.

Interestingly, while writers on physics tend to be sympathetic to Christianity, biologists are much less so. For anyone who wants to understand modern biology the work of Richard Dawkins (*The Blind Watchmaker*, *Climbing Mount Improbable*) and Stephen Jay Gould (especially *Wonderful Life*) provides an unsurpassed introduction. But Dawkins in particular writes from the absolute assurance that his own viewpoint is the only possible one. Anything else is not only unscientific but also irrational. Nonetheless, if we arm ourselves with both a thick skin and the understanding that Dawkins' anti-religious viewpoint is *philosophical* and only tenuously related to his science, then he can teach us much about the genuine power of the modern neo-Darwinian synthesis. The most remarkable single book on evolution is not by a scientist but a philosopher. Daniel Dennett's *Darwin's Dangerous Idea* surveys the whole field of evolutionary biology, its scientific and philosophical implications and its relation to the study of the mind and Artificial Intelligence. Dennett can only allow a small and circumscribed place in his grand scheme for religion, but aside from this, his grasp of the breadth of the subject is breathtaking.

In a few pages we cannot hope to compete with even the most basic of the books mentioned above. Instead, we shall attempt a brief sketch of a few important areas of science the study of which raised important philosophical and theological questions during the twentieth century. We shall see that the issues remain alive for us today.

The machine stops – from Newton to Einstein

To understand modern physics, and the shock which scientists received as the theories of relativity and quantum mechanics were developed, it is necessary to realize that at the end of the nineteenth century Isaac Newton's picture of the universe had been unchallenged for two hundred years. To all scientists working during the eighteenth and nineteenth centuries it was more than a picture; Newton had unfolded God's plan. Two brief couplets catch the sentiment:

> Nature, and Nature's laws lay hid in night:
> God said, *Let Newton be!* and all was light.

So wrote Alexander Pope; according to Sir John Squire, he was being over-optimistic:

> It did not last: the devil howling 'Ho!
> Let Einstein be!' restored the status quo.

In chapter 2 we saw that Isaac Newton's great achievement was to picture the universe as a huge machine, and to discover the mathematical equations which described how the machine worked. Although as we have seen Christian theology played a large part in preparing the way for Newton, his work raised problems:

1. If the world really is a machine, what is God's place? Newton himself believed that from time to time, God needed to intervene in order to keep the machine running smoothly. To others this suggested a faulty design. As Newton's contemporary Leibniz put it, Newton's God is an imperfect creator, a second-rate clockmaker. Before long, in any case, scientists came to a better understanding of Newton's laws which ruled out the need for any intervention in order to keep the mechanism running smoothly.

2. An alternative view suggests that God started the whole machine of the universe running – wound up the clock – or, created the conditions by which it came into existence. But can this Deist view of God do justice to the Christian understanding of a loving and involved creator?

3. Returning to our first question, if the world really is a machine, where do living things belong within it? Is the specialness of life an illusion, and all creatures simply machines, complicated but essentially mechanical. If not, how is life to be explained. If the world is a machine, can we any longer feel at home here? It was such considerations that lead Descartes to restate the philosophy of dualism. Existence has a mechanical component and a separate spiritual one. The difficulty is that, as science explains more and more of the world in simple, mechanical ways, the spiritual is gradually squeezed out of the picture. Does 'the Ghost in the machine', as Gilbert Ryle contemptuously labelled it, have any reality?

It has been necessary to take space to spell out the consequences of Newtonian physics because many non-scientists
assume that science still works with this *deterministic* view of
the universe: a place where everything runs like clockwork. This
is, however, not the case. Einstein's theory of relativity, and the
initially quite separate development of quantum mechanics have
replaced Newton's mechanical view of the universe.

We live on one planet in a vast universe. We can only imagine
how the universe might appear to other observers in other places.
Newton assumed that a complete picture was easy to draw: all
the observations from different places – different frames of reference – could be put together by imagining one special, universal
viewpoint, an absolute frame of reference. My way of seeing
might be distorted, but I could always check my partial picture
against a complete and final one.

Einstein's revolution[2]

Newton's theory implies that there is an absolute, correct, vantage
point from which the universe can be observed. Albert Einstein
(1879–1955) realized that this must be incorrect. There can be
no privileged perspective, all observers are equally handicapped.
The situation of each and every observer is relative. In fact, in
questioning our understanding of Newton's work, Einstein built
on the even earlier insight of Galileo – that the laws of physics
look the same from anywhere in the universe. For this to be true,
according to Einstein, the idea of an absolute reference point
must be sacrificed.

Newton's picture followed common sense, which was hardly
surprising as our senses have been formed in the same world
that Newton observed when formulating his laws. By contrast,
Einstein set out to imagine what must happen in situations very
different from those of everyday life, for example, when observers
themselves are travelling very fast. We should not be surprised
if common sense breaks down here, for this situation is totally
outside our normal experience. By the time Einstein began his
work, scientists using ever more powerful instruments could
indeed explore such exotic situations. Common sense has no rules
ready to apply here, but, once the first links had been made, it
would not be long before the exotic would begin to touch every-

day life. The various applications of atomic power are the best known situations where relativity has real effects in our ordinary world.

Einstein himself always explained the theory of relativity in theoretical, even philosophical, terms. By the end of the nineteenth century, however, scientists were also beginning to observe unexpected experimental results which seemed to contradict Newtonian mechanics. A whole series of experiments, including the classic measurements of Michaelson and Morley, had begun to cast doubt on the observability of the aether. These so-called anomalies could be explained more easily by the theory of relativity than by Newton's theory, and seemed to most people the deciding factor in favour of relativity. Einstein, however, always insisted that he had formulated his theory first, and only later realized that it solved these problems.

It is important to emphasize that the theory of relativity doesn't claim that everything is relative. What Einstein made clear was that the 'laws of physics' were less relative than our common sense understanding of space and time. The *Special Theory of Relativity* (1905) forces us to understand space and time as one single entity. To the usual three dimensions for space an additional dimension is added for time. The *Special Theory* also assumes that the velocity of light is constant, irrespective of the motion of the source of the light. From this follow the counter-intuitive results that so surprise us. Time will seem to pass at different rates to observers travelling at different speeds relative to each other, objects will seem heavier or bigger, and events that seem to one observer to happen simultaneously will happen at different times according to an observer travelling at a different speed. This intimate linking of time and space, concepts which until Einstein had seemed very different and entirely separate, also leads directly to the famous equation linking mass and energy, $E = mc^2$.

The *General Theory of Relativity* (1915) continued Einstein's work by linking together changes in motion (acceleration) and gravity. The effects of forces and acceleration cannot be distinguished. Clocks in strong gravitational fields (for instance, near very heavy objects, like stars, run slow) just as they do when accelerated to high velocities. Again Einstein cuts through our common sense feeling that these must be very different effects.

The General Theory allows us to picture gravity as changing the 'shape' of space. Einstein suggests that it is this curvature of space which 'explains' the effects of gravity. The common sense notion, which had first been formulated by Euclid and hardly been questioned since, that space is the neutral ground on which things happen, is replaced by Einstein with the notion that space is changeable and that changes in space lead to the other changes which we see taking place around us.

The word *relativity* is often taken to sum up the twentieth century, a metaphor for the denial that there are any absolute truths – everything is relative. The scientific theory doesn't support this view, but the feeling remains that if even science can be mistaken and exchange one theory for another, then what hope is there for any certainty? Some Christians have taken comfort in the fact that science has been shown not to be infallible. It may be better instead humbly to remind ourselves of the provisional nature of all human knowledge.

Einstein's work dents our faith in the reliability of human knowledge. If even science can be mistaken, then what can we be certain about? In addition, as we have seen, it also denies that we can rely on common sense. What is unquestionable for me here and now simply may not apply in different circumstances.

In the middle of the nineteenth century science had often been described as being 'organized common sense.' With Einstein, science moves beyond such notions: no longer could the ordinary educated person assume that their own experience would account for the whole universe. And worse was to come.

The strangeness of quantum mechanics[3]

As we saw earlier, when Thomas Huxley first read Darwin's *Origin of Species* he remarked 'How extremely stupid not to have thought of that.' This exemplifies one of the common views of science: once a new theory has been explained, the rest of the scientific community see in a blinding flash the power of the new explanation. Even relativity convinced a large proportion of the scientific community quite quickly, although the public were troubled by the way in which it seemed to contradict common sense.

From the beginning, quantum theory has been an exception to

this rule. In 1908 a professor of physics looked back at the time of his retirement:

> That such a hypothesis [the quantum nature of energy] should be advocated by men whose opinion deserves the most serious consideration, shows the restless turmoil which agitates the scientific thought of the present day.[4]

Ninety years later an international conference on science and theology witnessed a procession of senior physicists presenting papers on their own novel attempts to explain away the paradoxes of quantum mechanics. A book on the philosophy of quantum mechanics – and it is surely remarkable that there need to be books on the philosophy of quantum mechanics – talks without any conscious incongruity of a particular understanding of quantum mechanics as 'at most an interesting *heretical* alternative to the more *orthodox* Copenhagen viewpoint'.[5]

Why does quantum theory cause such difficulties for the scientific community? The reasons are to be found partly in the ambiguity and limitations which are central to quantum theory but are anathema to scientists. After all, the purpose of science is to understand the world and measure it accurately; quantum theory sets limits on just how much the constitution of the world can be pictured in everyday terms, and it provides a theoretical limit to the accuracy of our measurements.

At the end of the nineteenth century, physicists were faced with a number of problems. Some concerned how light was emitted and absorbed, especially by substances which absorbed light and then generated a small electric current (the photo-electric effect). Another set of problems concerned heat and how it was absorbed by solids. The experiments showed what happened, but how could mathematical equations be written to describe it? Light and heat have in common that they are both forms of energy, and it turned out that the solution to both these problems was to imagine that energy could only come in bundles of a particular size. It was all or nothing. Hence, while a gentle stream of energy could never knock an electron out of an atom to create the photo-electric effect, the electron could be displaced by a single bundle of the same amount of energy, arriving all at the same time.

So far so good. This picture causes no problems for our

common sense. After all, if matter is made up of atoms why not everything else? Unfortunately this is as far as common sense will take us. Physicists were shocked that energy came in bundles because they had spent much time experimenting on light, which was comparatively easy to examine and measure precisely in the laboratory. By the end of the nineteenth century the results were conclusive: the way in which light behaves can only be explained if it is made up of waves. Now a new set of experiments could only be explained if light behaved like a stream of particles. How could different experiments contradict each other in this way? An early joke was that light behaved like waves on Mondays, Wednesdays and Fridays and like particles on Tuesdays, Thursdays and Saturdays.

In fact, the real situation is more complex still: it is easy to arrange a thought experiment (the twin slit experiment) where light behaves as either particles or waves depending on how we look at the apparatus.[6] This introduces a second feature of quantum mechanics: the behaviour of the universe seems to depend on the way in which it is observed (or not). More disconcertingly for common sense, physicists soon realized that if light which seemed to be a wave could also be described as a particle, then all the particles which made up atoms, and therefore even atoms themselves, should also behave like waves. Sure enough by the early 1990s experimenters had succeeded in the difficult task of performing the twin slit experiment with atoms, proving that atoms 'travel like waves and arrive like particles' in the same way as light.

Even now, one hundred years after the first experiments, there is still no universally agreed explanation for this behaviour. The theory of quantum mechanics was agreed by the end of the 1920s and refining it has been one of the great projects of physics ever since. We can describe – in mathematical terms – the behaviour of the universe and make detailed predictions, but there is no easy way to put the maths into words.

Measurement and uncertainty

There is obviously an analogy here with relativity. As soon as our scientific investigation of the world moves away from the world we see around us, then strange things seem to happen. A moment's thought allows us to understand, if not to explain, what is happening. Our senses are the senses appropriate for creatures of our size living in a world like ours. By the end of the nineteenth century physicists had become skilful enough to explore parts of the universe very different from our world. Exploring the large scale and very fast moving lead to the Theory of Relativity; exploring the very small lead to quantum mechanics. At the atomic scale of quantum mechanics, we can no longer *see* anything. However, in order for human beings to investigate the atomic world there must be a connection between what is happening at that scale, and something which we *can* observe.

We can only picture what happens in terms of objects like those we see around us, but this picture breaks down at the quantum mechanical scale. The mathematical equations seem to describe very precisely what is happening at that scale, but for most people this does not provide a complete explanation. They want to understand what the mathematics is describing.

There is a genuine difficulty in linking the world of our senses to the atomic world. It may be helpful to remind ourselves that all scientific observation or measurement must involve interfering with whatever it is we want to measure. We probe or poke or shine lights. Usually once we become skilled at what we are doing we can be very careful not to disturb our subject. But at the atomic level, the smallest measuring tools we can think about will always be big enough to disturb the subject. Our 'fingers' are simply too big for the task and there is nothing else available.

The limits to measurement provide the context for *Heisenberg's Uncertainty Principle*. What we struggle to picture as the duality of particles and waves has the mathematical consequence that we can never precisely pin down the behaviour of very small entities (the same limits apply to everyday objects, but are usually so small as not to be noticed). For these objects – it is not really accurate to call them either particles or waves – the equations of quantum mechanics mean that pairs of properties are linked. The most important of these pairs is momentum (the product of the mass and the velocity of the particle) and position. The more accurately we know the position the less accurately we know the momentum of the particle. If we know either position or momentum precisely, then we shall be able to know nothing of the other. It might be tempting to think that we could settle for knowing position accurately, and build an accurate picture of the sub-atomic world from this; sadly the price for knowing the position accurately is a total lack of knowledge of momentum. The object may be at rest (unlikely) or moving with any speed in any direction. Our picture will dissolve before we can assemble it.

Suppose we want to take a picture of a fast moving train. We can set the camera to take a very short exposure which will capture the engine in sharp detail as if it were standing still, or we can set a longer exposure, and from the amount of blurring deduce the speed of the train. The blurred picture, however, will not allow us to see details such as the nameplate of the engine. This is only an analogy. For everyday objects there are other ways of measuring velocity or describing detail. At the quantum level, the only tools available are always intimately linked.

We have already hinted that quantum mechanics, unlike most of the other theories of physics, can be interpreted in various different ways. Indeed, Einstein spent his final years battling against the interpretation of the theory held by a majority of physicists. A few physicists, to whom Einstein might well have been sympathetic, interpret Heisenberg's Principle as a practical limitation to our knowledge, similar to the problems of measurement which we have discussed above. They refuse to accept that the Principle tells anything about the structure of the universe, although its practical consequences are unavoidable, and strictly determined. The majority of physicists, however, understand Heisenberg's Principle as a theoretical limit on our knowledge arising from the very nature of the universe.

Is there anything there?

Heisenberg's Principle is sometimes pictured as a 'Limit to Understanding': there is a quantum horizon beyond which accurate measurement becomes impossible, and without measurement there can be no scientific understanding. Most modern understandings of quantum mechanics go further. Not only can we not measure reality precisely beyond a certain limit, they would claim that there *is* no precise reality beyond this quantum limit. All the real and definite events of our world spring from an undefined world of possibilities which only become actual when measured in the human-sized world. Niels Bohr (1885–1962), who made many early contributions to quantum theory, worked in Copenhagen, so his understanding of quantum mechanics is usually known as the *Copenhagen Interpretation*.[7]

The Copenhagen Interpretation's lack of certainty, its denial of causation, and even the claim that the concept of a precise, picturable 'reality' is meaningless all fit very well with the instrumentalist philosophies of science which we have previously examined. According to this view, however, there remains a problem in describing how this quantum world of many unrealized possibilities crystallizes into the particular things and events which we can see and measure around us, without any ambiguity. How are the worlds of quantum and classical physics connected?

It is clear that quantum mechanics accurately describes the mathematics of the universe. Like all scientific theories it is fallible, but whatever replaces it will not be able to overcome this genuine paradox.

The gruesome thought experiment known as *Schrödinger's Cat* illustrates the point. Imagine a cat trapped inside a box with a flask of poison linked to a Geiger counter so that the decay of a radioactive atom would cause the counter to react and to break open the poison. The mathematics of quantum mechanics, and the statistics of radio-active decay, state unambiguously that we cannot predict the behaviour of a particular radio-active atom at any particular time, all that we can predict is the chance that the atom will have decayed after a certain time. After a short time it is not very likely to have decayed, left longer the chance of its decay increases.

At one point in time there will be an equal chance that the atom has decayed, breaking open the poison and killing the cat, or that the atom still remains intact, and with it the cat.

Now, when we open the box to look inside, the cat must be either dead or alive. Is it our act of opening the box that 'forces' the atom to decay (or not) and the cat to die (or not)? If we do not open the box, the state of the atom is described by a probability wave, here giving an equal chance of decay or not. But the fate of the cat is inextricably linked to the fate of the atom and so must presumably also be described by such a wave. This wave tells us that there is an equal chance of the cat's being poisoned or not. Therefore, according to the Copenhagen understanding of quantum theory, before we open the box, the cat is both dead and alive at the same time.

This thought experiment highlights the differences between the human scale world in which we live and the quantum scale world. It also highlights the *links* between our common sense everyday world and the strange world of quantum scale events: our world is after all composed exclusively of quantum sized bits and pieces. Finally, it illustrates the question we raised above: if we cannot picture the quantum world, does it really exist in any meaningful sense?

It may be that here once again the fundamental issue is one of scale. So long as our experiments were dealing with objects more or less the same size as ourselves, the role of the observer did not really affect the results. Once the scale is very different, then as human sized observers, we have to think very hard about our role. The problem arose with relativity and now confronts us in quantum mechanics. How is this very small (and therefore, to us, very strange) world connected to our everyday world? Do all the possibilities exist until they are measured, at which point one of them becomes real? If so, what makes the collapse of the wave function into a definite particle-like state happen? Is it the conscious human observer? Or the measuring apparatus? Is Schrödinger's cat conscious enough to be an observer itself? Or would a computer be adequate?

What does quantum mechanics mean?

We have already seen how terms such as orthodoxy and heresy fly about in discussions of the meaning of quantum mechanics. Let us consider two 'heretical' solutions before returning to orthodoxy.

It is well known that Einstein disliked the ambiguity and uncertainty of quantum mechanics. 'God doesn't play dice' sums up his unease with the theory and his demand for a different sort of explanation. For Einstein, there must be more than the chances and ignorance of quantum mechanics. Perhaps behind quantum theory there lies another theory which we have not yet discovered which will somehow explain the paradoxes of the theory in conventional terms. He was not alone in this. Karl Popper, the great philosopher of science, also sought a similar explanation of quantum mechanics. During the last years of his life Einstein developed an ever more complex series of thought experiments in dialogue with Niels Bohr and his colleagues in order to test the paradoxes of quantum mechanics. Einstein hoped to highlight the absurdity of quantum theory.

In fact, the EPR paradox (named after Einstein and his two collaborators, Podolsky and Rosen) can be tested by a thought experiment that was eventually performed. John Bell refined the thought experiment into 'Bell's inequality', and in the 1980s Alain Aspect carried out the experiment and proved that Einstein was wrong and that the paradoxes of quantum mechanics were physically true. Proving the EPR paradox seems to demand that once quantum mechanical objects have been connected they always remain connected. It is as if one object instantaneously 'senses' a change to the other. But this seems contrary to relativity theory itself, because it demands communication between the different objects faster than the speed of light – which is forbidden by the theory of relativity. A practical outcome of this is that any 'hidden variable' theory – that is, a theory which somehow lies hidden behind quantum mechanics and explains it – must itself be extremely complex, and must satisfy a set of conditions which are very specific and very hard to meet. The 'gap' left for such theories seems to get smaller with each new result. Despite years of trying we have little idea of what such a hidden theory might look like.

The second type of 'heretical' solution is known as the *many worlds interpretation*. This imagines that whenever there is a choice to be made, such as the decay of a radioactive atom in the Schrödinger's Cat experiment, then the universe splits into two. In one universe the atom decays and the cat dies; in the other it does not, and the cat lives. What we experience as the passage of time is a progression through a particular series of branching universes, the other branches represent *all* the possible outcomes of any event. This interpretation has recently become increasingly popular among physicists as it removes the difficult question of why an atom 'chooses' whether or not to decay. A moment's thought will show just how mind-bogglingly extravagant it is. There is a new universe, not only each time *I* make one decision rather than another, but whenever a neurone fires in my brain or an atom decays.[8]

The third solution is that offered by Niels Bohr and the Copenhagen interpretation. Fundamentally this states that the world is a very strange place which we can never fully understand, because the scale at which quantum events happen is so different from the scale in which our common sense is formed. This interpretation seems to demand that the cat really is both dead and alive whilst in its box. Only when the lid is opened must it either live or die. A more austere version of the Copenhagen interpretation is that quantum mechanics does not seek to describe the individual quantum states of the components of the world; according to this version, which seems to have been Bohr's own understanding, quantum mechanics only describes the combination of the experiment and the measuring device or observer. At all other times it has nothing to say: until observed the cat is *neither* dead nor alive.

According to the Copenhagen interpretation we cannot know the true nature of reality, but should not puzzle over this, because we can use mathematics in order to predict how the quantum world will affect our everyday existence. Many philosophers have objected to what has been seen as forced ignorance, but so far no experimental evidence has been forthcoming to oppose this interpretation of quantum mechanics. Einstein spent much time and ingenuity trying to disprove the Copenhagen interpretation but he always failed to shake its scientific basis.

One of my own teachers, Sir Rudolf Peierls, objected strongly to the use of the label 'Copenhagen interpretation':

> Because this sounds as if there were several interpretations of quantum mechanics. There is only one. There is only one way you can understand quantum mechanics. There are a number of people who are unhappy about this, and are trying to find something else. But nobody has found anything else which is consistent yet, so when you refer to the Copenhagen interpretation of the mechanics what you really mean is quantum mechanics. And therefore the majority of physicists don't use the term; it's mostly used by philosophers. [9]

However much this may be true for the physicist working on quantum theory, the rest of us, at least, cannot stop wondering what the world is really like. How can we picture it in our own inadequate ways? Quantum mechanics is immensely successful, but how much does it limit our understanding?

Theology and the quantum universe

It will be useful briefly to gather together some of the conclusions of the preceding sections, and to comment upon them.

Beyond common sense   We have seen that a change of scale makes a great difference to the shape of scientific theories, and the ability of non-scientists to understand them. The lay audience needs to put theories into pictures, because they do not possess the complicated mathematics needed to understand quantum theory, or even relativity. But this becomes increasingly difficult. Quantum mechanics suggests that this change of scale is fundamental and can never be easily overcome. Perhaps the human observer is eternally trapped in his or her limited perspective and can never fully appreciate the universe as a whole. The Uncertainty Principle sets limits to our ability to measure and therefore to understand the universe.

Duality and complementarity   Common sense gives us pictures of particles and waves and of the ways in which they behave. Quantum mechanics takes away those pictures. Either/or becomes both/and. Scientists and philosophers are divided as to whether this paradox goes beyond our inability to picture what is happening, but it is certainly true that the quantum world is complex and seems to require complimentary descriptions if it is to be understood in terms of our world. A simple reduction to something unambiguous will no longer suffice. Many theologians have made the analogy between objects being both particles and waves and the paradoxes of religion, such as the Chalcedonian definition of Christ as both God and human. Other commentators have seen the rise of the cubist school in art, at about the same time that quantum theory was being developed, as providing a good analogy: both abandon a simple, single explanation in favour of a multi-layered approach.

The rise of the observer   The paradox of Schrödinger's cat graphically demonstrates the importance of the observer. It is the observation which forces (or allows) the cat to be dead or alive. This is only a thought experiment, but enough real experiments have been performed to demonstrate that it is essentially true. Observation cannot be written out of quantum theory. Some theologians would wish to draw a conclusion from this: the universe needs human observers in order to be itself. There is need for caution here, and we shall discuss this topic again when we consider the Anthropic Principle.

God's Universe?   Newton's picture of the universal machine was easy to understand – and some aspects of the universe certainly behave like clockwork. But God is not a watchmaker. The real universe is much more intricate than a watch, and is not deterministic in the way Newton's followers imagined. A determined mechanism leaves little room for freedom, either human or divine. It may be that the interplay of law and chance suggested by quantum mechanics allows an openness which is more amenable to the presence and action of God. We will return later to this topic.

Einstein never accepted the uncertainty of quantum mechanics, hence his famous remark: 'God doesn't play dice.' His image is of God controlling each and every detail, but is this the only way to imagine the activity of God? An immediate response to Einstein came from a quantum physicist: 'Stop telling God what to do!' As God's creatures we cannot be sure of *how* the creator works in the creation; as Christians we are only sure that God *does* work with and for his creation.

Very small and very large

As we have seen, the science of physics takes our common sense observation of the physical world around us, classifies it and gradually extends the observations to realms far beyond our common sense and imaginings. In the twentieth century, in particular, physics has explored the structure of matter. Physicists have sought to understand the components of atoms down to the smallest scale possible.

There is still debate within the scientific community but it may be that the series of layers which physicists have described, from molecules to atoms and then through the various sub atomic particles, in fact comes to an end with the quarks which current theory assumes combine together in order to make these particles. Certainly there is very little suggestion of experimental evidence that the sequence continues like the layers of an onion. On the other hand, one hundred years ago atoms themselves were thought to be the basic building blocks, and seventy years ago it was believed that combinations of electrons and protons made up all matter. We need to keep an open mind.[10]

In the other direction, twentieth-century physics turned its attention to the very large. The old observations of astronomy were being brought together into the new science of cosmology which aimed to look at the universe as a whole and its origins. I am not going to retell the story of the discovery that the universe was expanding and so presumably had a beginning in time. The Big Bang theory has now been universally accepted as part of physics. This gives the universe a history. It also means that the attempt must be made to trace the history back to its origins. This is, of course, the subject of Stephen Hawking's bestselling *A Brief History of Time.*[11]

Why are the first few moments of our universe's existence so significant? At that stage everything that composes the universe was contained within an unimaginably tiny space; and incredible developments happened in smaller periods of time than we can imagine. The theory of relativity shows that the dimensions of space and of time will be distorted by the great forces involved. It is difficult to untangle precisely what happened in those first few moments. Hawking's suggestion that there need be no 'beginning' is simply one of a number of suggestions. The important point to grasp is that at this stage of the universe everything was in the melting pot. For physicists today cosmology and particle physics – the study of the very small and the very large – come together in exploring those first few moments. All the theories of physics are needed to explain, and perhaps themselves be explained by, what happened at the birth of the universe, if it indeed had a birth.

A theory of everything?

When Stephen Hawking became Lucasian Professor of Mathematics at Cambridge in 1980, following in the footsteps of Isaac Newton, he entitled his inaugural lecture 'Is the end in sight for theoretical physics?' Hawking's suggestion was that both the laws and the state of our universe might be explained in terms of a few simple equations. Once physicists understood what happened in those first few moments after the Big Bang, everything else would fall into place. In 1980 Hawking hoped that this might be achieved within a few years, and that theoretical physicists might thus think themselves out of a job! In *A Brief History of*

Time, he seems to imply that we would then understand not just physics but everything:

> So long as the universe had a beginning, we could suppose it had a Creator. But if the universe is really self-contained, having no boundary or edge, it would have neither beginning nor end: it would simply be. What place then for a creator?[12]

The hope of physicists is that they can derive one neat equation, or, more realistically, a set of equations, from which a complete explanation may emerge. At present relativity and quantum mechanics are both needed to explain the universe, and how to make the two very different theories fit together is by no means obvious. One of Stephen Hawking's contributions to science has been to try to iron out these problems. He has also attempted to remove the need for a beginning of the universe in time.

It is important to remember that a Theory of Everything is only an attempt to unify the theories of physics; it does not deal with the new properties that emerge at different levels of complexity. Some scientists seem to assume that a mathematical description of reality is exactly the same as reality. We will want to deny that this is the case. Obviously it could not be true theologically, but it may not provide a complete *scientific* explanation either. Finally, even if Hawking's theory removes the need for a beginning, it does not remove questions about the origin of the laws and boundary conditions which allow the universe to exist at all.[13]

Darwin's dangerous idea

We saw in an earlier chapter how Darwin developed his theory. What Daniel Dennett calls *Darwin's Dangerous Idea* was to link together the natural variations that occur in all living creatures with the struggle for survival.[14] If only a very small proportion of all living things survived long enough to breed successfully, then it was likely that those that did breed would be better fitted for life than those excluded, hence species might change in the way that domesticated plants and animals were deliberately changed by selective breeding. Thus Darwin demonstrated a powerful and universal principle which could explain in general terms many of the features exhibited by plants and animals in the natural world. At the time Darwin wrote he did not understand *how* natural selection worked. It was only after his death when Mendel's work on genetics became generally known that a possible mechanism for natural selection was discovered.

The twentieth century saw biologists combining the insights of Darwin and Mendel in the so-called New Synthesis (or neo-Darwinism) of the 1930s and 40s, in which Theodsius Dobzhansky, Julian Huxley and Ernst Mayer spelt out the physical links between the chromosomes in each living cell and the genes by which genetic information was passed from one generation to another. The discovery of the role of DNA in the 1950s completed the picture by identifying the precise chemical mechanism by which living cells could reproduce and transmit the genetic material.

This work of the physical listing and mapping of genetic ends to physical causes still continues through the human genome project and much other research. It is worth remarking just how subtle and complex are the links between the chemicals which compose the DNA and their results in the genetic make-up of future generations. It has taken forty years from the discovery of DNA for the first simple genes to be unambiguously located at certain positions within the DNA molecules. Roughly the same amount of research has been needed before genetic engineering has become a practical reality, bringing to public attention a number of difficult ethical issues. It is important to stress the vast amount of scientific hard work involved in these developments. Scientists sometimes get carried away and assume that once a theoretical possibility has been suggested it can become an everyday reality tomorrow. We should not be overawed by such pronouncements. Almost all science involves painstaking hard work; often theoretical possibilities prove to be practical false trails. It may be that some inherited characteristics, which an individual acquires through his or her genes simply cannot be mapped in any straightforward or useful way. Other characteristics may involve an impenetrable mixture of inherited and other causes.

More than one hundred and fifty years after Darwin first conceived the idea in his notebooks, Darwinian science is only now beginning to provide direct links from the basic building blocks to living creatures. Darwin's contribution to science was not a directly practical one. Darwinian biology does not provide a 'recipe' in the way that chemistry might, or detailed mathematical predictions in the way that physics often does. What evolutionary biology does do is to tell the most reasonable stories and hence provide economical and plausible explanations. The fact that molecular biology suggests a particular physical mechanism by which the theory works is important but not crucial. As we have already emphasized such physical confirmation was never available to Darwin and yet his theory received widespread acceptance in his lifetime.

Dennett's claim in *Darwin's Dangerous Idea* is that single-handedly Darwin gave a new shape to the whole of biological science with his theory of evolution by natural selection. The vast scope of the subject made it inevitable that Darwin himself could not fill in all the details. Some of his own ideas would be proved wrong, and some only properly understood with the discovery of DNA and the New Synthesis. Nonetheless, and this is what makes Darwin a great scientist, rather than a philosopher, he illustrated his vast overall picture with many detailed studies of the application of his idea to specific parts of the natural world. Dennett explicitly compares the scientist's *faith* in Darwin's idea with religious faith, although for Dennett the great difference is that Darwin's idea is constantly being tested by its practical application to ever wider, and ever more detailed areas.[15]

When we considered the philosophy of science we noticed just how hard it is to replace one scientific theory with another. Darwin's work is a good example of this. Many of his detailed proposals were simply wrong (for instance, Darwin suspected that some organisms could pass on learnt improvements to their offspring; later work entirely rules this out in any simple sense)[16]. Darwin's failure to appreciate the importance of Mendel's work meant that he could never fully justify his theory. Nonetheless, the overall picture which Darwin described allowed others to fill in the details. Once the details had been described, the framework could be re-examined and modified. This is far from the clear-cut image of hypotheses proposed and tested which figures in the popular pictures of science, but it remains a rigorous process. All scientific theories are open to improvement and even to being overthrown, as we have seen with Newton's physics. Nonetheless any theory that seeks to replace the neo-Darwinian synthesis must explain the same range of facts.

I spoke of Darwin's theory as a powerful and universal principle. We need now to examine *how* powerful and *how* universal. For Dennett and many others, including Richard Dawkins, Darwin's idea is all that is necessary to explain the whole development of life from its earliest origin to the complexity of human society. They suggest that the concept of favourable variations selected through competition explains the full diversity of living things.

The universality of natural selection

Dennett sees evolution as an algorithmic process. Algorithms are very general, foolproof, mechanical principles that apply to a wide variety of situations. Mathematical equations and computer programs are algorithms, but the concept is more general and applies anywhere where, to use Dennett's definition, mindless procedures produce guaranteed results. Teaching a child a road safety drill until the child applies it automatically – without thinking – at any curbside is a similar process.[17]

Is evolution by natural selection an algorithm? It certainly has some of the necessary characteristics. The process seems to apply universally to all life forms available for us to study. It also seems to produce guaranteed results, not in the sense that we can predict how a given species will evolve – all sorts of chance factors can influence this – but, in the sense that it predicts that competitive pressure will always lead to selection.

Charles Darwin himself never assumed that natural selection was the only cause of evolution. Once his successors understood the mechanism of genes and inheritance, however, it has come to seem that the single principle of natural selection could account for the natural world as we see it surrounding us today. Ever since Darwin's times religious writers who accepted evolution have often wished to qualify Darwin's work by asserting that whilst the fact of evolution is accepted, the mechanism could be guided by God, as easily as by natural selection. One of the reasons why an algorithmic solution appeals to those writers who advocate it is to make clear their belief that evolution is not guided in any sense, but proceeds by means of a blind process. Hence, the assertive titles of Dawkins' books: evolution proceeds because of *The Selfish Gene* or *The Blind Watchmaker*.

I do not want to discuss this issue in detail here, but one point is worth emphasizing. Natural selection has a great explanatory power. There is nothing to stop the theist invoking God's involvement in the process, and of course the Christian doctrine of creation proclaims God's intimate involvement with the whole of his world.[18] However, natural selection seems to provide an adequate explanation: we may choose – as a matter of faith – to see God's involvement here as everywhere. Science, on the other hand, does not *need* to invoke anything other than natural selection in order to explain the processes and results of nature.

This confusion is what appears to lie behind the dogmatism of much of the writing of Richard Dawkins and others. They are jealous for the independence of science. For them, the possibility of a religious explanation seems to deny the adequacy of the scientific version. Much Christian defensiveness about evolution seems to spring from the same root. If Darwin can succeed in explaining the living world then God is unnecessary. The nature of explanation is a complex issue, but it does not appear unreasonable to allow that natural selection may indeed explain the form of the world, without necessarily providing a complete and satisfactory explanation. Unsympathetic commentators, however, may well ask what else there is to explain. We shall return to this point.

A more serious objection to labelling natural selection as an algorithm lies in the assumption that algorithmic processes are independent of the material through which they work. A simple calculation performed with pen and paper, or on a pocket calculator or by a supercomputer will give the same result. Is natural selection independent of its medium in this sense? We can see that in some ways it is. Darwin borrowed Malthus' original work of human populations and applied it to the whole of the natural world. Richard Dawkins' computer games simulate many of the characteristics of life, without themselves being alive.[19] But is this enough? Such questions lie behind two of the great scientific debates of our time.

Many of the proponents of Artificial Intelligence claim that the basic processes of thought can be mimicked on a computer. For them the connection of mind and brain is unimportant – all that counts will be to reproduce the correct algorithms on a computer and the machine will be intelligent, and perhaps even 'alive'.[20]

The second debate is that begun by Richard Dawkins when he tried to understand human culture. Darwin himself assumed that evolution could explain culture and morality. This debate has continued in the work of the sociobiologists. No doubt much of our behaviour is determined by our genes, but human nature is complex and, on an evolutionary timescale, has developed very rapidly. Most scientists have not been convinced that genetic natural selection can explain all its intricacies. Dawkins therefore suggested the concept of the *meme*.[21] In the same way that the gene was selected in the physical world, so the meme would be selected in the mental world which had now become so important for humanity. Dawkins and others have made use of this idea to tell stories about the development of human culture. In a sense they are like Rudyard Kipling's *Just So* stories. They aim to provide a scientific explanation for the behaviour of human beings: why are we moral, why we compose music or marry.

If natural selection really is an algorithmic process then the development of the concept from genes to memes is a comparatively small step. Conversely, if natural selection is intimately linked to its physical circumstances, then there is no particular reason to suppose that the evolution of culture follows a similar pattern to that of the body. In particular the concept of the gene as an indivisible building block is linked to the physical form which life takes. There is no scientific reason to suppose that cultural evolution possesses such building blocks.

Are elephants nothing but atoms?

Peter Atkins is a physical chemist working at Oxford. He believes science involves the peeling away of appearances in order to expose the simple core of reality. Science means asking simple questions which always possess simple answers. He explains his beliefs in the first chapter of his book *Creation Revisited*, which is called 'Obvious Things':

A great deal of the universe does not need any explanation. Elephants, for instance. Once molecules have learnt to compete and to create other molecules in their own image, elephants, and things resembling elephants, will in due course be found roaming through the countryside. The details of the processes involved in evolution are fascinating, but they are unimportant: competing replicating molecules with time on their hands will inevitably evolve.

Some of the things resembling elephants will be men. They are equally unimportant ... Their special but not significant function is that they are able to act as commentators on the nature, content, structure, and source of the universe ... .[22]

An atom is not alive, and amoebas are not conscious. It is perhaps not so entirely obvious as Atkins supposes how elephants and human beings are derived from such building blocks. Atkins' philosophy is an extreme form of reductionism. In one sense reductionism is an essential method of science. One of the techniques of scientists will always be to attempt to understand the complex in terms of the simple. To break down everything into its component parts. Atkins goes further than this and assumes that all explanation will always be in these terms. An elephant does not need any explanation because it is nothing but its component parts. To describe the atoms is to describe the elephant. This philosophy has been christened *Nothing buttery* by its critics.[23]

Unlike Atkins, many scientists no longer expect that everything will be explained in terms of cells, or the movement of atoms. New properties emerge as complexity increases. A living cell is not simply explained by chemical reactions and the movement of atoms; humanity and human behaviour cannot simply be reduced to physical explanations. The modern understanding is more open to the different dimensions of human life, including the spiritual.

Arthur Peacocke has written extensively about a *hierarchy of levels*.[24] His contention is that complete understanding cannot be achieved through Atkins' simple building blocks, but rather by understanding that significant different properties emerge at different levels of complexity. Four levels are often distinguished: The physical world; living organisms; the behaviour of living organisms; human culture.

It is important to be clear about the claim that is being made here. It is not disputed that human beings are composed entirely of ordinary chemical elements which obey standard physical laws. In that sense, Atkins' picture is quite correct. There is no room for mysterious qualities to enter into the description. Life *is* a property of the physical elements which make up living things. However, to assume that this provides a complete scientific description is misguided. To insist that life, living creatures and all of human culture is nothing but a few chemical compounds is to misunderstand the complexity of the world around us. Atkins and others who take a naive reductionist position fail to appreciate that to describe a house in terms of the bricks of which it is composed or a home as an assemblage of rooms is not to give a complete scientific description, but instead to rule out what is most interesting about the object.

Peacocke talks of *foci of interest* and *levels of complexity*. Different sciences have developed which concentrate on the different levels and develop tools and descriptions which are appropriate to their own subject areas. In terms of physics or chemistry an elephant may not need explanation, but to pretend that a complete description of an elephant is fascinating but unimportant, as Atkins does, is to betray the subtlety both of the universe and of science.

In attempting to explain the complexity of these issues Daniel Dennett has coined the phrase *'reverse engineering'*.[25] When we take something apart, we can appreciate how each of the components fits together, and what function it has. Knowing the machine – or creature – from which we started, it is comparatively easy to describe how it works, and why the parts are assembled in the way they are. No further explanation is necessary. If we begin at the other end of the process, however, there is a different story. Any child who has taken a clock to pieces will know that dissection and construction are by no means reversible processes. The difficulty is multiplied if we consider not a set of specific parts, but the more basic building blocks. These are unformed pieces of metal, or atoms, in the case of the clock. They are cells, or complex organic chemicals, of living organisms. Dennett would be the last to suggest that any non-physical processes are at work here. The point is simply that Atkins is wrong: elephants *are* interesting, because their form is *not* predictable from the basic materials.

The need to give scientific space to different levels or hierarchies of explanation is still disputed, but is increasingly accepted as a real part of the complexity of our world.

'Top down' and 'bottom up' causation

The defence of the integrity of different levels of explanation has led many scientists and philosophers to speculate concerning the nature of causation. The classical scientific picture is of understanding causes by understanding the effects of combining the simplest possible building blocks. This is the picture which Atkins describes. An understanding of the genuine novelty of emerging complexity at different levels of organization leads to somewhat different conclusions. The old assumption of science working exclusively with 'bottom-up' causation has to give way to the possibility of 'top-down' causation.[26]

The work of Ilya Prigogine has shown that even some chemical reactions depend on the whole system of which they are part and not simply on what is happening around them. These chemical systems are far more simple than any living organisms, so as Peacocke notes, their behaviour seems to question the whole trend of reductionist explanation. Prigogine entitled his popular description of the work for which he won a Nobel prize, *Order out of Chaos*, and this is indeed a good summary of its consequences.[27] If such insights are true for comparatively simple chemical systems, then it seems likely that they will also be an important part of any complete description of living systems.

According to the traditional picture of 'bottom up' causation, science explains the world by referring everything back to the simplest possible units. Many more recent explanations, at least in the biological sciences, have begun to take account of the complexity of the whole system under consideration, alongside the behaviour of its component parts. The scientific value of 'top down' causation is being recognized. We should welcome this development, which comes from within science, as being sympathetic to the complexity of complete explanations. It values wholeness and not simply the building blocks of the world. Explanation involves relatedness, not only the properties of individual parts.

There are obvious theological analogies. Both quantum mechanics and the possibility of 'top down' causation may have implications for the pictures and analogies we use when seeking to describe God's action in the world. We shall consider this point in more detail at the close of the chapter. Before that we will use the concept of levels and hierarchies to help us appreciate the efforts of science to understanding the working of the human brain.

Studying the mind and the brain

Arthur Peacocke uses the concept of a hierarchy of levels to remind his readers how the scientific study of the human brain or mind can begin from a number of different perspectives.[28] The neurosciences (neuro-chemistry and anatomy, neuro-physiology and biology) begin from the physical components of the brain, attempting to discover how electrical impulses and chemical reactions influence and underlie all human thought patterns. Using the language of reductionism, these sciences seek to understand by working upwards from simple building blocks.

Sociobiology and behaviourism attempt to link these physical causes with patterns of behaviour. They hope that by linking the simple blocks together an understanding of human behaviour will result.

At a higher level of complexity, cognitive and experimental psychology begin with human thought and behaviour. Sociology and social anthropology are largely concerned with the behaviour of groups of individuals and the explanation of cultural patterns. They are less concerned with working upwards from simple beginnings, and might be said to work sideways across a particular level of complexity as they seek to map the reality of human behaviour as it emerges at this more complex level.

Lastly, philosophy is more directly involved with the study of the mind and the brain than with any other aspect of science. This is one of the few areas of science where scientists seem to accept the legitimacy of the involvement of non-specialists. The very nature of the enterprise of attempting to study ourselves and what constitutes human existence inevitably has profound philosophical consequences, and may also need philosophical guidelines. Still following Peacocke's terminology, we might say that philosophy seeks to understand by working downwards from general principles to the specifics of human behaviour.

The ghost in the machine

The list of individual and different approaches above demonstrates the enormous task which faces scientists studying human thought and behaviour. The human brain is the most complex single object known; the human mind the most subtle. What is the relation between the two?

Dualism attempts an answer by supposing that the physical and mental belong to two separate worlds. The physical brain somehow provides a home for the spiritual mind. The philosopher Gilbert Ryle coined the phrase 'The ghost in the machine' to encapsulate the problem with this popular solution. If mind and brain are composed of entirely different types of stuff, how can there be any links between them? Enough is known of the effects of chemicals and drugs on the mind, or of the way in which injuries to the brain cause profound mental changes to demonstrate that the mind is intimately dependent on the brain.

Ryle's own solution was to suggest that dualism makes a fundamental error by assuming that the mind and the brain are different things. For Ryle the mind is a consequence of the activity of the brain. It is not different and separate but rather *the sum of* all the activities of the physical brain.

Until Darwin, philosophers tended to deny the possibility of the emergence of something as complex as the human mind from something as simple as the brute matter of the physical universe. Common sense is once more in question here. Intuitively it seems obvious that nothing can come from nothing and that therefore mind is needed to produce mind. Darwin suggests an alternative picture. He claims that gradual increases in complexity, which can be built upon, lead slowly but quite naturally to the emergence of new properties.[29]

Much Christian theology still assumes that the old philosophical tradition is correct. We may feel instinctively that to grant the natural origin of the mind is to concede too much: to sweep away the Ghost in the Machine is to deny the value and reality of the spiritual dimension of life. Paul Davies and John Gribbin suggest a different perspective. In a book largely devoted to a description of the physical universe, they note, as we have, the oddness of the combination of humanity and the machine. Physics, they insist, has now moved on from Newton's picture:

In place of clodlike particles of matter in a lumbering Newtonian machine we have an interlocking network of information exchange ... [W]e can see that Ryle was right to dismiss the notion of the ghost in the machine – not because there is no ghost, but because there is no machine.[30]

The picture with which we are presented then, is of the mind as an emergent, but genuinely new and different property of the physical universe, existing in a physical universe which is genuinely its home. Angela Tilby, whose popular television series, *Science and the Soul*, explored similar ideas, has written movingly of the sense of alienation which human beings often felt in Newton's machine.[31] To abandon the dualism of spirit and matter as different things is not to deny the reality of the spiritual, but is instead to claim that the divisions between the two are purely artificial.

Theologically a strong case can be made that the incarnational nature of Christian faith is better expressed through a unified picture of a universe in which mind naturally belongs, than by the old divided dualistic universe where what was most important – human mind and spirit – was divorced from the everyday stuff of the world. After all the Christian message is that God became human, not that he visited the world as a disembodied spirit.

The evolution of culture

If Darwinian evolution by natural selection is alone sufficient to account for the development of matter into complex brains, it remains clear that with the emergence of consciousness something changed. The speed of development of human culture and its comprehensiveness argue that we cannot simply describe the development of humanity in Darwinian terms. We have already discussed Richard Dawkins suggestion as to how cultural evolution might move beyond physical natural selection, and memes might replace genes. We should probably be suspicious of any single explanation and look instead to a battery of partial descriptions, written from particular perspectives. Arthur Peacocke sums up the change neatly in his phrase: '"Evolution" becomes "History".'[32]

John Wright, although writing from a Christian perspective, is more positive about sciences such as sociobiology, behaviourism and psychodynamics than many apologists. He calls them 'windows into the mind'. Christians should not be afraid of scientific explanations, which seek to explain human behaviour in physical terms; there is much to be learnt from them. But the sheer complexity both of the mind and of human society suggests that these sciences cannot provide a complete explanation. They may each provide a window explaining a part of what we are. Any complete explanation will need to rely on the best insights from each together with much else.[33]

It will be helpful to conclude this chapter by gathering together some of the points which we have discovered when looking at the individual sciences.

Change and development

It is remarkable that first from geology and biology, as we saw in chapter 3, and later from physics and cosmology, as we have seen in this chapter, modern science paints the picture of a changing and developing universe. Two hundred years ago it was assumed by most naturalists that the living world which they observed was essentially the same as that which God created at the beginning of time. Even a hundred years ago the physical universe similarly seemed to be in a steady state.

Scientists are not yet able to make links between the different kinds of change pictured by physics and biology, and perhaps there are no scientific connections. Nonetheless it is remarkable that where the world around us once seemed stable and unchanging, it is now pictured as a place with a *history* (and a future); and a history moreover which it is the business of science to describe.

To take one other large-scale feature of the universe, it seems clear that both the physical and biological aspects of the universe exhibit a pattern of increasing complexity. In cosmology this stretches from the formation of the first particles of matter through to the evolution of galaxies, and in biology from the basic buildings blocks of the viruses to the complex mammals. In both cases what we observe tells a remarkably similar story.

Again, as yet there is no scientific explanation for this. The overview that we have been assembling in this chapter is of the application of broad, general laws, together with the emergence of different levels of complexity at various points. This picture certainly provides a framework within which structures of increasing complexity may emerge and receive a certain amount of protection once they have emerged. Such generalizations might suggest that there is a simple inevitability to the universe, a Theory of Everything waiting to be discovered. The real picture is more complex.

Chance and chaos

The clockwork universe has been rendered obsolete by quantum mechanics. Whether by a limit on what we can ever know about the nature of reality, or because there is no fixed reality to be known, Heisenberg's Uncertainty Principle guarantees the uncertainty its name suggests. In one way or another, quantum mechanics insists that chance and the prediction of probabilities replace Newtonian certainty in our description of the universe.

In biology Darwin's theory of natural selection also emphasizes the role of chance. In a famous book, *Chance and Necessity*, Jacques Monod pictured the whole of existence as being the result of chance: 'Pure chance, absolutely free but blind, at the very root of the stupendous edifice of evolution.'[34] Monod insisted that the involvement of chance ruled out any possible meaning for the universe. In place of religion Monod settled grimly for a cosmic pessimism. Stephen Gould, in *Wonderful Life*, gives a similar high profile to chance. Gould rejects the usual picture of an almost logical development from the simplest life forms to human beings, and instead stresses the role of chance in wiping out whole families and kingdoms of exotic living things. He suggests that the creatures that survived the mass extinctions might have been very different. The toss of a coin has determined the form of life on earth.[35]

At the quantum level, and at the biological level, modern science insists on the role of chance in the evolution of our universe. Chance has also entered science through the development of chaos theory. In chaos theory scientists seek to explain a number of very different phenomena ranging from the behaviour of simple types of pendulums to global weather systems. Chaos theory is surprising because it is *not* an exotic new field of science. It seeks to describe everyday events – the dripping of a tap or the shape of clouds. The mathematics it uses is exactly the same as that of Newton and classical physics.

The sole difference with clouds and dripping taps is that the equations that describe them do not give easy and clear cut answers like those of Newton's equations. Similar situations do not give the similar results that scientists have learnt to expect; instead two similar beginnings can give wildly different results. Hence the name chaos theory.[36] Unlike quantum mechanics the mathematics is simple, and the effects are familiar in our everyday world. Scientists often understand so-called chaotic systems very well, but they still cannot predict exactly how the systems will behave. They know the range of possibilities, but not which particular one will occur. Chance plays a large part. The world's weather, to take the most familiar example, is governed by well-known laws, but the number of different factors involved and the sensitivity of the weather systems to small changes mean that accurate long-term prediction will always be impossible. The picture of the flapping of a butterfly's wing affecting the weather halfway across the world is not a fanciful one.

God of chance

David Bartholomew has made a detailed study of the importance of chance for both science and theology.[37] He notes that scientifically we can use the term in three different ways:

1. When we say that something is caused by chance we may mean that there are causes present which we don't yet understand. Sooner or later science will tease out what is responsible. Some Christians might want to add that *some* events may be caused, but not by anything which science can analyse. By faith they may wish to insist that some events may not be due to chance, but to God.

2. A scientist may invoke chance to signify agnosticism about why a particular event happened. Perhaps there are direct causes, perhaps not, perhaps we shall never know. This is one interpretation of the role of Heisenberg's Uncertainly Principle. Some scientists have seen it as leading to a theoretical agnosticism, a definite limitation on scientific knowledge.

3. The third way of speaking of chance is the most surprising. This is to insist that some events may genuinely be due to chance and nothing else. It may be pure chance whether or not the radioactive atom decays and Schrödinger's cat dies. There may be no mechanism to discover, no unknown equations to formulate; science may simply have to stop at this point and wait to observe what happens. If the event is genuinely due to chance no firm prediction will ever be possible.

In the past, most writers, whether friendly towards religion or more hostile, have regarded the role of chance in the universe as evidence against the involvement of God. How can God be the Creator if the universe depends on chance? Monod's brave, and open-eyed cosmic pessimism has often seemed more realistic. Recently, however, there has been more interest in the way in which God might use chance.

It is possible to imagine that God works underneath the chance and uncertainty that we observe in the universe. Our investigations can never penetrate down to quantum levels, but perhaps this is where God is active. Bartholomew quotes the physicist, G. D. Yarnold:

> Every electron is held in existence by God. Every electron moves in exact obedience to God's Will. If, as we believe, physical science really has reached the fundamental level beyond which it is impossible to trace back the causal sequence any further, then may not this be the very point at which God's control over the universe is exercised? . . . Are not the extremely rare departures from the statistical regularity . . . the occasions of the direct personal action of God in a universe in which he usually acts impersonally?[38]

This position is always open to the Christian but it does raise its own problems. The first is the familiar issue of free will. If every electron, at every moment, is under God's direct control then can there ever be any genuine freedom anywhere in the universe? Christians will want to accept that each electron is held in existence by God. To assert as much is simply to restate the doctrine of creation, but how far can God influence the behaviour of the electron, without his interference being detected?

This raises the second problem. Physicists cannot penetrate to the quantum level, but they do possess sophisticated theories and methods which can detect how behaviour at this level influences the everyday world. All their searching has failed to detect what are known as 'hidden variables'. If God does affect the behaviour of the universe in this way, he hides his action scrupulously. If this is indeed how God works, he acts only occasionally and within the overall predictions of quantum probabilities. For God to act in such a limited and hidden way might seem somewhat demeaning for the creator of the universe, 'a rather hole-and-corner sort of providence', as Polkinghorne puts it.[39]

An alternative is to suggest that God allows the chance nature of quantum mechanics and natural selection to sort through all the possibilities open to a created universe, rather as a dealer might deal endless decks of cards until an interesting hand appeared. Peacocke suggests that this would be an efficient way for God to create a meaningful world, without having to be in such close control that freedom is excluded from the world.[40] Other writers remain suspicious of the wastefulness that seems to be involved, but Peacocke's picture does take seriously the modern scientific emphasis on chance in a way that most theologians fail to do.

Whatever our judgment of particular proposals it is important that we emphasize the fact that we are certainly not living in a simple, or simplistically determined universe. Both science and theology need to embody the possibility of chance. We shall return to this point again.

The anthropic principle: A new argument from design?

Why does the universe take the form that it does? This is obviously one of the basic questions of science. The previous sections have shown that modern science is inclined to give a large role to chance when it comes to discussing what happens within the universe and to account for the variety of living things. But why is there an organized universe at all, rather than a chaotic soup of the basic building blocks?

If there is to be a universe which is anything at all like the one we know, then certain conditions are required. One of the great successes of modern cosmology has been to understand with some precision what those conditions are. As Russell Stannard puts it: 'A universe coming into existence kitted out with some *arbitrary* selection of physical laws, would have virtually zero chance of being suitable for the development of living creatures.'[41]

Our universe has developed because of a number of 'coincidences'. First, the Big Bang must have been the correct size. Too violent and matter gets no chance to come together into stars. Too weak and the newly-formed universe collapses back into itself before stars can develop into solar systems with planets and the possibility of life. Next, carbon – the basic building block of organic chemistry and hence life – must be formed somehow. This is a complex process that must take place within stars, and only happens under very precise conditions. Thirdly, the carbon must be distributed from the centres of stars around the universe, again only possible though an unlikely set of coincidences. Finally, the balance of the different forces that bind stars together, and allow nuclear fusion (the process that releases energy from the stars) must be exactly right to allow the stars to burn over the long period necessary for the development of life.

At first sight these coincidences seem so unlikely as to be impossible by pure chance. Together the odds against them all happening seem overwhelming. The so-called *Anthropic Principle* draws our attention to this fact, and offers possible explanations. The Principle comes in a number of different forms. The *Weak Anthropic Principle* simply notes that, of all the possible universes, only a very few could support observers like ourselves. The fact that we are here and observing the universe greatly limits the range of possibilities. It might be that there are many universes. As observers we would never be in a position to know about any of the other universes, because this is the only universe in which we are present; the only one we can ever observe. A similar argument imagines a succession of slightly different universes existing one after another until this one came into being. It is worth noting John Leslie's remark that many universe theories are very wasteful.[42] It may be philosophically, or even scientifically, neater to assume that God has arranged the coincidences in order to facilitate a universe in which thinking observers would eventually develop. This line of argument is known as the *Strong Anthropic Principle*. It claims that the form of the universe is significant, because it has been designed as a home for humanity. In the nineteenth century Darwin's theory of evolution by natural selection finally removed the old Design Argument from the sphere of science. Does the Anthropic Principle herald the return of a new Argument from Design for the twenty-first century?

Scientists are unhappy with coincidences. The fact that the form of the universe depends on such an unlikely set of coincidences prompts questions: Are the 'coincidences' really that, or are they somehow linked? Perhaps the equations that govern the behaviour of stars are derived from some theory that also governs the force of the Big Bang. This is the sort of scientific musing that lies behind the quest for a Theory of Everything. The Anthropic Principle points to our scientific ignorance concerning the cosmological coincidences. To scientists this is both profoundly unsatisfactory, and a stimulating challenge. The coincidences provide a potentially rich field of research.

The Anthropic Principle has received much discussion by recent writers on science and religion. It has both fervent advocates and strident critics.[43] Those who strongly advocate the Principle believe that the coincidences described above are so different that they can never possibly be explained together by one scientific theory. They believe that they are also so unlikely that it makes much more sense to invoke God to explain them than simply to leave them as mere coincidence. Opponents tend to be more cautious about the power of science to explain the unlikely. After all, who expected Darwin to turn round the old Design Argument to demonstrate the reasonableness of natural selection? Ultimately, although a Theory of Everything does *not* explain everything, it might succeed in showing that only one universe is possible. Angela Tilby makes a highly relevant comment here:

> The scientist's task is to explain the world without invoking the transcendent. This is why scientists use God as a kind of cipher, a word to encompass the undiscovered. The whole purpose of their task is to make the word redundant, to 'know the mind of God' [to use Hawking's famous phrase].

She goes on to make a useful distinction:

To explain the world without reference to God does not disprove God, it simply demonstrates that God is not to be invoked simply as an explanation for things.[44]

For all these reasons, I am sceptical about the value of any of the versions of the Anthropic Principle as an apologetic tool. The weak form of the Principle may be useful to help highlight some fascinating questions on the frontiers of current science, but it seems to me unhelpful to attempt to find God's purposes in any direct way behind a set of currently unexplained coincidences.

As we have seen, physics does seem to be moving towards a set of very simple explanations for the state of the universe. In his 1980 lecture 'Is the End in sight for Theoretical Physics?', Hawking was a little over-optimistic; he hoped that the work might be completed by the end of the twentieth century. Nonetheless great simplifications have been achieved. Quantum mechanics is being brought ever more closely into agreement with relativity. Particle physics and cosmology clearly share a common agenda. Physics is well on the way towards building a single, coherent and comparatively simple picture of the whole universe, which stretches from the very small to the very large. There will be surprises on the way – the universe undoubtedly contains things of which we have never dreamed – but the broad brush stokes of a complete picture can already be discerned.

We may guess that the complexity which we find around us in the universe will soon be explained in scientific terms. Beginning with an initial set of simple equations, a Theory of Everything, or something just a little bit more complex, physics will describe the evolution of the physical universe. The emergence of more complex structures and the building blocks of life will be fully mapped out by the chemical sciences. And life itself will be seen as an inevitable consequence of the operation of the simple laws of physics and chemistry. Once that crucial step is passed, the operation of natural selection will explain the diversity of living forms up to the emergence of human consciousness, when it will probably be accepted that other factors become more important.

Angela Tilby's point is an important one. God is not to be invoked in place of a scientific explanation. Much of the sorry history of the relationship between science and religion has been characterized by the fear of religious people that God must be just this sort of explanation or will count for nothing. Equally, much of the suspicion of religion by scientists is derived from their assumption that 'God' is being used to bar investigation or to protect ignorance or vested interests.

The strangeness of science and the love of God

Most laypeople experience the oddness of science for the first time when they encounter the effects of Einstein's Theory of Relativity. Many scientists find relativity comparatively easy to accept, because the mathematical equations it uses are a straightforward extension of classical mathematics. For scientists, strangeness often enters with their first consideration of the consequences of quantum mechanics, the theoretical limit to how much we can know of the structure of the universe, and the ever stranger thought-experiments, most of which sooner or later seem to be confirmed in the laboratory. The emergence of complexity from simplicity, and consciousness out of brute matter according to the theory of natural selection, provides yet another assault on our notion of common sense.[45]

There is a lesson to be learnt. The broad general explanations which provide such powerful tools in the scientific understanding of the universe often do not correlate easily with our own mental furniture, built up from our day-to-day experience. Common sense can only apply to common experience, and we cannot describe the whole universe in such simple terms. The universe has a breathtaking range of complexity and novelty.

The scientific pictures of the living world and the physical universe which we have built up in this chapter are suggestively similar. Science is now close to understanding the general laws which govern the development of forms of life, and of the physical world. In both cases the laws work in an open way, the particular form of the universe or of plant and animal life seems not to be determined by the equations, but to be the result of chance.

This might be unsettling. Does an all-powerful creator really work in this way? Some Christians have wanted to claim that the uncertainty of quantum mechanics, or the chances of evolution, allow for the hidden hand of God closely directing the process. Some are confident that, through an anthropic principle,

God has arranged that the universe will develop as a suitable home for human beings. Others suggest that God may actually work through the chances of the world by using the myriad possibilities in order to achieve his purposes, in co-operation with the world which he has created.

The modern scientific understanding of the universe as *both* open *and* lawlike is much more sympathetic to a religious dimension than the old mechanistic approach. An open universe allows for new possibilities and genuine novelty, it allows space for an openness to real human choice. A universe of consistent, if flexible, laws demonstrates God's reliability, and allows that human beings can develop the capacity to understand the universe, and through the universe to glimpse some brief vision of its creator. Our understanding of this universe as open yet lawlike may suggest a God who is loving and constant and yet who allows his creatures a measure of freedom and space for their own creativity.

Our common sense notions of how God acts cannot be expected to survive such an explosion in our knowledge, any more than common sense can any longer serve as a reliable guide through science. Just as the Christian understanding of God as Trinity broke open the old ethical monotheism, so new understanding of what the universe is, and how it (and we ourselves) came into being will inevitably change our understanding of the action of God. Such considerations belong to the next chapters. For the present we will simply quote from one of the few contemporary theologians to rise to the challenge, the hymnwriter, Brian Wren:

> Are you the friendly God, shimmering, swirling, formless,
> nameless and ominous, Spirit of brooding might,
> presence beyond our senses, all-embracing night,
> the hovering wings of warm and loving darkness?
> If hope will listen, love will show and tell,
> and all shall be well, all manner of things be well.

> Are you the gambler-God, spinning the wheel of creation,
> giving it randomness, willing to be surprised,
> taking a million chances, hopeful, agonized,
> greeting our stumbling faith with celebration?
> If hope will listen, love will show and tell,
> and all shall be well, all manner of things be well.[46]

Chapter 7

Relating Science and Religion

In the book of Acts, Luke describes Paul standing at the Areo-pagus, the traditional place of meeting between the philosophers and the people of Athens, and preaching the gospel of Jesus Christ. Paul has clearly taken the trouble to learn something about his audience, and to speak in terms that will make contact with their beliefs and preconceptions:

> For as I went through the city and looked carefully at the objects of your worship, I found among them an altar with the inscription, 'To an unknown god.' What therefore you worship as unknown, this I proclaim to you (Acts 17.23 NRSV).

Paul goes on to develop his argument in terms of God as the creator of the world and humanity, that for which all people search. He quotes 'some of your own poets' in support of his case. What is remarkable here is just how different the content of this speech is from most of the other speeches in Acts, with their emphasis on the particularity of God's dealings in history with the Jewish people, and with God's recent mighty acts in Jesus Christ.[1]

We do not know how successful Paul's speech was. Many commentators claim that it was a failure, at least in part because Paul tried too hard to express the gospel in terms familiar to the Greeks. Other commentators, like the Athenians, reserve their judgment.

Already in this first encounter, though, we see many of the

great missionary and apologetic issues being raised. How far is the gospel message changed when it is translated into a new language? Does translation involve simply the finding of equivalent words in a different language, or the finding of equivalent ideas in a new culture? Can the Christian message take over philosophical concepts in order to make its reception easier, or must potential new converts always be taken back into the original world of Jewish thought forms in which the gospel was first preached? Only one hundred and fifty years after Paul, Tertullian asked: 'What indeed has Athens to do with Jerusalem?', a question which has haunted the church through the years.

Mission: dialogue and assimilation

We all of us have some picture in our mind of the expansion of Christianity out of its Palestinian Jewish setting, and into the wider world. A picture of Jewish ideas meeting Greek ones, and of the religion of God's revelation meeting and coming to terms with the dominant intellectual world view of the age. Our creeds, the traditional formulations of christology and the doctrine of the Trinity, all took the form with which we are familiar as the theologians of the first few centuries sought to explain their beliefs in a world dominated by Greek ways of thought, and to defend those beliefs against misunderstanding, misinterpretation and deliberate perversion. The twentieth-century philosopher A. N. Whitehead spoke of Christianity as 'a religion in search of a metaphysic'.

If Christianity is 'a religion in search of a metaphysic', can that metaphysic be found only through philosophy or must we be prepared to ask of each culture where an appropriate partner is to be found? Even to raise such questions is to suggest the accommodation or compromise with 'heathen' views which Tertullian reacted so strongly against. But, as Paul himself had discovered, this is one of the perennial risks of a missionary faith. Historically, great reformulations of Christianity were undertaken in their various ways by the Greek Fathers, by Augustine, by Aquinas and the Scholastics and by the Protestant Reformers, as they sought to make sense of the philosophical temper of their times.

The last two hundred years have faced Christians with a new

question: Should the rise of science have any effect? Do the philosophers still have a monopoly not only on the most basic questions but also on how to ask them? Does the very fact of the success of science in learning how to explain the world have any consequences for Christians?

These are genuinely new questions. For most of its history, Christianity was involved in dialogue with different schools of philosophy, seeking to discover the best way to talk about God and the world. Where in the past the dominant language of intellectual discourse was philosophical, it is now scientific. The public perception of science is often confused, suspicious or simply downright wrong. But it is there, and the theologian, apologist or evangelist cannot merely disregard or condemn it. Scientific languages may be impoverished and much less able to speak in generalities than philosophical languages, but they are here to stay, and the theological task is always the same – to understand, to interpret and to translate. How can value and meaning be mediated to an alien culture?

How do science and religion relate to one another?

A large part of this chapter will be taken up in examining two different schemes which attempt to provide models of the relationship between science and religion or theology . This exercise is important for three reasons. First, it is valuable to discuss the insights of each model in its own right. The different ways of describing the relationship bring into focus different emphases and different problems.

Second, the different schemes help to uncover the complexity of what is being claimed when it is said that an interaction between disciplines is possible. It can be tempting to speak of the relation between science and religion as if it were obvious that there must be a relation, but Mary Midgley questions this assumption: 'should an elephant try to be like a concrete mixer?'[2] We shall need to justify our assumption that comparisons can be made between science and religion.

Finally, by considering more than one model, we shall suggest that no single scheme can be anything other than an attempt to model or picture a very complex reality.

Ian Barbour is one of the most respected commentators on the relationship between science and religion. He suggests four general categories to describe the ways in which science and religion relate to each other: conflict, independence, dialogue and integration.[3] We shall need to consider each in detail before returning to consider the assumptions which lie behind Barbour's scheme.

Conflict

When we traced the history of the relationship between science and religion, we saw that 'conflict' was by no means the only way to describe the relation. Christianity could just as easily be seen as a spur to the rise of science, and apparent conflicts were often between different interest groups rather than between the formal armed camps of science and religion, which rarely existed except in the public imagination. The popular 'conflict' books of the nineteenth century have long given way to a series of comparative books which acknowledge twentieth-century realities. To take an obvious example, notice the similarity in the titles of recent sets of Gifford lectures: Arthur Peacocke's *Theology for a Scientific Age* and Ian Barbour's *Religion in an Age of Science*. The titles have a slightly defensive tone, acknowledging the fact which we discussed at the start of this chapter, that the common perception is that the twentieth century was a scientific age, and that other ways of thinking must be accommodated to this fact.

In some quarters, however, it still seems as if there is a battle to be fought. Given the great explanatory success of science it is not surprising to find that there are some scientists who assume that the methods of science are the only valid methods to be used for analysing the whole of human life and experience. Because the methods of science have proved so successful in disclosing the structure of the world, it is claimed, they can be generalized into a metaphysic which will then be used to assess whether or not any other way of organizing knowledge is legitimate. This philosophy is usually known as *scientism*. Some who hold this view would go further, and regard religion in itself as a threat to the practice of science or even to the well-being of humanity.

We have already seen how Jacques Monod described the theories of modern biology under the title *Chance and Necessity* and wrote of 'Pure chance, absolutely free but blind, at the very root of the stupendous edifice of evolution'. For him the scientific description had the most wide-reaching implications: we now have 'biological proof of the absence of a master-plan'.[4] Richard Dawkins takes a similar position. He is positively evangelical in his anti-religious attitude. Dawkins wrote, in one of his frequent letters to the newspapers, commenting in fury on Susan Howatch's funding of a post at Cambridge to study the relation of science and theology: 'Theologians don't do anything, don't affect anything, don't achieve anything, don't even mean anything.' A few days later, the 'Peterborough' column in the *Sunday Telegraph* made the obvious point:

> Why does he rage so furiously against theology, a thing in his view so obviously bogus and on the way out? Can it be that he is not so entirely certain of his invincible rightness as it seems? Does he even sometimes suffer, like other mortals, from doubts, intimations of worlds unrealized which will not go away, however often they are triumphantly refuted?[5]

A similar logic, that either science or religion must triumph, but that they can never coexist, would seem to motivate many Christian fundamentalists and creationists who often see themselves as being in an opposing camp to science. Their case is that God has laid down laws in scripture and that these apply to the whole of the universe. These laws, being God given, are normative for scientific as well as religious purposes.

Creation Science or Creationism, starting from this premise, seeks to demonstrate that the structure of the world and the diversity of living organisms can be derived from 'scientific' theories that do not deviate from biblical principles and have no need of the theory of evolution by natural selection as developed by modern biology. The various battles between the 'Creationists' and 'Evolutionists' in the United States are well known. States have been induced to pass laws demanding equal prominence in teaching evolutionary and creationist science. At the time of writing, all these laws have been successfully challenged by the Supreme Court, but the campaign continues.[6]

Ian Barbour points out the similarities of the arguments used to justify creationism and scientism. It is assumed that one simple set of rules can govern the whole of creation and human life. Both positions are reductionist because they assume the universal application of a set of principles discovered or revealed in one area. Biblical 'laws' can be applied to scientific descriptions of the natural world, or scientific laws to whole of human experience. In Barbour's words: 'Both positions fail to observe the proper boundaries of science.'[7] The fundamental assumption that scientific discoveries can threaten the foundations of religion lies at the heart of the conflict, and will need to be examined carefully.

Independence

In 1972, at a time when the creationist debate was just beginning to come to prominence, the American National Academy of Sciences passed a resolution which was intended to settle any possible argument between science and religion:

> Religion and science are ... separate and mutually exclusive realms of human thought whose presentation in the same context leads to misunderstanding of both scientific theory and religious belief.[8]

Science and religion are two entirely separate domains of human endeavour and there can be no useful contact between the two. The resolution quoted above owes a good deal to pragmatism: we might picture both camps retreating to lick their wounds after the indecisive battles of the nineteenth century. John Habgood had written a few years earlier of 'the uneasy truce between science and religion'.[9] In addition, however, there are good theoretical reasons for accepting the separation of science and religion. Much of Western thought has allowed for a metaphysical dualism between spirit and matter, stretching from the general Greek distaste for all things bodily to Descartes's influential proposal to place the human mind at the centre of all certain knowledge, surrounded by a mechanical creation.

If a dualistic division is accepted then the realm of matter is the natural domain of science, and the realm of the spirit that of religion. A similar separation is pictured in the image of the two books, that of nature and that of revelation, through which God reveals the truth about himself and his actions. This picture was used by Galileo, but originated centuries earlier. The scientist can discover some of the truth, including some truths about God, by studying the world that God has made, but the complete truth about God only comes through the revelation given through the scriptures.

We can see here the beginning of a distinction between the doctrine of creation and that of redemption. The potential problem raised by the fact that the scriptures do make scientifically interesting statements can be neutralized by assuming that the scriptural authors were divinely inspired in matters of doctrine, but also that they were real people of their time, and so fallible in all other areas. Conversely it may be assumed that at the end of time God will reconcile any apparent conflicts.[10]

Independence and spheres of interest

The different spheres of approach can be applied in a number of other ways. The methods of science can be said to apply to the sphere of fact; whilst those of religion apply to areas of feeling or relationship. Martin Buber, the Jewish philosopher, taught of the essential difference between I-It relationships, those between a person and a thing, and I-Thou relationships between people.[11]

Such concepts have been developed by existentialist writers in particular, but a much larger group of Christians would want to claim that their relationship with God is the supreme example of an I-Thou relation, and that this relation will need to be described in ways which go beyond the scientific description of the world. The scientific description consists of objective, neutral knowledge. Human experience, let alone human experience of the divine, is subjective and personal in nature. Unlike the subject matter of science and scientific experiments, experience is not repeatable – at least, not in a cold measureable way, and its object will not be the acquisition of an ever greater body of fact; instead it will result in a loving relationship, or the call to action.

Thomas Torrance, while denying the distinction between the realms of science and religion, arrives at a similar conclusion. For him, theology takes its place among all the other sciences, but each individual science has its own method.[12] The appropriate method for astronomy is not that of molecular biochemistry or that of theology. The scientific way is to apply our basic human rationality in particular situations. We must acknowledge both the unity of knowledge and the diverse realms of nature.

Torrance's vision is essentially of a series of parallel disciplines, each worthy of the name science so long as they conform to certain basic standards, but each retaining a firm control over the subject matter under discussion, and equally, being undertaken in very different ways according to the character of that subject matter. For Torrance theology is inevitably a special case because he insists that God's truth breaks into the discussion, or *interrogates us*, rather than being interrogated *by us*.[13] It is difficult to imagine how a theology which has been formulated in this way could be compared to any other discipline.

From a different starting point some philosophers, inspired by Wittgenstein, have pointed out that human beings use language in very different ways depending on the context. They claim that our public lives consist of a number of different 'language games', and it is not at all clear how language used in one context can easily relate to a new context. Scientific language and religious language perform very different functions. We have already seen that postmodernist philosophers arrive at a similar conclusion:

From the perspective of deconstruction, there is nothing upon which we can ground an argument for evolutionary biology as opposed to fundamentalist creationism, since both are discourses, with their blindnesses and their insights, and neither one can be said to be more or less accurate than the other, there being no pathway open from the text to the world.[14]

The postmodernist programme allows science and religion their own independent existence, but as John Habgood's phrase suggests, the truce between science and religion is *uneasy*: uneasy because the subjects in fact do meet at various points. Ian Barbour concludes:

The independence of science and religion represents a good starting point or first approximation. It preserves the distinctive character of each enterprise, and it is a useful strategy for responding to both types of conflict mentioned earlier.[15]

Like Barbour, we will want to stress that such a strategy is only a starting point. Independence inevitably leads to a privatized version of religion, or to one that stresses the doctrine of redemption to the exclusion of any real interest in creation. Equally, we have demonstrated that science is not the totally objective enterprise that it was once thought to be. Sooner or later, we are likely to feel the need for dialogue between science and religion.

Dialogue

The rise of Western science was bound up in a complex, but on the whole positive way, with the assumptions of Western Christian society. Earlier we likened the relation of Christianity and science to that of parent and child: after the initial nurturing phase, when strong parental support is required if the fragile infant is to survive, come the inevitable phases of rapid growth to independence followed by the equally inevitable adolescent rejection of parental values. Only in mature adulthood can a dialogue take place between autonomous equals.

There is in fact no clear dividing line between a model of dialogue and that of integration, which we shall discuss in the next section. Dialogue tends to assume two distinct bodies of knowledge or spheres of influence which meet only at certain boundaries. This raises difficult questions. Is there a way to communicate? To whom does disputed territory belong? Are the two entities really independent equals? Integration, on the other hand, suggests that finally there is one way of seeing reality, one sphere, one body of knowledge and that the task is to integrate everything which at present appears to be separate into one neat category.

The task of dialogue will be to construct bridges and pathways between the subjects; to discover ways of translating the language of one into that of the other. J. R. Carnes in his book *Axiomatics and Dogmatics* attempts to consider the whole fields of both science and religion. His aim is to see if the two very different areas can in fact be compared. He likens scientific data to religion and religious experience, and the theories of science to the systems of theology. This helps Carnes to suggest which parts of the subjects should in fact be in dialogue. Thus 'Science', as a complex of interrelated theories, should be in dialogue with the developed systems of systematic theology, rather than the raw data of religious experience. Carnes also demonstrates just how difficult is the task of dialogue. It is surprising to learn that very few of the theories of the different branches of science have been formulated in such a way as to make them fully compatible with each other – this is the discipline of *axiomatics* of Carnes' title. Formal comparison with theology – *dogmatics* – is infinitely more complex.[16]

Those who make use of the conflict and independence models tend to suggest a sharp separation between the hard, objective methods of science, and the subjective methods of theology. Such a distinction has been increasingly challenged. Physics has traditionally been seen as the most objective of all sciences, yet the development of the theories of quantum mechanics meant that modern physics had to take seriously the concept of the observer, not simply as a passive spectator, but as an important – and essential – part of the experimental arrangement. In quantum mechanics, and in ways which are still hotly debated, the observer changes the experiment. The theories of physics can be seen to have been in advance of, and to have prepared the way for, more recent changes in the philosophy of science.

The similarities between science and religion

The work of Michael Polanyi, Thomas Kuhn and others has meant that recent writers on the philosophy of science tend to stress the similarity between the practice of science and theology, instead of their differences. Both involve the selective judgment of skilful practitioners who must persuade a professional community of the value of their work. Both involve a mixture of the objective and subjective; both involve data and its interpretation. Both have a proper place for tradition and authority.[17]

As we have seen, these changes have led some commentators, sociologists foremost amongst them, to suppose that science is in fact an irrational enterprise having little connection with any possible external reality, only justified by its impressive internal consistency. Others, though, have welcomed the humility which the loss of its exulted and absolute status has brought to science (and scientists). The scientific enterprise can still be justified by describing the theories of science as providing the most reasonable explanation available. The difference between competing scientific theories is no longer that one is true and another false, but that one is a closer approximation to the truth than another.

The new approaches often make extensive use of probability, rather than absolute proof. Using the language of approximation to the truth and probability leads several recent writers to note the similarity between this approach to science and modern descriptions of religion and theology.[18]

It may be that new choices are opening up for philosophers of religion. In the past, Aquinas' formal arguments were used to provide proof for the existence of God. At the opposite extreme the *fideists* cared for nothing except the personal commitment in faith of the individual believer. Today a number of writers stress the significance of the ordered and comprehensible universe in which we find ourselves, and suggest that the most reasonable explanation for its existence is that it was created by God. A leading exponent of this approach is John Polkinghorne who has written a series of books culminating in his Gifford lectures, *Science and Christian Belief.*

We must not attempt to press such arguments too far. There are still differences between science and religion or theology. Science is not a complete lifestyle in the way that all religions must be; great as is the investment of professional scientists in science or one of its paradigms, the faith of a religious believer is of a different kind. Fact and experiment play a decisive role in science which is rarely echoed in theology. Remember Jesus' words at the end of the parable of Dives and Lazarus: 'neither will they be convinced even if someone rises from the dead' (Luke 16.31 NRSV). Religions and their followers have an almost limitless capacity for adapting or ignoring awkward facts.

What has changed, as we have seen in the last few chapters, has been the growing appreciation of the difficulty of obtaining proof even in science. The need to use concepts such as verisimilitude or approximate truth has led to a wide understanding that science and theology are not such totally different subjects as they once seemed. There are still, of course, major differences. Academic theologies are not the same as the beliefs of the average religious follower; and unlike the data of science, religion can find its own voice, often at odds with that of the theologian. Nonetheless, the fact that skill, commitment and faith are now acknowledged to play an important part in the success of science argues well for future dialogue between the subjects. The methods of science and theology are not opposed or qualitatively different;

they are better understood as being at different points on a spectrum.

Integration

Models of independence and dialogue both assume legitimate separate areas of interest for science and religion. Models of conflict and integration, despite seeming to be at opposite ends of the scale, are similar in that each assumes that there are *no* separate areas of interest. The conflict model claims that either science or religion must oust the other. Integration demands that they must be reconciled and interwoven with one another.

The arguments for the existence of God

Traditionally the formal 'proofs' of the existence of God set out to perform a similar function. Natural theology used such proofs to demonstrate rationally the existence of God. David Pailin treats both the traditional proofs and their modern equivalents in *Groundwork of Philosophy of Religion*.[19] Some of the proofs begin from moral or philosophical considerations, but others start from a consideration of the natural world, and these are relevant to our discussion.

The cosmological argument dates back to the early Greek philosophers, but addresses one of the fundamental questions which science seeks to answer. When we look at the world around us, it is full of many different kinds of objects. Why are they there; why do they take the form they do; where do they come from? We also see movement around us: what started the heavens in motion, and why do they continue to move?

The philosophers pictured a chain of cause and effect stretching back in time. This object comes from that, which in turn originates in . . . At its most basic the cosmological argument insists that the chain must stop somewhere, and that the 'first cause' or the 'final mover' is God. This universe could have taken many different forms, but beyond all the chance and accident of our world lies the necessary reality of God. This question is no longer simply the business of the philosophers, however, and as we saw in the last chapter modern scientific cosmology directly addresses this question. The concept of a Theory of Everything seeks to answer it. Stephen Hawking's infamous remark about doing away with the need for a creator addresses exactly this question.[20] Our previous discussion suggested that Hawking has too simplistic a view of the matter. It is difficult to believe that it will not always be possible to ask a question that science cannot answer. In this case: who created the laws and boundary conditions necessary for Hawking's universe without beginning or end?

Hawking's theory, however, does help us to understand some important points. Firstly, the place of science is not fixed. Science will continue to expand, attempting to answer questions that were previously the province of philosopher and theologian. Secondly, the whole chain of the cosmological argument, which seemed so obvious to the Greeks, may no longer convince us. Hawking's work might suggest that it is not clear any longer that there has to be a first cause. Perhaps the infinite series which the Greeks so disliked does provide the only possible explanation. After all, other mythologies picture the universe as eternally renewed, like the serpent eating its own tail. Even if we accept the need for a prime cause, there is little to link this philosophically necessary 'god' with the first person of the Trinity.

The argument from design notes that the world in which we live seems to be ordered and to work to some pattern. How could an eye originate by chance? As Paley suggested, if someone finds a watch on a heath, it is only reasonable to infer the existence of a watchmaker. But even before Paley wrote, David Hume had attacked the argument: the order which we claim to see may in fact be natural to the system. The universe is not a watch and we should not imagine that what is true for the one must also follow for the other. Why stop at the watchmaker, Hume implies. Those who use the argument for design will claim the Designer who made the watchmaker is God: why do we not claim that the Designer was made by a Super-designer and so on for ever?

Soon after Paley had written, the theory of evolution suggested plausible alternative mechanisms to account for the so-called evidence of design. What had seemed a strong argument for the necessity of divine intervention in the universe, in order for it to make sense, suddenly became the strongest evidence for the power of natural processes to explain the whole of the natural world.[21]

The teleological argument at first sight looks similar to the argument from design, and indeed the design argument is often treated as a special case of the teleological one. The difference is that the design argument begins with the details of the world and argues from them to the need for a creator. By contrast, the teleological argument asks us to consider the whole of reality, and whether it has a purpose. It is almost beyond belief, claim those who find this argument persuasive, that the world should have emerged with such a structure through the random interaction of blind forces.

Some commentators see the *Anthropic Principle* as a version of the teleological argument, which seeks to put a similar case in purely scientific terms. Others identify it more closely with a rehabilitated argument from design; as we have suggested, the boundaries between these arguments are blurred.[22]

All versions of the teleological argument assume that we, as humans living within the universe, can know enough about the total structure of reality to draw overall conclusions about the purposes of God. As Christians we may well wish to claim that such insights have been revealed to us, but as scientific observers, this claim is an immense one to make.

In fact, none of the so-called proofs are of the sort that would convince a sceptical observer. Nor do they threaten the Christian demand for a personal response in faith. What they may be able to do is to reassure the believer that there is nothing inherently irrational or improbable about theistic belief. Several recent books and articles make this point.[23] It may be that the experience of Paley and Darwin has made theologians too reluctant to draw conclusions from the natural world. It should be perfectly natural for Christians to understand that the world is the way it is because a loving God has made it so.

Scientists as theologians

Arthur Peacocke represents a modern and moderate approach to a model of integration. In *Theology for a Scientific Age*, Peacocke deliberately begins by outlining a simple and non-specialist picture of science. Theologians, he suggests, should be aware of at least this much science before they attempt to write theology. The question at the heart of his work is whether theology needs to be 'modified and enriched by the impressive perspectives on the world that the natural sciences now give us'.[24]

Peacocke's answer to his own question, which is worked out in the remainder of his book, seems to be that our doctrines will indeed need to be reinterpreted in the light of the scientific contribution. So, for example, he reviews the subtly changing meaning of the virginal conception, as increasing scientific understanding of the processes of human reproduction became available, and suggests that unless modified a simple statement of the doctrine today would convey a very different meaning from that originally intended, tending to detract from Jesus' true humanity rather than to emphasize his divinity.[25]

It is instructive to compare Peacocke's approach with that of John Polkinghorne. Polkinghorne sees his primary task as being to justify the basic doctrines of theology, by demonstrating their compatibility with the results of science.[26] So, for example, whilst he notes the difficulties, he suggests that the doctrine of the virgin birth can still form a useful part of Christian belief, and be held with integrity by an informed scientist.[27] Thus, following our classification, whilst Peacocke's thought tends towards integration, Polkinghorne's tends towards the dialogue model.

John Polkinghorne has considered three 'scientist-theologians' as he calls them in *Scientists as Theologians*. The trio is Polkinghorne himself, Peacocke and Ian Barbour. The three are particularly important to the study of the present state of the relationship of science and religion, not least because it is to them that theologians tend to turn when they wish to learn more about science.[28] All have made a similar journey, from a formal training in one of the sciences to a later concern to make use of their scientific experience in the service of theology. It may seem surprising that Polkinghorne does not include John Habgood, the former Archbishop of York, among his scientist-theologians. Habgood was a physiologist before training for the priesthood, and wrote an early book on the relationship, *Religion and Science*. His later work, however, has tended to concentrate on the ethical implications of science, about which he has spoken extensively in the House of Lords. Since his retirement, Habgood has begun to write again more directly and in more depth about the theological implications of science.[29]

For Polkinghorne, the crucial distinction to be made when considering the relationship of science and religion lies in the difference between consonance and assimilation. He defines himself as seeking consonance between the doctrines of religion and the theories of science, whilst Barbour seeks a much greater degree of assimilation of religion to science. Polkinghorne places Peacocke somewhere between himself and Barbour. The categories of consonance and assimilation are similar to those of dialogue and integration, which we borrowed from Barbour.

Integration and Process Thought

Barbour himself would probably agree with Polkinghorne's classification. He is sympathetic to Peacocke's work, but believes that it does not go far enough.

> [Peacocke] gives us vivid images for talking about God's relation to a natural order whose characteristics science has disclosed. But I believe that in addition to images that provide a suggestive link between scientific and religious reflection, we need philosophical categories to help us unify scientific and theological assertions in a more systematic way.[30]

Barbour moves on to talk of a *systematic synthesis* between science and religion, both of which find their place within a comprehensive metaphysics. For Barbour this is to be found in Process philosophy, which he believes provides a large enough canvas to be sympathetic and fair to the insights of both disciplines. It is difficult to do justice to Process Thought in a few lines, as it has been extensively developed in different ways by individual thinkers. A short extract from Barbour's summary gives the flavour:

> Process metaphysics understands every new event to be jointly the product of the entity's past, its own action, and the action of God. Here God transcends the world but is immanent in the world in a specific way in the structure of each event. We do not have a succession of purely natural events, interrupted by gaps in which God alone operates. Process thinkers reject the idea of divine omnipotence; they believe in a God of persuasion rather than compulsion . . .[31]

Barbour's approach seems attractive, but we should be aware of its underlying assumptions. Barbour makes considerable use of

Process philosophy, but this rests on very questionable assumptions about the nature of reality. Is the world really composed of the entities and events which are proposed by Process Thought? More fundamentally still, Barbour assumes the superiority of philosophy over both science and theology, when he suggests that the task of our endeavour is to seek a mediating position, superior to that of both science and theology. Barbour sees philosophy as the only possible candidate for such a task. Peacocke by contrast implicitly denies the priority of philosophy. In the future the relation of science and religion may be a rather more direct one.[32]

Different maps: dimensions of relationship

Conflict, independence, dialogue, integration. Barbour's scheme conjures up pictures of territory to be occupied, boundaries to be mapped out, negotiations to arrange. The language is that of diplomacy between sovereign powers. A description of the nature of the interaction itself provides the essence of the scheme. It is important to realize that any description will impose its own logic from outside on to the reality of the situation. At least part of what we find is shaped by what we ourselves bring to the situation.

The point may become clear if we consider another scheme which, according to its authors, seeks to describe in much more general terms than Barbour the dimensions of the interaction between any pair of disciplines.[33] The use of the word 'dimension' ought to remind us of the dimensions of time and space. Although they sound familiar and easy to picture the four dimensions of the space-time continuum are in fact beyond the limit of common sense visualization: visually we can only picture three dimensions! Another difference from Barbour is that this scheme deals with the relation between disciplines, which means that we are now considering the relation between science and theology, both in some sense, organized bodies of knowledge, rather than Barbour's more ambitious interaction between science and religion. Science and religion may turn out to be very different creatures: the one a highly disciplined body of fact and theory; the other so amorphous as to be practically beyond definition. The approach here is to consider four dimensions, which it is claimed, are common to the systematic study of any subject:

Approach   When we begin 'to do' science, what questions are we attempting to answer? Is it the case that science sets out to ask a series of 'How?' questions about the world, while theology instead tackles the 'Why?' questions? If it could be shown that this was exclusively the case, then there would be no interaction between the approaches of science and theology. Whether or not their subject matter was the same they would have different interests.

It is often remarked, for instance, that a biological description of the mechanics of sexual intercourse has little in common with a discussion of Christian love and marriage. On the other hand this illustration does show that the separation of How and Why is only part of the story. Christian marriage *does* assume the biology of sex; and a complete biological description will have comments to make about the psychology of attraction and the utility of permanent pair bonding, which will intrude into the ethical sphere.

Language   We have already seen that many philosophers, following Wittgenstein's lead, have described how language is used differently in different contexts. The language of theology may simply be incompatible with that of science. Certainly the technical languages which are needed for the study of any discipline at an advanced level are difficult for the non-specialist to understand.

It may well be that this is not simply a question of jargon and the inability of professionals to communicate. The use of different languages may suggest a limitation in our ability to describe the whole of reality. Perhaps each language can only be used for part of the task, or alternatively perhaps the whole concept of an external reality in any simple sense is misleading. 'Reality' may be shorthand for the artificial construction of each language group as they use their language; another group's reality may be very different.

Attitude   The objective scientist only committed to hard fact, and prepared to abandon cherished theories at the first intimation of an unexpected result, is as much a figment of the imagination as is the subjective theologian, defending dogma by twisting all facts to fit into the inherited tradition. Nonetheless, religion demands an approach of critical commitment which is inevitably different from that demanded by science. The theologian and the scientist ought to have different attitudes to the subject matter of their disciplines. Philosophers of science from Polanyi onwards have, however, insisted that the difference is one of degree rather than kind.

Object   What is it that theology studies? What does science seek to understand? It may be that the world is composed of two realms: the eternal and the spacio-temporal, the supernatural and the natural, or however we seek to define them. If the concept of dualism is in fact correct then the objects of theology and science are totally separate, and there can in principle be no conflict because there is no overlap of interest.

It ought to be clear by now that these four dimensions are not simple polar opposites, but in fact represent a complete spectrum of approaches, some sympathetic to interaction between disciplines; others denying any possibility of dialogue. Our own position has been to suggest that the attitude of the theologian and the scientist to their work ought to be different, but that the difference is only one of degree. On this model, the correct professional approach of scientist or theologian can easily be situated at slightly different positions on the same line for each of the four dimensions considered.

It will be useful to remind ourselves of our purpose in examining different ways of modelling the relation between science and religion. Different models provide different insights into the issues; they demonstrate the complexity of what is being claimed when it is said that an interaction between the disciplines is possible. Finally, by considering more than one model we have suggested that no single scheme can be anything other than an attempt to model or picture a very complex reality.

Science and theology: from obstacle to aid

From all that we have learnt about the history of science, we might well expect that scientists will remain somewhat suspicious of any outside influences on their work. Thomas Huxley wrote with biting clarity about the situation at the start of his professional life, as it seemed to him, looking back from the close of the nineteenth century:

I had set out on a journey, with no other purpose than that of exploring a certain province of natural knowledge; I strayed no hair's breadth from the course which it was my right and my duty to pursue; and yet I found that, whatever route I took, before long, I came to a tall and formidable-looking fence. Confident as I might be in the existence of an ancient and indefeasible right of way, before me stood the thorny barrier with its comminatory notice-board – 'No Thoroughfare. By order. Moses.' There seemed to be no way over; nor did the prospect of creeping round, as I saw some do, attract me. True there was no longer any cause to fear the spring guns and man-traps set by former lords of the manor; but one is apt to get very dirty going on all-fours. The only alternatives were either to give up my journey – which I was not minded to do – or to break the fence down and go through it.[34]

Huxley and his colleagues played a large part in the assertion of the independence of science from all non-scientific considerations, and the professionalization of science. This had a profound effect on all disciplines. As Mary Midgley puts it 'historians, philosophers, theologians and scientists all withdrew further and further into their respective classrooms, taking their various pupils with them.'[35]

Midgley highlights a real problem here. It is no longer possible for most of today's scientists to take an professional interest in the concept of knowledge as a large map. Ever increasing specialization is bound to make heavy demands. There is more and more basic material to digest before the aspiring scientist becomes fully literate in a discipline. Limitations on time, but perhaps also the lack of inclination, mean that few of today's scientists have the understanding of the historical and philosophical background to science and its theories that was commonplace at the time of Einstein and Bohr. In *Science as Salvation*, Mary Midgley forcefully suggests that many scientists, when they do emerge from their own specialisms, have a tendency to treat everything outside science as intellectually inferior or even irrational. It is still often assumed that science can solve all problems. This blinkered vision can lead to strange, humorous but sometimes also dangerous results: The idea of a scientific salvation from the end of the world can be laughed away, but Midgley fears 'an unrealistic, mindless exultation of [the] intellect – narrowly conceived as searching for facts – and a corresponding contempt for natural feeling'.[36]

Some of the results of contemporary scientists emerging, almost as innocents abroad, to discover the age-old questions of philosophy and theology are well known:

> It may seem bizarre, but in my opinion science offers a surer path to God than religion. Right or wrong, the fact that science has actually advanced to the point where what were formerly religious questions can be seriously tackled, itself indicates the far-reaching consequences of the new physics.[37]

and, the most notorious of all:

> [We] shall all – philosophers, scientists and just ordinary people – be able to take part in the discussion of the question why it is that we and the universe exist. If we find the answer to that, it would be the ultimate triumph of human reason – for then we would know the mind of God.[38]

We can easily make fun of all this, and these particular arguments are not hard to demolish. Both Davies and Hawking are physicists, professionally trained to describe the intricacies of the physical universe. They seem to assume, almost without argument, that an understanding of certain physical realities is the same as an understanding of everything that is, including the complexities of the human mind. But if we listen with a little more sympathy we hear genuine questions being asked, and not necessarily glib answers being delivered.

For Davies at least, ultimate questions arise out of the study of physics. This is surely a sign of hope. It may not say anything about the structure of the universe. Those who have studied the so-called Anthropic Principle are divided as to whether it is a pointer from within physics to questions that are by definition beyond physics, or whether it is simply the glorification of our ignorance into a spurious scientific principle, which like all arguments from gaps in our knowledge will in its turn be circumvented. The contemporary writers whose work we have met in this chapter are divided on the issue. Midgley is suspicious, whilst Peacocke and Polkinghorne cautiously welcome the Anthropic Principle. Perhaps rather than describing the nature of the universe such questions in fact remind us of universal *human* expectations and aspirations. If so, of course, they are indeed the stuff of theology. Paul Davies himself has commented on this:

> I recently asked a Jesuit why so many theoretical physicists were preoccupied with theology. He replied that other scientists turn to theoretical physics when they are stuck, but theoretical physicists have nowhere else to turn but theology.[39]

According to Midgley the result of modern specialization in science is that, to use her map-making analogy, modern maps show fine detail correctly but by concentrating on the small scale, fail to map out the whole terrain, and so no longer provide the route maps needed for actual journeys.[40] This has practical consequences. The more practitioners in different subjects are isolated from one another, the more they rely on their own resources. Midgley calls her book *Science as Salvation*, and notes the unfortunate and perhaps catastrophic consequences of scientists cut off from any understanding of other than scientific resources. Not knowing of any real world beyond the scientific, they cannot look beyond science for help in the solution to their problems; conversely they assume that all problems have scientific solutions. For them science is the only possible salvation.

'The queen of the sciences'?

There are, however, other voices to be heard. We can give just one example from within the physical sciences. Chris Isham is a professor of theoretical physics. At a conference organized by the Vatican Observatory to commemorate the three hundredth anniversary of the publication of Newton's *Principia*, he treated a mixed audience of scientists and theologians to a tough and rigorous exposition of 'Creation as a Quantum Process'. Isham does not see any simplistic relation of the disciplines of science and theology, certainly not one that could be resolved by the simplistic absorption of scientific results or theological presuppositions, but

> My reasons for presenting the ideas underlying a modern scientific theory stem rather from a belief that philosophy and theology are indeed the 'queen of the sciences' and, as such, are

charged with the awe-inspiring task of overseeing *all* modes of enquiry and of cohering them in a unity of vision that is both emotionally and intellectually satisfying.[41]

Isham, writing as a physicist, is probably too optimistic about the power of theology and philosophy to act in a disinterested way. Past history demands that theologians display a certain humility. Nonetheless, we will wish to affirm as basic theological assertions that there are maps of 'reality', that theologians can help scientists to understand the significance of their work, and that scientists can help theologians to understand and therefore glorify God's creation. Isham's vision is fundamentally correct. To seek a unity of vision is an inescapable consequence of taking seriously the biblical witness to a God who both creates and sustains, who remains involved with the creation, and the development of science to its present state of sophistication.

However, we need to add a cautionary note, which applies to the whole notion of the possibility of a useful relationship between different disciplines. Science has been so very successful over the past couple of hundred years because it has deliberately restricted itself. The old jibe about knowing more and more about less and less has a kernel of truth. By limiting, and simplifying and not looking over the garden fence, scientists have managed to make an incredibly complex and confusing world comprehensible. By considering ideal cases they have formulated laws which, on experiment, are discovered to approximate to the workings of the real world.

There is a major problem here. When you take something apart the sense of the whole is lost. However much he cries afterwards the boy who pulls the wings off a fly can never recreate the living insect from the dismembered parts. The separate directions of individual sciences will inevitably diminish interest in the complete whole of creation and in God its creator. Hence, the importance of a theology of creation, as a possible *theological* answer to the questions raised above by Midgley and Isham. Once we lose our sense of the wholeness and unity of the world, it is easy to lose our wonder in it as creation. It then becomes so much easier to take what we have for granted, as ours, and to lose sight of the delicate balance between one part of the creation and another. It becomes much easier to justify the use and exploitation of 'creation', because we no longer view it as one creation, but simply as the sum of its parts. And if the world no longer has the unity of a creation, then we no longer need to see ourselves as its stewards.

An important task of theology is precisely this: to try to make sense of the whole. But we must be under no illusion as to the difficulty of the task. Specialists are specialists in narrow subject areas exactly because an overview of the whole is so difficult. It takes so long simply to absorb the necessary facts and techniques, let alone to gain the attitude and outlook of a scientist. Beside the professionalism of the specialist, any theologian will look like an amateur.

The task, however, is a crucial one. We have discussed elsewhere the issue of *reductionism*. At each level as we break things down into their component parts something essential is lost. The mind is not just the sum of the brain's operations; the living creature is not just the sum of the chemicals of which it is composed; the world is not just a vast treasure trove to be endlessly mined without consequences. These integrative tasks are not unknown to the scientists as they seek accurately to describe the world, but it is the specific task of the theologian to celebrate the wholeness of God's creation; to describe God's love for it and involvement with it. In a similar way, it is the task of any Christian to live in the world remembering that it is God's creation, and that, redeemed by the love of God, she or he is God's steward, the priest of creation.

Chapter 8

Doing Theology in a World of Science

Theology cannot just be left to the theologians, as is made clear by the recent spectacle of a distinguished theologian writing over three hundred pages on God in creation with only an occasional and cursory reference to scientific insight.[1]

John Polkinghorne is here criticizing Jürgen Moltmann's *God in Creation*. This is a much admired contribution to systematic theology, which in many ways fulfils the promise of its subtitle, 'an ecological doctrine of creation'. But Polkinghorne is correct to complain that Moltmann makes very few references to the contemporary understanding of the world as developed by modern physics and cosmology.

In the last chapter we looked at various suggestions that have been offered to provide a theoretical framework within which to understand the possible interactions between science and religion. In this chapter I want to discuss the attempts of some contemporary theologians to meet the challenge. We shall soon see that their work does not fit easily into any of the theoretical categories. To ask whether theologians have been able to take account of science is to engage in dialogue with different theologians, who have their own specific concerns, and who are more or less well-informed about the state of contemporary science.

This chapter will be more messy and less organized than most of the remainder of the book. It seeks to engage in a genuine dialogue with individuals working today, and that is never a neat process. Nevertheless, at the end of the chapter we shall feel confident enough to make some specific suggestions as to how theologians, and religious believers in general, should approach the world of science.

Specialists and amateurs

At the end of the last chapter we noticed an obvious difference between theology and science. While science tends to ever greater specialization, the task of theology remains to synthesize. Whilst many scientists are properly occupied in discovering ever finer detail, many theologians continue to attempt to redefine the broader picture. The success of science as a progressive discipline has often been attributed to this narrow concentration. At the same time theology can be seen as preoccupied with endlessly refighting old battles.

Like almost all the differences between science and theology which we have discussed this is not a question of absolute opposition, but rather of different positions on a spectrum. Many of the tasks of theology do demand particular technical specialization – we would have little sympathy with a New Testament scholar without the necessary knowledge of Greek. Equally, ecology and other interdisciplinary sciences demand a wide overview. However, we should not disguise real differences. Polkinghorne's criticism of Moltmann, quoted above, is justified, but we would not criticize scientists for not taking into account Moltmann's theology in their laboratory work. We would, of course, expect them to have studied the fundamental issues involved when making ethical decisions or writing on the implications of science.

In this chapter we shall consider the work of a number of theologians who strive in their work to develop a broad picture, making use of the insights of science. By definition this is exposed and dangerous territory. The theologian cannot be an expert in all areas of science, and so is open to the attacks of those who know their own specialities intimately well. Equally, the theologian cannot simply defer to the opinions of an expert scientist. Judgments have to be made, and these will be personal and often disputed.

Perhaps theologians cannot win. John Polkinghorne complains of Moltmann's lack of scientific reference. Wolfhart Pannenberg, by contrast, has always taken the scientific worldview very seriously. In *Towards a Theology of Nature* and in his *Systematic Theology* he seeks to develop his idea that the spirit of God can be described helpfully in terms of field theory, an integral part of physics since the work of Faraday and Maxwell in the nineteenth century. Ironically, Polkinghorne is as critical of Pannenberg as he was of Moltmann:

> Wolfhart Pannenberg seems to think that modern field theory offers a way of thinking about spirit, though to a physicist a field is about as spiritual as a tenuous gas![2]

Such critical dialogue, although sometimes painful, is both justified and necessary. What can sometimes seem unfair is the assumption by many writers on popular science that theologians can be lambasted for their lack of scientific understanding, but that no preparatory training or reading is necessary before engaging in theological speculation.

The pope and the scientists

It may seem unexpected to devote part of this chapter to Pope John Paul II, but in 1992, John Paul II issued a formal rehabilitation of Galileo. The event generated world-wide publicity and comment. It was, however, simply the best publicized of a number of papal gestures. John Paul II is often characterized as a conservative, traditionalist pope, but in the area of the relations between the church and science his pontificate has been remarkable for its open-mindedness about the errors of the past. As Michael Sharratt points out, the formal rehabilitation of 1992 was as much the rehabilitation of the authority of the church as of Galileo. Here was the church saying sorry and making a firm promise of amendment for the future.[3] 1996 saw the publication of a message to the Pontifical Academy of Sciences, declaring that Darwin's theory of natural selection was 'more than just a hypothesis.'[4] And earlier, in 1988, the Pope had used the conference organized by the Vatican Observatory to commemorate the three hundredth anniversary of the publication of Newton's *Principia* to review the relationship between the church and the sciences.

Despite an early failure of communication reported by Stephen

Hawking in *A Brief History of Time*, it seems clear that John Paul does not make the mistake of Pius XII, who enthusiastically welcomed the Big Bang theory, as supporting a biblical view of creation. The Big Bang *may* be good science, and *may* support biblical doctrines, but when Pius XII wrote, the Big Bang was simply one theory among others. If Hoyle's explicitly atheistic Steady State theory had been successful in scientific terms, where would this have left the church? Equally, as Stephen Hawking demonstrates, the Big Bang theory does not *necessarily* support a doctrine of creation, at least in any straightforward way. To assume that scientific theories give direct support to doctrine, or indeed oppose it, is to have failed to learn the lesson of Galileo.[5]

By contrast, John Paul calls for genuine dialogue. There must be a strong relationship between science and religion, but neither can dictate to the other. His message to the conference marking the anniversary of Newton's *Principia* is worth quoting at length:

Theology is not to incorporate indifferently each new philosophical or scientific theory. As these findings become part of the intellectual culture of the time, however, theologians must understand them and test their value in bringing out from Christian belief some of the possibilities which have not yet been realized . . .

If the cosmologies of the ancient Near Eastern world could be purified and assimilated into the first chapters of Genesis, might contemporary cosmology have something to offer to our reflections upon creation? Does an evolutionary perspective bring any light to bear upon theological anthropology, the meaning of the human person as the *imago Dei*, the problem of Christology – and even upon the development of doctrine itself? What, if any, are the eschatological implications of contemporary Cosmology, especially in the light of the vast future of our universe? Can theological method fruitfully appropriate insights from scientific methodology and the philosophy of science?

Questions of this kind can be suggested in abundance. Pursuing them further would require the sort of intense dialogue with contemporary science that has, on the whole, been lacking among those engaged in theological research and teaching. It would entail that some theologians, at least, should be sufficiently well-versed in the sciences to make authentic and creative use of the resources that the best-established theories may offer them. Such an expertise would prevent them from making uncritical and overhasty use for apologetic purposes of such recent theories as that of the 'Big Bang' in cosmology. Yet it would equally keep them from discounting altogether the potential relevance of such theories to the deepening of understanding in traditional areas of theological inquiry . . .

Science can purify religion from error and superstition; religion can purify science from idolatry and false absolutes. Each can draw the other into a wider world, a world in which both can flourish.[6]

The Pope's programme is both thorough and radical. We are cautioned not to be tossed around by the changing fashions of science at the cutting edge, but to wait until theories have gained wide acceptance. The church must not simply pick and choose theories such as the Big Bang, which suit its theology. Equally, it must be prepared to offer reasoned criticism where it seems necessary: 'religion can purify science from idolatry and false absolutes'.

The questions raised in the second paragraph of the quotation above are startling in their comprehensiveness. Cosmology may be able to assist us in the same way that the early chapters of Genesis were moulded by the intellectual climate of their times; evolution may help us to understand ourselves, and our relation to God, as well as the development of the church's teaching.

Finally, the plea is made that theologians equip themselves properly in this area. We might contrast this hope with the hostility that Derek Stanesby reports from other quarters: 'When I pressed one of my esteemed colleagues [on the Church of England Doctrine Commission] about the importance of scientific knowledge for theology he replied that he simply did not have time to acquire such knowledge.'[7]

We shall see in the remainder of this chapter how some contemporary theologians measure up to the challenge set by the pope.

The science of theology

Two theologians who have both taken science very seriously, but make use of it in markedly different ways, are Thomas Torrance and Wolfhart Pannenberg. Both are aware of the complex nature of the interaction between science and religion and both possess the necessary technical expertise to address the issue at a number of different levels. As we shall see, they pursue entirely different strategies.

Thomas Torrance: the givenness of all knowledge

Thomas Torrance has been systematically sympathetic to the scientific enterprise over many years in a way unmatched by almost any other theologian. The titles of many of his books reveal this interest: *Space, Time and Incarnation*, *Space, Time and Resurrection* and the influential, *Scientific Theology*. In addition Torrance has edited two important series of books exploring different aspects of the relationship between science and theology: *Theology and Scientific Culture* and *Theology and Science at the Frontiers of Knowledge*. In the general introduction to the latter series he writes:

> We must now reckon with a fundamental change in the generation of fundamental ideas. Today it is no longer philosophy but the physical and natural sciences which set the pace in human culture through their astonishing revelation of the rational structures that pervade and underlie all created reality.[8]

At the very centre of Torrance's thought is the conviction that what we can know rests on what is *given*. Theologically our knowledge of God is graciously revealed to us:

> Christian theology arises out of the actual knowledge of God given in and with concrete happening in space and time. It is knowledge of the God who actively meets us . . .[9]

Similarly our scientific knowledge rests on the givenness of the physical world. In the same way that Torrance is a realist in his theology, so his philosophy of science is also based on realism.

He believes that science is constantly attempting to describe what is already present, rather than constructing a picture of the world. In neither case is this a simple process, because Torrance insists that we must look beneath the surface content to find the deeper reality within. According to a recent commentator, this allows Torrance to insist on the ultimate co-ordination of science and theology whilst respecting their own particular subject matter.[10] So, the theological investigation of God in Creation can provide a framework for (natural) science; the work of science in turn enables theology to understand the scientific method – which theology can then use in its own way; science can enlarge our understanding of God's world, and also begin to ask fundamental questions concerning the universe as a whole.

This co-ordination, however, is at a very deep, even remote, level. In practice, time and again, Torrance emphasizes that theologians and scientists must work with the givenness of their respective subject matter. Through the grace of God, God himself, or the universe, may be known. Reality actively gives itself and also provides the means by which it is known; we actively respond by learning to explore reality in the appropriate way. Torrance here uses Polanyi's insights: the skill of the explorer – theologian or scientist – is to use the correct tools in the proper ways and to learn to see what is there to be seen. Torrance's debt to Polanyi is acknowledged clearly in *Belief in Science and Christian Life*.[11]

Science and scientific theology

As we noted earlier it would be an over-simplification to categorize Torrance as merely arguing for the independence of science and theology (theology is usually his preferred equivalent to science rather than religion).[12] At the very deepest level he sees a co-ordination between science and theology both in terms of content and method (though, on principle, these are never sharply divided in Torrance's work). Torrance's model of the relation of science and theology has been described in terms of the dynamic interaction of 'cultural solar systems' which enables a positive and mutual regulation of choice as the subjects are in dialogue with one another.[13] The sheer complexity of this definition is characteristic of Torrance. Nonetheless, as a broad generalization, our original point can stand.

For Torrance, there is no science; there are only the sciences. There is no scientific method; only methods that work in specific situations. There is a scientific way, which is to apply our basic human rationality in particular situations. We must acknowledge both the unity of knowledge and the diverse realms of nature. Theology and science can consistently illuminate each other, but such insights tend to be at the level of analogy, or to be described as complimentary approaches to the same problem. Natural theology is to be rejected as using the wrong method. God chooses to make himself known in revelation, in grace, and to start to look for him in nature is simply to start from the wrong place.[14] Even this brief summary illustrates Torrance's solid rooting in his Reformed tradition and especially the influence of Karl Barth, whose work Torrance has translated into English.

Contingency: the independence and dependence of creation

An important concept for Torrance is that of the *contingency* of the created world. Contingency is not an easy term to define but, as used here, it means that everything that has been created not only depends on God, but depends on *God's free grace*, so that nothing which has been created had to exist, in any logical sense. The creation is not necessary, everything takes the form which it does because God wills that it should do so. The idea of contingency allows an independence to the world which makes science both possible and necessary. This is because it implies that there is no 'logical bridge' between God and the world. We cannot discover God within the world, and so the sciences have their own genuine autonomy which cannot be threatened by or threaten that of theology:

Since there is no logical bridge between God and the world, there is no logical reversibility between them. If there were such a relation, knowledge of the created world and knowledge of God would be clamped together in such a way that we would derive knowledge of God necessarily and coercively from knowledge of the world, while knowledge of the world even in its natural operations would not be possible without constantly including God among the data.[15]

Torrance seeks to guard against two difficulties. He wants to defend the freedom of God to act graciously in any way that God chooses, totally unconstrained by external considerations. At the same time, he wants to defend the practice of science from any *a priori* conclusions. In his view our knowledge of God cannot, and must not be allowed to, affect the way in which science is conducted, or the conclusions of the sciences. The concept of a contingent world, made and dependent upon God, but separate from God allows Torrance to achieve his goal. This is achieved at a price, however, because for Torrance the proclamation of a creator God is almost entirely separated from our practical knowledge of God's creation.

The second difficulty against which Torrance seeks to provide safeguards is the claim that any interaction between the subject matter of science and theology restricts the freedom of God. Is Torrance correct that such a connection would imply that knowledge of God derives 'necessarily and coercively' from knowledge of the world? To answer these charges we need to return to the doctrine of creation, and one of the major preoccupations of contemporary theology.

Jürgen Moltmann and others have pointed out that there is a paradox in our concept of creation. For God, who is all in all, the act of creation is in itself a limitation.[16] In creating, God chooses to allow space for the created order; God chooses not to allow God's presence to overwhelm the creation. By creating this creation rather than some other created order, God has made actual only one among an apparently infinite set of possibilities. If this train of reasoning is correct, then it is not the potential knowledge of God to be derived from the created order which limits God, it is the fact that there is a created order to be investigated that provides the limitation. By the act of creation God defines Godself; by creating this world God is further defined. But these are not human, philosophical or logical restrictions which presume to instruct God how to be God. Rather they are part of the gracious activity of God whereby God reveals Godself not only as redeemer but also as creator of this world. Far from being an inappropriate restriction on the sovereignty of God, this understanding forms part of the gospel proclamation of a God who loves the world that he has made so much that he suffers for it and in it. Thus the claim that a positive relationship is possible between science and religion, and that it has a definite theological content, belongs together with the more general re-evaluation of the attributes of God, and in particular of God's supposed impassibility, which has proceeded in recent years. As Paul Fiddes has written: 'God has made the world as it is *because* he chooses to suffer with it.'[17]

Torrance can be criticized for the complexity of his language and the density of his discussion. Given the vast subject matter with which he works, and his desire never to relax the rigour of his argument, this is understandable. A more telling criticism is that Torrance's preoccupation is with the Theory of Relativity – the last great monument of classical physics – rather than with quantum mechanics, which raises a very different series of questions for theology, as we shall see later in this chapter. The theoretical consequences of relativity and classical physics (Torrance rarely strays beyond physics) are perhaps more easily compatible with Torrance's philosophy than those of quantum theory.

To sum up: Torrance sees theology as one science among many others, but if the different sciences are so different in method and subject matter is there really a useful common currency to the concept of science? In a revealing aside, Torrance speaks of his presuppositions:

> If I may be allowed to speak personally for a moment, I find the presence and being of God bearing upon my existence and thought so powerfully that I cannot but be convinced of His overwhelming reality and rationality. To doubt the existence of God would be an act of sheer irrationality, for it would mean that my reason had become unhinged from its bond with real being.[18]

For Torrance, like Barth before him, the revelation of God made known in and through Jesus Christ will overwhelm all other sources of knowledge of God. The danger of theology seeking to make use of the results of science is that this is to look for God in the wrong place, and using the wrong tools.

Wolfhart Pannenberg: the importance of contact with the real world

Wolfhart Pannenberg begins his *Systematic Theology* with a discussion of the ground of theology, which is directly relevant here:

> But what does it mean that for the most part dogmatics does not formally discuss the truth of Christian doctrine but presupposes it? It means that dogmatics does not expressly, or at least systematically, make the truth claim of Christian doctrine one of its questions; it simply accepts it . . . If the theses of Christian doctrine do not make the world's questioning of the reality of God, its contesting and rejecting of this reality, a question which is put to its own Christian truth-consciousness, then these theses will not make contact with worldly reality but will hover above it and will not, therefore, be true.[19]

Pannenberg is here claiming that the neo-orthodox programme of Barth and Torrance chooses to isolate itself from an objective debate as to the status of the truth-claims which it is making. This may have been a necessary strategy in Barth's time, with the church facing challenges both from liberal criticism and from totalitarian attacks on its sovereignty. But, as Pannenberg suggests, it cannot provide a final answer to the question of involvement with other disciplines or with the real world. Whilst each subject must claim a measure of methodological independence, to claim total independence from the wider scientific world, is, in the end, to demand an unproductive isolation.

Defining a relationship of relative independence between academic disciplines was a major concern of Pannenberg in his *Theology and the Philosophy of Science*. There he sought to understand scientific explanation, in a much more unified sense than Torrance would allow, and to redefine the place of theology within intellectual life. He characterized much post-Enlightenment theology as seeking independence:

> [O]n the whole theology in recent times has tried to find a basis more or less exclusively in the idea of man's subjectivity and self-understanding. This has inevitably meant a theological interest in seeing the anthropological and historical sciences

autonomous and independent of a natural science which seemed no longer to offer theology a purchase of any kind.[20]

But for Pannenberg, this is too much of a retreat into subjectivity and relativism: 'One gains the right to be irrational at the expense of losing the right to criticize.'[21] If theology is content to connect the question of God only with a theory of humanity then the doctrine of creation will simply wither away. More hopefully Pannenberg sees signs that science can begin to attempt the task of connecting the parts to the whole; and that scientific explanation is not to be conceived as the understanding of the novel in terms of the known. Instead new understanding will be won in terms of new, wider frames of reference.[22] In this enterprise theology, especially in its close connection to history – one of Pannenberg's great preoccupations – can indeed now be accommodated into the scientific enterprise.

After *Theology and the Philosophy of Science*, Pannenberg continued to study the subject, writing on a wide range of the technical issues involved, including a set of 'Theological Questions to Scientists' before incorporating the results of his research into his *Systematic Theology*. Here Pannenberg engages in major discussions of inertia, evolution, and space and relativity.[23]

Pannenberg's thought is highly complex, but he makes a fundamental distinction between descriptions of the world based upon interacting particles and those based on fields of force, the distortion of which we recognize as particles. For Pannenberg, God cannot be described as one object among others and so it is difficult to describe God adequately in a model where particles are fundamental. In a field model, on the other hand, Pannenberg believes that the extensive nature of the field corresponds well to God's omnipresence.[24] Ted Peters, who is sympathetic to Pannenberg's theology, notes just how radical his claim here is:

> Pannenberg rushes in where two-language angels have feared to tread. He does not say that spirit *is like* a force field. He says spirit *is* a force field. There is a directness and a literalness here that seems to throw caution to the wind.[25]

This is exactly the criticism that Polkinghorne makes. For him, Pannenberg is placing too much weight upon a particular interpretation of field theory. Polkinghorne does not accept that the theory implies what Pannenberg wants it to mean. We have here a theologian, well read in the theories of science, attempting to make direct use of scientific understanding in his theology. He is being criticized by a scientist, who is well versed in classical theology, for misinterpreting the true meaning of science. Such dialogue ought to provide for fertile and creative growth in understanding.

Torrance takes science seriously, but insists that the very act of taking a discipline seriously inevitably leads to an assertion of the separateness of its subject matter, and hence a certain reserve in the questions which can be legitimately asked by one discipline of another. By contrast, Pannenberg insists that different disciplines can ask direct questions of each other, and appropriate each other's results in a comparatively straightforward way. The theories of science are here in continual and fruitful dialogue with the theories of theology.

The case for a new metaphysic

Langdon Gilkey: nature, reality, and the sacred

Can the interaction possibly be as simple as Pannenberg suggests? The radical American theologian, Langdon Gilkey, thinks not. He begins his exploration, however, from a very practical personal experience of the 'creationist' legal battles in the United States in which he was called as an expert witness. This provided him with the opportunity to observe both parties to the court battles at close quarters. Gilkey did not find the spectacle edifying.[26]

From this experience Gilkey deduces that it is dangerous to import religious language too easily or too directly into everyday life, as Creationism seeks to do. To succeed in this would be to introduce an infallible element into ordinary experience. Religious certainty cannot be examined or contradicted. A society which accepted such a valuation for religious statements would soon be forced to reject all science, for science is based on observation rather than revelation.

But if the Creationists are dogmatic, Gilkey finds a comparable dogmatism among the scientists. In his view, they possess a set of useful methodological rules, which choose to simplify the world by considering only physical entities, and ignoring anything else. Because these rules have proved so successful in extending scientific understanding, many scientists – and especially those involved in the Creationism trials – are willing to leap far too quickly from their useful rules to sweeping general conclusions which declare that there *is* nothing else apart from the physical. This is to confuse methodology and ontology. *How* we can learn to understand the world, the necessary techniques and short cuts of science, becomes confused with *what* the world must consist of, the new dogma of scientism. If our methods choose to ignore everything but the physical it is not surprising that we only observe the physical in our experiments!

In Gilkey's view *both* religion and science draw upon resources outside themselves to understand themselves and to communicate their content. Theologically, he is in some ways an old fashioned liberal, stressing the importance of the symbolic nature of truth:

> [T]he articulation of ... religious disclosure is not through factual propositions but by means of symbols: in narrative, metaphors, and analogies; in symbols that signal a 'doctrine', for example, creation, providence, revelation, incarnation, and so on.[27]

Gradually, Christianity has been reinterpreted as it came into contact with the results of modern science. Gilkey gives the example of the reinterpretation of the doctrine of the Fall by, for example, Reinhold Niebuhr, Tillich and Ricoeur. The scientific account of human origins has clearly influenced doctrine here. For Gilkey, these changes represent an advance for religious truth, and one that has been paralleled in science with the development of quantum mechanics and the new philosophy and sociology of science:

> As scientific knowledge has shown itself – now here is a mystery! – as more and more trustworthy, its relation to its real object has become less and less clear.[28]

Thus science and religion may be more similar than they realize. Both now stress the importance of symbol – direct, unambiguous knowledge is elusive. Both also stress the importance of the observer – all our knowledge is mediated through human agency. In addition Gilkey claims that both need a wider cultural framework in order to be understood and communicate, although both often fail to recognize this fact. He illustrates his point with numerous examples of the absolute ignorance of philosophical questions shown by most modern writers on popular science:

> All of the cosmologies [used in a broad sense] discussed herein manifest what can only be called an 'unyielding dogmatism' on issues relevant to teleology and religion, that is, on ontological or metaphysical issues.[29]

This poses a problem because it leads to those involved being forced to make absolute choices. On the scientific side, if only the physical counts, then science will inevitably be atheistic. On the religious side there has been an inevitable reaction to the atheism of much science in the growth of Creationism.

A modest and hesitant natural theology

So, Gilkey begins to develop what he calls a modest and hesitant natural theology. This is not a natural theology in the sense that it learns all that it knows about God from the natural world. Instead Gilkey seeks to intertwine theological and scientific insights. He suggests a number of elements derived from scientific pictures which are sympathetic to his proposed theology.[30] The first of these elements is *the importance of dynamic processes*. In contrast to older world views contemporary science understands the universe as continually developing and changing. Secondly, science now pictures the universe as *a defined but open system*:

> Necessity and order, on the one hand, and contingency and openness on the other hand, seem mysteriously mated and balanced in the stream of process ... Thus the microscopic level seems to prepare the way for the self-direction and the interaction of the organic level and the determinate-indeterminate character of history.[31]

This balance of order and openness, with the universe organized into different layers, allows for continuing novelty. Finally, Gilkey claims that science suggests that the universe as a whole demonstrates in its increasing complexity *an order of increasing value*. Gilkey's list is similar to the list that we ourselves made at the conclusion of chapter 6, after we had reviewed some of the general tendencies of contemporary science.

Gilkey suggests that a scheme of this sort probably could be agreed by scientists and theologians alike, the scientists perhaps without fully appreciating that it is already a metaphysical scheme, indeed one that owes much to Alfred Whitehead and Process Theology. To this basic, agreed framework, Gilkey would add a more explicitly metaphysical aspect, which he calls an 'inside' dimension. He argues that even now science does not fully appreciate the importance of the observing subject, or the importance of subjects in relation to one another. A complete description of the universe must include an understanding of the role of the consciously observing scientist. Gilkey also argues that science alone cannot properly explain the existence of order and complexity within the universe.

Gilkey's claim is that science needs the wider base which 'metaphysics' can provide both in order to understand itself, and to communicate beyond its own boundaries. For him, it is at this wider level that religion will find its natural place, rather than in any interaction at the level of particular theories. At the level of descriptive theories, nature can hint at God:

> God is thus the unconditional power to be – yet present in each puff of existence; God is the transcendent ground of freedom – yet creative in each quantum jump as in each human decision; God is the eternal source of order amid novelty, uniting the determined past with the possibilities latent in the open future.[32]

To limit God to this level, however, would be to deny what is, for Gilkey, the most important aspect of religion. For him, God is most fully known in our religious experience. Thus it is appropriate that Gilkey concludes his book with a simple and conventional statement of his own Christian belief. For Gilkey, the centre of understanding is God known in redemptive love. The mystery is that this love is revealed in both experience and nature.

It may be illuminating to remind ourselves of the movement

of Gilkey's argument. He began with the practical. Observing science and religion, or rather scientists and religious people, making what to him seemed grandiose and unsubstantiated claims, he suggests that neither science nor religion is in fact so directly connected to reality as either would suppose. Gilkey's own solution is to claim that the overall world view suggested by science, especially when bolstered by additional, but in his opinion reasonable, metaphysical assumptions, leads to a picture which is open to the important role of the human subject (as an observer in relationship). Without this perspective, science has only a partial view. Equally, religions also mislead themselves if they do not understand that all their insights (revelations) must be mediated through fallible human observers.

For Gilkey, religion cannot make direct claims with absolute authority, but can provide a powerful integrating tool at the metaphysical level. This is its most helpful level of operation, and at this level, the Christian world view provides a picture which is both sympathetic to the scientific view, but also enriches the scientific picture.

God's ways with the world

Dan Hardy: 'a detailed view and a wide vision'

This section discusses the work of Dan Hardy, an American theologian who has spent much time working in England. Hardy's importance lies in his attention to detail and in the way in which he seeks to draw pictures which have wide implications for the status of both theology and science, whilst always paying full attention to detail. His work is an example of how very intricate technical work can open up new possibilities, at the same time remaining true to its origins. Unlike the wide schemes of some of the scientific populists, Hardy keeps his feet firmly on the ground.

Dan Hardy works with a vast canvas, striving to uncover the profundity of *God's Ways with the World*, the title of his recent collection of essays and sermons. It is significant that a theologian whose essays deal with highly complex technical material includes in a single volume both theological essays and a selection of his sermons. Hardy's theology is to be a theology for the church. He seeks to bring together again 'faith, theology and other disciplined forms of life and thought'.[33] At first sight, it might seem that he is undertaking a similar project to that of Ian Barbour and Langdon Gilkey, who attempt to achieve a new synthesis through the construction of a new metaphysics, suitable for today's understanding. Hardy would certainly be as suspicious as Langdon Gilkey of the over simple moves of religious or scientific fundamentalists. But he is equally suspicious of moves like Gilkey's which seek to interpose a mediating metaphysic between science and religion.

In fact Hardy sees the task in a rather different light. His title may give the clue: there can be no easy synthesis of how God relates to the created order; instead we must speak of the plurality of God's *ways* with the world. My opening image of a canvas is misleading; we should perhaps substitute that of a cubist painter struggling to convey in a two-dimensional portrait something of the complexity of the human body and soul.

To take a different image, one of Hardy's essays begins by invoking the secure world view of Mozart or Bach. The society in which they lived allowed them a firm belief in God and God's creation as an answer to the whole of life, which then flows over into their music. He compares this vanished certainty with the fragmentation of our contemporary experience. His own preferred image for the contemporary understanding of creation is a poem by Micheal O'Sidhail describing the creation in terms of the improvisations of a Jazz club:

> I watch as swarms of dust in the spotlight,
>
> swirls of galaxies, and imagine he's blowing
> a huge balloon of space that's opening
> our world of order.[34]

The disjointed grammar of the poem reflects our situation. Unlike Mozart, we live in a world of 'private pinholes'[35] through which we see only a small part of whatever whole there may be. Our pinholes allow a blinkered vision, and we are foolish to imagine that we can impose a simple coherence on all that is real from such a limited perspective.

For Hardy, unlike Gilkey or Barbour, there can be no mediating theories, or new foundations. Process Thought does not provide a new metaphysical foundation, and nor does Fundamentalism. Instead we must seek to reconstruct the connections of theology and science (and all the other serious disciplines), whilst retaining the distinctiveness of each.[36]

Different vantage points

Hardy's central demand is that we must recognize that both the sciences and theology have valid contributions to any picture we wish to paint. Thus far his method seems similar to that of Thomas Torrance with his understanding of separate but equally valid sciences – including theology – exploring the universe in different ways suitable to their own different subject areas. Hardy moves beyond this, however, when he insists that the separate contributions of the different sciences must be brought together and allowed to interact.

On the one hand Hardy seeks to avoid the trap of Torrance's equal but separate sciences, and thus to avoid Pannenberg's criticism that such a theology will hover above world reality insulated from questions of truth and falsehood. On the other he strives to avoid a unity which is bought at the price of over simplicity. Science has often been guilty of reductionism, the claim that because a limitation of method has worked in certain areas then the methodology of denying all but simple physical causes must be applied everywhere. In a similar way, theology has also been guilty of making grandiose claims. Hardy notes that, in practice, the larger the claim, the smaller the subject areas in which it is useful. Large claims lead to narrow, self-contained understanding, only accepted by a few.[37] Creationism with its claim to regulate science via God's revelation in the Bible, and absolute reductionism, of the type described by Peter Atkins, provide clear examples of vast claims accepted in their entirely by comparatively small groups. The so-called 'Strong Programme' of the sociology of science which we examined earlier provides another example.

In contrast to this, Hardy insists on the validity of many different vantage points, each with its own context. Each context, in turn, must have its own ever widening series of contexts. For Hardy there is also what might almost be described as a dialogue between vantage point and context, which continually deepens understanding, and continues in an open-ended way. As if this was not complex enough there are further dimensions of richness. The contexts are not isolated; as they widen out they will inevitably intersect with the contexts of other vantage points. Finally, the whole picture should not be seen as static but is constantly changing. Hardy has a dynamic vision, always open to genuine novelty. No illustration can do justice to the subtlety here, but we might imagine a modern collage sculpture, in which each of the assembled parts brings its own history, but gains depth from its neighbours in the assemblage. To equate more closely to Hardy's vision, the artist would need to be continually adding new components!

The richness of the universe

Thus for Hardy, any vision of a universal theory, the GUTs and TOEs of the physicists, for example, is illusory. Of course these theories may be valid in their own domains, but always there will be a wider context and other viewpoints. Thus any laws we propose will have a limited validity. The application of any law may be immensely broad, but still its validity is limited to something less than the sum total of reality. Always remembering, of course, that such a description of reality is never less than complex, and that we can never pin down permanent boundaries. The great achievement of such an approach is to generate a richness of description that somehow rings true with our experience of the universe. It is worth entering into the struggle to master the complexity. Here is an example of Hardy's method:

The fact that explanation by physical laws and explanation by evolutionary laws open into each other, and both may open into others, illuminates the much-discussed difference of inanimate matter from animate, and animate from human. There is nothing in each kind of explanation to suggest that others are necessary, just as nothing in inanimate matter would lead us to expect that there is also animate ('an event of zero probability' says Monod) and nothing in either that would lead us to expect human life: this is the 'closure' of the theories from each other. But the closure in each case is a relative one in an open, unknown situation – their background. And that fact would lead us to consider the theories as related to each other – however difficult this interrelation is to discuss.[38]

This is a highly theoretical approach, but Hardy can use his general approach to generate specific theological insights. For example, he develops the position above as part of a discussion of what it means to describe the human being as creature. Having noted the difficulties of theorizing about human life from within, and the usual scientific dismissal of the validity of such approaches, he can use his theoretical approach to describe the openness of humanity to a purely scientific description (we are, after all, composed of cells and atoms), whilst at the same time presenting a strong case for the 'closure' of humanity, that is, its distinctiveness relative to its physical surroundings.

This is not to suggest a non-natural origin for human beings, 'What does require such talk is the open situation in which they exist, in which we have seen theories producing relative closures, thereby differentiating various elements (physical, animal, human) from the open background.'[39] Of course, the validity of this approach can always be denied, and it is easy for one authoritarianism to breed others. As we keep noticing, crude reductionism can quickly lead to the response of religious authoritarianism. What Hardy argues for is an open horizon, where the closures of particular theories or laws are understood as relative. For him, the danger is in fixed boundaries.

Interweaving science and theology

To sum up: Hardy denies the validity of bringing science and religion together via a new universal metaphysic. Instead he presents a picture of complex viewpoints understood in their own, fluid contexts. No one viewpoint can ever gain superiority over others; instead a more direct interaction is possible. So, unlike most other theologians, Hardy does not dismiss out of hand the speculations of Frank Tipler, whose book *The Physics of Immortality*, controversially attempts a secular and scientific eschatology. As Hardy says:

Like this account or not, it is emblematic of what must be achieved in a direct approach to the task of providing a combined account of current understanding of cosmology . . . with theology . . . If we wish to argue otherwise than does Tipler (or those whose arguments he uses), we must do so with the same comprehensiveness of argument.[40]

In the end, Hardy believes that Tipler's account is impoverished by trying to say something about everything, and hence, in fact, not saying enough about anything. Nonetheless, for Hardy the future lies in dialogue with Tipler, and in the attempt to provide a better account than he can:

> Cosmology as thus seen must be the context for our understanding of theology today, not only surrounding it (the conventional meaning of context) but interwoven with it (the etymological meaning of context) – as much so as ancient Hebrew and Greek concepts have been . . . The *substance* of science should interact with the *substance* of theology.[41]

The significance of Hardy's perspective is that it is always demands a direct dialogue between the 'theories' of science and religion, building on this direct interrogation without insisting that each submit to the moderation of some particular metaphysical scheme. Thus, at least in principle, such an open approach should make it possible for more participants holding a wider range of presuppositions to be drawn into an open dialogue. It also denies the demands of the philosophers that dialogue must always obey some external set of philosophical rules. At the same time Hardy can provide a sympathetic but in the end devastating critique of those who would construct new pseudo-religious world views simply from within science itself.

A conversation with postmodern science

Dan Hardy's picture of the interweaving of content and context runs through the attempts of Peter Hodgson and Sallie McFague to reinterpret theology in the light of our contemporary understanding of the world. As Hodgson writes:

> Context and content are in fact always intertwining, and each presupposes the other . . . [We cannot] responsibly reconstruct

the central themes of Christian theology (God, creation, nature, human being, sin and evil, Christ, Spirit, redemption, eschatology, etc.) without constantly attending to the very issues raised by science and ecology, liberation struggles, and encounters among the religions.[42]

Hodgson's *Winds of the Spirit: A Constructive Christian Theology* and McFague's *The Body of God: An Ecological Theology* represent two of the most thoroughgoing of recent attempts to incorporate the contemporary scientific world view into theology. McFague is blunt:

[T]he picture of reality coming to us from contemporary science is so attractive to theology that we would be fools not to use it as a resource for reimaging and reinterpreting Christian doctrine. My project will be centrally concerned with this very matter.[43]

It is useful to treat the two writers together here because their way of using science is very similar. Both write of *postmodern science* as a new scientific paradigm, which has replaced the (old) modern scientific world view. McFague and Hodgson repeat the picture of science having its roots in the mediaeval world view, coming of age through the Newtonian paradigm, and now moving into a new paradigm born from relativity and quantum mechanics.[44]

Their picture of science is similar to the one which we have developed in the course of this book and a number of familiar themes reappear. For example, the mediaeval view of an unchanging world was replaced by Newton's picture of vast numbers of particles continually in motion, but unchangeable in themselves. This picture is now being replaced by that of an emergent, developing universe with its own history. The mediaeval understanding of explanation in terms of purpose, was replaced by Newtonian determinism, which is in turn giving way to a more complex interrelationship between law and chance, structure and openness.

Both Hodgson and McFague emphasize the significance of the possibility of finally moving away from the reductionist atomism of Newton, where significance was sought exclusively in the smallest component parts of the universe. In its place they seek a new holistic understanding, stressing the significance of relationship and arrangement alongside reductionism. Holism may be hinted at by quantum mechanics, evolutionary theory or the replacement of body/mind dualism, to give only the most important examples.[45]

Sallie McFague: the 'view from the body'

McFague is careful to explain that the scientific evidence remains ambiguous. It can still be read as confirming the old mechanistic model, or as open to a new organic one. She justifies her reading in favour of organicism, in both theological and scientific terms. The old mechanistic reductionism may continue to provide a useful method, but holism may in fact provide a more accurate and even, more objective, description of the universe:

> The important issue here is situated or embodied knowledge resulting in a stronger objectivity, and therefore the possibility of humane scientific projects. The 'view from the body' is always a view from somewhere versus the view from above, from nowhere: the former admits to its partiality and accepts responsibility for its perspectives, while the latter believes itself universal and transcendent, thus denying its embodiment and limitations as well as the concrete, special insights that can arise only from particularity.[46]

This is a distinctively postmodern reading of science. It no longer simply accepts as neutral a scientific picture of the world; instead McFague feels free to evaluate the correctness of different possible understandings of science before she adopts one of them as part (and only part) of her case for the adoption of a particular model of God's relationship with the world.

For both of these writers, the development of a theology of nature opens up the possibility of a conversation between natural science, theology, and the other pressing concerns of today's world, which range from the ecological crisis through the collapse of the superpowers to the end of patriarchy! Science becomes an important resource for theology, but not one to be accepted uncritically. In fact, both theology and science attempt to construct appropriate models and metaphors, using metaphorical language rather than simple direct statements, and therefore both need the skilful use of interpretation and judgment.[47] McFague likes to speak of the need to take risks, to choose to make a wager on the value of one particular model:

> Theological constructions are 'houses' to live in for a while, with windows partly open and doors ajar; they become prisons when they no longer allow us to come and go; to add a room or take one away – or if necessary, to move out and build a new house.[48]

Models are not direct descriptions of reality, but they do help us to understand ourselves and our relation to God and the universe. Thus McFague advocates that the church should reappraise an organic model both of the universe and of relationship. We share one body with all creation, though we must never see ourselves as the head; that would be to fall into the dangers of earlier uses of the model. We must learn to think in a less hierarchical way – the body in her model is not a human body. The same model can be used for God. The risks are obvious, and she takes great care to distance herself from the charge that she is merely developing a new pantheism.

Great dangers may be balanced by great rewards. Potentially, claims McFague, her model has the ability to help humanity to integrate itself with the material world in a more appropriate way than Cartesian dualism could ever allow, and also to help Western Christianity to reclaim a vision of the immanence of God. Like all good models, this one suggests a number of different areas for exploration. For example, to envisage the world as the body of God is to suggest a re-evaluation of ourselves as bodily creatures. The model can thus provide a stimulus to Christian anthropology, and perhaps above all to our understanding of the incarnation, for as McFague pointedly writes: 'If Christianity is *the* incarnational religion, its treatment of embodiment, nature, and women is very strange indeed.'[49]

Peter Hodgson: the possibility of a new constructive theology

In *Winds of the Spirit*, Hodgson sets himself a different task. In a fragmented world, he asserts our need to learn to think systematically. Without systems we continually have to reinvent and reorganize everything. We must never forget the human and essentially limited nature of all our systems. It is especially important in an age that has taken such a negative attitude to the possibility of any meaningful systems that we find the courage to take up the constructive task once again.

> Perhaps the reality of God has always been connected in some fashion with a threefold human search: for wholeness (some would say wisdom or knowledge), for love (some would say life), and for freedom (some would say liberation). God engenders the search, corresponds to the search, *is* the search, fulfils the search.[50]

As he seeks to build a constructive theology out of this search, Hodgson draws extensively on the picture of science which he has developed. So, for example, in his discussion of 'the Creative Being of God' pride of place is given to the image of *energy*: it is God's energy which drives the processes of creation. The same section discusses the role of chance in natural selection, noting the problems raised by Monod's description of the process as 'blind chance', noting also Peacocke's proposed solution in terms of God making use of chance to run through a sequence of possibilities. Hodgson insists that chance can only be the *instrument* of creativity, God's creativity itself cannot be explained scientifically: 'Any reference to "creativity", whether viewed as purposeless or purposive, entails a metascientific perspective.'[51] There is a similarly thorough use of relevant scientific material throughout the book.

For Hodgson, science is an important context for constructive theology. It is both a tool and a discussion partner; not to be used uncritically, but emphatically not to be ignored.

Hodgson and McFague have learnt their science almost exclusively from Barbour, Polkinghorne and Peacocke. Nonetheless, they move significantly beyond those writers in their ability to create genuinely novel theology which makes use of science as an important resource, but does not allow science to dictate the entire theological agenda. Whilst learning from (postmodern) science, and integrating many of its insights into their world view, they generally succeed in retaining their autonomy, employing their judgment to choose between differing interpretations of the science they seek to use.

Frameworks for dialogue

The relationship between science and religion or theology is complicated, and we saw in the last chapter how difficult it is to describe one framework into which all points of view can be fitted. The more detailed studies of this chapter have illustrated how varied are the ways in which contemporary theologians have taken up the challenge.

In the last chapter we examined Ian Barbour's widely-used description of the relationship in terms of conflict, independence, dialogue and integration. According to Barbour's scheme, we can picture Thomas Torrance seeking a detailed dialogue, but from a starting point which claims independence for each of the partners. What seems at first sight a somewhat inflexible stance may in fact provide an effective strategy; dialogue can often be fruitful when each partner is under no illusion where the other stands.

Against this, however, it is difficult to imagine how a dialogue from independence can lead to change for either party. By contrast, Wolfhart Pannenberg begins his dialogue from a position much closer to the boundary with integration. For him there must be genuine points of contact between different disciplines, which will allow him to adopt scientific formulations, such as field theory, in his restatement of Christian theology.

Sallie McFague and Peter Hodgson clearly belong in the integrationist camp, but the very readiness with which they seek to make use of scientific material does mean that they regard themselves as able to evaluate the material on their own terms and not simply to accept it at the scientists' valuation. For them, a significant dialogue will take place concerning the correct meaning and importance of wide-ranging scientific theories, alongside the more familiar dialogue over the effects of science on theological doctrines.

Langdon Gilkey is perhaps best pictured as an integrationist with a similar perspective to Barbour himself. Like Barbour, Gilkey adopts a version of Process Thought. Gilkey is usually careful to point out, however, that science and religion make their most important contributions at different levels within the overall metaphysical scheme, science tending towards the practical investigative level, religion towards the level of overarching world views. Thus direct contact between science and religion tends to be reduced. What in one reading looks like a simple integrationist model can be read in a different way as being a model of independent disciplines, not unlike that of Torrance.

Such ambiguity may help to explain why Hardy is suspicious of all grandiose schemes: for him, the relationship is in the detail. Only when examined in great detail and with respect for the methods of the other partner can similarities and consonances between science and religion be anything other than suggestive coincidences or analogies. Hardy's careful concern suggests that we must address in the next section a persistent underlying question.

Do we need metaphysics?

A continuing theme running through the last two chapters alongside the particular models suggested for the relationship between science and religion has been whether or not we need to involve philosophy and metaphysics in the dialogue.

This question seems to be at the root of a dispute between the two foremost British scientist-theologians, John Polkinghorne and Arthur Peacocke. Polkinghorne takes the importance of metaphysics for granted:

> Theology is the great integrative discipline; it is metaphysics practised in the presence of God . . . Science does not determine theological thought but it certainly constrains it. Physics provides the ground plan for the edifice of metaphysics.[52]

For Polkinghorne, the important arguments will all take place at this level. Hence the reason for his persistent suspicion of Peacocke's work: 'I have to say that I feel that Peacocke has always been somewhat reticent about the metaphysical basis of his thought.'[53] The comment is accurate, but Peacocke might regard it as a compliment rather than a criticism, as he seems not to acknowledge the need for any additional metaphysical framework:

> Study of this interaction [between science and religion] . . . has impelled me to evolve a theology that has been refined, as far as it lay within my powers, in the fires of the new perceptions of the world that the natural sciences have irreversibly established. Such a theology needs to be consonant and coherent with, though far from being derived from, scientific perspectives on the world.[54]

Can the disciplines of theology and science speak directly to each other or do they inevitably need a metaphysical structure within which to talk? Dan Hardy's comment 'The *substance* of science should interact with the *substance* of theology'[55] has an attractive straightforwardness. But we must not forget the danger of such a stance. In a thought-provoking essay, Nicholas Lash has complained that we are all victims of an old model based on the ideal of the neutral observer:

> If there is but *one* way – namely, through disciplined observation – by which we can come to know *anything* . . . then we seem stuck with a tale of two sources of truth, two districts in which truths may be 'observed'. But all such dualisms eventually crumble before the practical acknowledgement of the comprehensiveness of the territory of scientific investigation . . . Thus science becomes, in fact, not 'partner in dialogue' to theology, but mediator of the latter's truth.[56]

Lash is right to point out the danger. From the time of John Tyndall's demand in the infamous Belfast Address (1874) that 'science claims the entire domain of cosmological theory' to Richard Dawkins impatient: 'Theologians don't do anything, don't affect anything, don't achieve anything, don't even mean anything,' the perceived success of science has meant that it may overwhelm all other ways of thought.

As both Hardy and Gilkey have observed, one authoritarianism tends to breed others in response. Creationism and the use of scientific reductionism as a philosophy perhaps deserve each other as sparring partners.

The difficulty with the response of those who interpose a meta-physical system between science and religion is that our society does not possess an agreed philosophy. Any system we introduce will be unacceptable to many of our potential dialogue partners. Although Gilkey attempts to build his version of Process Thought on insights shared by scientists and others, he soon moves beyond this common intuition into suggesting that his particular under-standing, based on Process Thought, will facilitate the dialogue. Few will be able to accept this as a level playing field.

Thus, my personal preference is for the more direct interaction advocated by Hardy, and practised by McFague, Hodgson and Peacocke, rather than the more indirect metaphysical approach of Gilkey, Barbour and Polkinghorne. If we accept that there can be a direct interaction between science and theology, we must be careful, however, not to be seduced into simply accepting science as the mediator of theology's truth. As Lash remarks:

> [W]e are as close to the heart of the sense of creation in considering and responding to an act of human kindness as in attending to the fundamental physical structures and initial conditions of the world.[57]

How important is science for theology?

The last section raises again the question of just how important science is for theology. The theologians discussed in this chapter are by no means typical of those writing today. Many well-respected and competent theologians simply ignore the implica-tions of science.[58] But it seems to me that Pannenberg's criticism here is unanswerable: 'One gains the right to be irrational at the expense of losing the right to criticize.' Unless we engage with other disciplines our truth-claims will hover above reality – impregnable, but also isolated. To give only one example: What does the Christian doctrine of the Fall, and the associated claims that death came into the world through sin, mean in the context of an evolutionary perspective? Arthur Peacocke puts the point clearly:

> Biological death was present on the earth long before human beings arrived on the scene . . . So when St Paul says that 'sin

pays a wage, and the wage is death' that cannot possible mean for us now *biological* death and can only mean 'death' in some other sense. Biological death can no longer be regarded as in any way the *consequence* of anything human beings might have done in the past, for evolutionary history shows it to be the very *means* whereby they appear and so, for the theist, are created by God.[59]

Against the traditional separation of Creation and Fall, evolutionary theories suggest gradual development and the inevitability of the presence of physical death in the natural world. Here at least, the theories of science impinge directly on the doctrines of the church.[60]

Taking stock: a constructive encounter?

Many theologians ignore the scientific age in which we live, and those who take account of science do so in very different ways. Are there any general points to be learnt from the contemporary encounter of theology with science?

Simple explanations are usually wrong. When T. H. Huxley confidently proclaimed 'one kind of knowledge and one way to get it' in the middle of the nineteenth century, it was still possible that the methodological reductionism of science might prove triumphant and sweep away the validity of all other explanations. At the end of the twentieth century it is quite certain that complete explanation always requires more than the application of a simple reductionism.

A powerful way of expressing this is Dan Hardy's talk of 'open' and 'closed' horizons. To be open is to be transparent to explanation in one direction only: there is nothing else, this is the sum total. By contrast all interesting features of the universe are closed, in the sense that explanation from one direction does not exhaust the possibilities of understanding. Human beings, for example, are 'closed' to reductionist explanation. Explanation in terms of atoms and their interaction will explain much, but to ignore the mystery of the closure of certain features of the human being to this sort of explanation is to deny oneself the possibility of a rich and expanding understanding of the true nature of the universe.

Human skills must not be discounted. Michael Polanyi was one of the first people to alert us to the importance of the exercise of ordinary human skills for the success of science. Since then many writers have built on his insights. The results of science are the more remarkable for arising out of the careful exercise of human skills: commitment, determination and judgment all play their part in the apparatus of working scientists. This has important consequences:

1. It helps to demystify science. Like all disciplines the sciences have their techniques, their specific methods and their technical languages, but the sciences as a whole need not be held in special awe simply because of their undoubted success. They form one group of disciplines among others.

2. In the same way we do not need to apologize that theology also requires the exercise of judgment and skill, or that it uses its own jargon. Theologians frequently disagree and come to differing conclusions, but this is simply what we should expect from any community of scholarship. The nature of the subject matter with which the sciences deal *is* different from that with which theology engages, but the difference is one of degree rather than kind.

3. The necessity of the exercise of skill and judgment within both science and theology, hints that our attention should focus not simply on a fixed body of objective material, but also on these human attributes, which have traditionally been ignored as more subjective. In fact they form part of any complete picture. What theology has always known but has sometimes been reluctant to bring into the academic debate – the importance of personal and interpersonal qualities – now confronts us both from a consideration of the practice of science, and from the formulation of, for example, quantum mechanics.

Experts have limited value. It is important distinguish between two different but equally necessary, and equally skilled, intellectual tasks. The specialist, by definition, can only be an expert within a narrow field. The sum total of knowledge continues to increase, and the human brain can only absorb so much material. By contrast, the generalist will seek to bring together the insights of different experts, hoping eventually to arrive at a new synthesis of knowledge. By and large in this book, we have been concerned with specialist scientists and generalizing theologians. The task of the systematic theologian, to use the common modern name, will be to evaluate the results of the specialist – whether in biblical languages or physics. The systematician must weigh one report against another, and, not infallibly but with humility, attempt a sketch of a larger picture. Experts are invaluable, in their place.

Metaphysics may be more trouble than they are worth. In the face of scientism and creationism, there is a real temptation to seek out a metaphysical or philosophical framework which accurately puts both science and theology in their respective places and seeks to arbitrate between them. By now, the impossibility of this task should be clear. Our society does not possess an agreed metaphysic, and in such circumstances any proposed solution simply becomes part of the problem. What remains essential is a clear-eyed search for hidden assumptions behind grand proclamations. We need to understand the temptation for scientists to turn a supremely successful methodological rule into an ontological conclusion, or the temptation for theologians to claim absolute status for their own particular understanding of the ways of God.

A direct interaction between disciplines is possible without hidden metaphysical assumptions. What is indispensable, however, is skilful, serious participants, who accept the possibility of complexity, or, in Hardy's sense, the 'closure' of parts of the universe to their own cherished methods.

The world is contingent, but not accidental. The form of the world in which we find ourselves cannot be deduced by logical necessity. Science is necessary in order for us to understand why the world is the way it is. We have already discussed the relation of this assertion to Greek and Christian thought. Fundamental to a correct understanding of the Christian doctrine of creation is the assertion that God created this world in this way, by whatever means, out of God's free love and grace. In other words, God chose to create this world. A further assertion is necessary, however.

In whatever way the world has arrived at its present state, it seems clear that chance has played a large part. Nonetheless, we make the claim that the form of the world is not accidental. A theology of nature is possible, whereby we can make certain assertions about the character of God from the form of the world.

Torrance talks of there being no 'logical bridge' between God and the world. The key assertion here is that this is only true in one direction. We may not say that God *must* have created this world, and for these reasons. However, we *may* say that given the world in which we find ourselves it is reasonable to make this set of assertions about God.

An analogy here – or perhaps more – is to be found in the debates surrounding evolution and natural selection. It seems quite clear that it is impossible to deduce the form of the living world today from the earliest and simplest forms of life on earth; too much depends on chance. On the other hand, given the present form of the living world we can trace a logical path back to the earlier forms by means of what Daniel Dennett has called 'reverse engineering'.[61] My claim is that something similar is possible in the case of God and the creator's relationship to the creation.

Thus, finally, we can justify our claim that *science provides an important resource for theology*. We have seen that the case for the practical separation of theology from scientific influence can be made not only by those with little knowledge of or inclination for science, but also by theologians as sympathetic and well-informed as Thomas Torrance, but we have rejected their case, and instead found in science a rich resource for theological understanding.

On the other hand, there is no easily established and uncontroversial account of science which can simply be taken over by theologians. We need to use our own judgment in order to assemble a package of the 'best-established general features of the scientific accounts', to borrow Arthur Peacocke's phrase. The skill that theologians must master is to learn how to make use of science without letting science dictate the entire agenda of theology. For, as Sallie McFague says, there is a general trend to scientific thinking today which 'is so attractive to theology that we would be fools not to use it as a resource'.

Chapter 9

Creation Waits: Making a Theology for Today

At the heart of science lies the attempt to understand and describe the world around us. Christians claim that this world has been created by God. Throughout this book we have argued that there are links between these two statements. In this final chapter we shall look more closely at how what we believe might be affected by our claim that science and theology meet and indeed overlap at certain points.

Making or discovering?

A few years ago the first pictures of a comet colliding with one of the planets were sent back to the earth from a space probe. They were greeted with great media interest, and a few days later the following letter appeared in *The Times* with the heading 'Beyond Belief':

> Sir, I never cease to marvel at the sense of purpose and design evident in the universe. How is it, for example, that the fragments of a distant comet, invisible to the naked eye, manage to crash into the planet Jupiter in strict alphabetical order?[1]

There is an important lesson here for both scientists and theologians. We look around us and attempt to describe an ordered universe. At least some of the apparent order which we claim to have discovered has in fact been imposed on the raw material by our own intelligence. We label the fragments of comet and impose our own perceptions upon them; too often we go on to assume that the view through human eyes is the only possible one. Paul Davies and John Gribbin make the point neatly: 'If history is anything to go by, nature has a nasty habit of deceiving us about what is real and what is invented by human beings.'[2] Both theologians and scientists need to learn humility about their achievements and their limitations. What seems obvious to us may only reveal the limited viewpoint from which we pronounce eternal truths.

Nonetheless, as we saw in the last chapter, one of the gifts which theology may be able to offer to science is the possibility of a glimpse of the wider picture. Scientists are nearly always experts in only narrow fields; that is how they become experts. Theologians may look like amateurs in comparison, but they can help the experts to learn where they belong on a larger map.

The world of science

We can expect that within a few years science will provide us with a self-contained picture of the world. A TOE or Theory of Everything will describe the development of the universe. It will give a fully scientific description of how the universe developed from the moment of the Big Bang, through the development of the physical universe into energy and the particles of matter, and the particles into galaxies, star and planets. If Stephen Hawking's speculation is correct the theory will also explain or explain away the Big Bang itself, turning it from the singular event at the start of everything into a necessary consequence of the theory.

The great hope of scientists is that the theory will then connect with their understanding of the conditions necessary for the origin of life, providing a convincing picture of the seamless progression from the geology of the early planets to the biochemistry of life. From there the path is already fairly well mapped by evolutionary biology tracing the development of more and more complex organisms by natural selection.

A further connection will link the hints of emerging consciousness in the higher mammals to the experience of consciousness in humans, thus providing an unbroken chain of scientifically understood links between the Big Bang and human thought.

This Theory of Everything is for the moment science fiction.

The outline of what it needs to explain is well understood by physicists, but the mechanics of how the explanation will work remains tantalizingly elusive. Some commentators take comfort in this, and it is true that from the 1870s onwards when scientists were first beginning to understand the full explanatory power of Darwin's work, they assumed that the secret of life was just beyond their grasp. Some of the Victorians boasted that another ten years work or so would see all explained. Well over a hundred years later life still remains elusively just out of reach. Nonetheless as we suggested earlier it would be unwise to allow any of our faith to rest on such an insecure foundation. The likelihood is that the scientific connections will be made sooner rather than later.

Theories of Everything, however, are not really theories of everything. Our theory above may explain away the coincidences that lie behind the Anthropic Principle, or it may not. Being able to produce a scientific description of the history of the universe, and humanity's place within it, may uncover the unsuspected links between separate theories: the size of the Big Bang, the formation and distribution of carbon, the balance of the nuclear forces. The very unsuspectedness of the links, however, means that our speculation is simply speculation. If it was anything more we would have discovered the sought-after new theory for ourselves. Alternatively, a new and complete theory may not be able to make these connections and may throw into even sharper relief the unexpectedness of the coincidences. The Anthropic Principle might survive the arrival of a Theory of Everything in even better health than today.

It is also the case that such a theory might (or might not) explain the trend towards increasing complexity which we observe both in the physical universe and in the living world. Present physical and biological theories understand and explain the mechanism behind the increasing complexity of the universe as time has passed since the Big Bang. We saw Daniel Dennett label this kind of understanding 'reverse engineering'. In some ways the current state of scientific explanation is close to the old simplistic division: Science *does* understand 'how' in both these cases. 'Why' is a much harder question, but – and this is where the old distinctions fail – 'why' has become a genuinely scientific question. The present state of knowledge means that we can understand the mechanisms which lead to the complex structures – living or not – of which the universe is composed. For the present though, scientists do not have a convincing argument as to why both the physical universe and the living world are made up of these complex structures rather than much more simple ones. But this does not mean that we need to resort to God or any other non-scientific explanation. The search is on for a scientific reason as to why the way the universe has developed is the only possible way, the *necessary* way for this universe to develop under these conditions.

A gospel *from* strength *to* strength

In the previous section we have explored the current state of science, and the gaps which remain to be filled. To use the word 'gap' is to sound a note of caution as to any possible role for theology here. Earlier we noted Angela Tilby's strong warning that 'God is not to be invoked simply as an explanation for things.' To use God as an explanation is at once to trivialize God: God is about much more than things and their causes. It is also to assume that God is most naturally named in times of human weakness: scientists can't explain this – God must be the answer. But, as early as 1874 John Tyndall was making the bald assertion that: 'Science claims the entire domain of cosmological theory.'[3]

There is a most important lesson to be learnt here. God should not be invoked as an explanation out of weakness, but out of strength. Interestingly, and beginning from a totally different starting point, Peter Selby's reflection on sin, morality and world debt, *Grace and Mortgage*, invokes Dietrich Bonhoeffer to come to a similar conclusion. Selby summarizes Bonhoeffer's conditions for a Christian faith which can remain true to Christ today:

Christian faith has to address a world in which its everyday activity is undertaken largely on secular assumptions; and the gospel has to address human beings in their strength rather than creating and then exploiting a sense of weakness.[4]

Bonhoeffer's challenge to the church was to proclaim God without relying on the failure of secular assumptions or the weaknesses of humanity. A gospel *from* strength *to* strength as we might summarize it. God, in God's strength, speaking to humanity in the strength of all our very real achievements should be one of the aims for theology today. The use of Bonhoeffer's work here will ensure that we never forget the other crucial strand of twentieth-century theology. An apologetics from strength must be matched by the proclamation of the theology of the cross, which Bonhoeffer summarizes in a telling phrase: only the suffering God can help.

Beyond common sense

As we discovered when looking at the theories of contemporary science, common sense only applies to common experience. When we come to attempt a description of the whole universe, from the very small to the very large, any description in simple, common sense terms is bound to fail. The universe is a complex place, full of novelty. When scientists move far beyond the scale of the everyday world, it ought not to be surprising that they become like strangers constantly facing the unfamiliar.

Common sense only applies to common experience. Like the scientific exploration of the universe, the phenomenon of early Christianity forced its first adherents to move beyond the familiar into ground breaking, novel territory. Here is Wayne Meeks writing about the Revelation of St John:

> The moral strategy of the Apocalypse, therefore, is to destroy common sense as a guide for life . . . so long as one does not disturb the public order or wilfully affront one of the symbols or agents of her sovereignty, Rome is a powerful but benign presence. That is the common sense and from it follows a quiet and peaceable life. The vision of the Apocalypse shreds and rips away that common sense with as much violence as that with which John sees the sky itself removed.[5]

Common sense is just that: a generalization from the common experience of day-to-day living. Both science and God break through the boundaries of common sense when we consider the full sweep of the universe on the one hand and God's love for it on the other.

Science and the creator

If we are to test whether science and theology can speak to each other from strength to strength and without the reassuring certainties of common sense, an almost unavoidable starting point is provided by the doctrine of creation.

We saw earlier that one of the consequences of the difficult relationship between science and religion in the nineteenth century has been that most theologians have chosen not to discuss God's creation in scientific terms. As usual Karl Barth's dismissal of the issue is magisterial. When studying Genesis, Barth writes, he had expected that he would need to tackle the scientific issues:

> It was my original belief that this would be necessary, but I later saw that there can be no scientific problems, objections or aids in relation to what Holy Scripture and the Christian Church understand by the divine work of creation ... There is free scope for natural science beyond what theology describes as the work of the Creator. And theology can and must move freely where science which really is science, and not secretly a pagan *Gnosis* or religion, has its appointed limit.[6]

Quite apart from the fact that scientists fought many of the battles of the nineteenth century precisely in order to escape from being told by theologians where the limits to their subjects were, Barth's summary dismissal of the relevance of science is unhelpful. It is a commonplace of language to speak of the *created* order, or the *creation* within which we live, but we need to remind ourselves that the very fact that God creates is Good News. The existence of anything and everything, so often taken for granted, ought to provide a key part of the proclamation of the gospel of God's love.

Stephen Hawking may be correct, and the common sense demand that we make for science or God to explain the beginning of the universe may be simply another example of common sense leading us astray when confronted with the strangeness of the real universe. It does not follow, however, that his rhetorical question, 'What place then for a creator?' must receive the negative answer which Hawking expects.[7] If there is indeed no beginning the place for a creator is just what it has always been: To create the conditions which allow the universe to exist – the universe may have existed at all times, but God's love extends beyond time. Theology has also always understood that the work of creation continues as God sustains the universe, moment by moment, through its whole existence. In the words of the mediaeval mystic Mother Julian of Norwich:

> And he showed me more, a little thing, the size of a hazelnut, on the palm of my hand, round like a ball. I looked at it thoughtfully and wondered, 'What is this?' And the answer came, 'It is all that is made.' I marvelled that it continued to exist and did not suddenly disintegrate; it was so small. And my mind supplied the answer, 'It exists, both now and for ever, because God loves it.' In short, everything owes its existence to the love of God. In this 'little thing' I saw three truths. The first is that God made it; the second is that God loves it; and the third is that God sustains it.

We have seen time and again that the great danger of ignoring science is that theology then has nothing significant to say about the whole created order. In Pannenberg's words such a theology hovers above worldly reality but never makes contact with it. There can be no genuine dialogue, nor the possibility of mutual enrichment: 'One gains the right to be irrational at the expense of losing the right to criticize.'[8]

God's love on a cosmic scale

The gospel tells of God's work in the lives of individuals. The gospel is also proclaimed in and through our human fellowships and societies, and in challenging those societies and their structures. If the Christian understanding is correct, however, God's love cannot be limited. Our understanding of God is inadequate unless it encompasses even the largest conceivable scale. Evangelism, for example, is not the proclamation of the Christian gospel if it merely calls individuals to repentance and conversion, without setting its proclamation within the context of the creative love of God for the whole universe which God's love has brought into being. This argument raises a serious question: Is the Good News which is experienced in the lives of individuals also manifest and discernable in the totality of creation? If so, what do the investigations of science have to say to the theologian and to the evangelist?

When Karl Barth dismissed the usefulness of science for theology, his primary motivation was to remind Christians of the dangers of liberal theology. He believed that the dominant theology of his time had fallen into the old trap of natural theology, forsaking God's gracious revelation for 'the hints remaining after the Fall'. Barth's warning must not be forgotten, but at the same time we will want to stress the importance of the doctrine of creation. Jürgen Moltmann has been justifiably criticized for ignoring the science of creation, but theologically his instincts are correct when he writes with persuasive power of God the creator: 'Out of his free love he conveys and communicates his goodness: that is the work of sustaining his creation. His love is literally ecstatic love: it leads him to go out of himself and to create something which is different from himself but which none the less corresponds to him.'[9] Thus, unless the Fall left the creation utterly stripped of the presence of God, we should expect to find hints of that presence around us. The task of Christian proclamation will always include the naming of God wherever God is to be found.

To see the creation as merely the stage upon which God's great acts of salvation are played out is an unfortunately demeaning view of the created order. The central tenet of an incarnational religion is not of a visit from a strange God, but of God who can make Godself known through the ordinary material of the creation. In the words of Charles Wesley:

> See the eternal Son of God
> A mortal son of man
> Dwelling in an earthly clod
> Whom heaven cannot contain!

Incarnate once, God is unlikely to have been or to remain totally detached and inscrutable at all other times. Indeed, as we have seen, historians of science increasingly favour the view that the rise of modern science itself owes a great deal to the perception of the Christian faith that the universe is God's creation, and therefore that the investigation of the creation is a proper and important way of discerning God's glory and celebrating it. This insight, which saw the universe as God's creation, was coupled with the understanding that the creation was contingent upon, but separate from, God. This second insight, again derived from a Christian understanding of the relationship of God to the creation, was equally important for the rise of science. A certain separation between God and the world was necessary; too close a relationship would have proved fatal to science. If, for instance, the world had been understood as God's body, it would have seemed dangerously impious to probe its structure by investigation. Biblical monotheism, as opposed to pantheism or atheism, provided a favourable theoretical background for early scientific investigation.

The biblical doctrine of creation

It may be useful at this point to remind ourselves of the biblical roots of the doctrine of creation. It is helpful to begin, not from Genesis, but from the central section of the book of Isaiah. The prophet of consolation and hope in exile reminds God's people that God always has been, and always will be, both their creator and their redeemer:

> Thus says the Lord, your Redeemer,
> who formed you from the womb:
> I am the Lord, who made all things,
> who alone stretched out the heavens,
>   who by myself spread out the earth . . . (Isa. 44.24).

The biblical witness begins with the sense of a relationship to God. God is the God who makes a covenant with his people; who chooses them to be his own; who acts for them in history; who carries them out of Egypt and establishes them in the promised land; who punishes them, but will never forsake them; who brings them back from exile.

Day by day God's people live with the reality of a relationship to God; with the sense of being redeemed. From that experience of God they begin to ask and to answer other questions. The day-by-day experience of the activity of God is developed and expanded. The God who is experienced as caring for them now must also be the God who formed them in the womb, and before that formed the world.

As time goes on their understanding of the scope of God's activity is widened; God himself is perceived on a grander scale. He is not simply one tribal God among others, but is the one true God, and creator of the heavens and the earth. And as the vision of God expands, so quite naturally all questions come to be answered by reference to him. Commentators on the Hebrew Bible tell us that there is a fundamental difference between the Jewish pictures of creation and the seemingly similar myths from the surrounding tribes. These myths tell the story in the same sort of way but the Bible is alone in firmly insisting on God as the cause and implementer of it all.

The central emphasis of the Jewish tradition, which Christians have inherited, is of the one true God as the author of all things. Later theologies wrestle with the implications of this doctrine for questions of suffering and evil, but the Bible is clear that God alone is the creator of the universe. God it is who brings order out of chaos; a creation out of nothingness. We can argue as to the status of the Genesis stories and the other pictures of creation embedded in the Bible. Did their authors understand them as myth, as – to use an anachronistic modern category – literal fact, or did they see them as roughly equivalent to 'science': the best explanation for the origins of humanity and the world available at the time? Perhaps all of these; perhaps none. What is striking is that the Jewish authors pictured the coming into being of a *uni*verse, one harmonious creation brought to its completed form by God alone. As we have repeated, such a picture both encouraged the early development of science and, in its broad outline, is perfectly in harmony with contemporary developments in science. Indeed, it might be thought that a Theory of Everything stands in close agreement with the Jewish proclamation of the one God who made heaven and earth.

Creation – from old to new

There is far more to the Hebrew Bible than this simple outline can suggest, but the relation between redemption and creation is fundamental, and carries us on into the Christian witness of the New Testament. The New Testament continues the history of

God's involvement with creation. From the prologue to John or the first chapter of Colossians which spell out the cosmic importance of Christ, to the stories of the passion which remind us of the cost of God's involvement. Christians might say that what we see in general terms in the Hebrew Bible for us is spelt out in the New Testament. This is how deeply God is involved with God's creation; this is the cost of its redemption.

Although the central emphasis of the New Testament is on the work of Jesus Christ, the New Testament is not simply about the redemption of humanity. In Romans, Paul reminds us that the creation itself hints at the truth about its creator:

> Ever since the creation of the world his eternal power and divine nature, invisible though they are, have been understood and seen through the things he has made (Rom. 1.20 NRSV).

Other translations of the verse make Paul's point more strongly using phrases such as '*clearly* seen'. In the light of the struggles by Christians through the years to make sense of God's relation to the creation, Paul might be somewhat overoptimistic here! Later in Romans, Paul goes on to state the important truth that the future of the universe is bound up with our own future (8.19–24):

> For the creation waits with eager longing for the revealing of the children of God; for the creation was subjected to futility, not of its own will but by the will of the one who subjected it, in hope that the creation itself will be set free from its bondage to decay and obtain the freedom of the glory of the children of God . . .

The letter to the Colossians claims that our saviour is also the first born of creation through whom and for whom all things were created (1.15–16). Throughout their writings, John and Paul remind us of God's love for the world, and of God's attempts to reconcile the world to Godself – though perhaps they only mean the human world. Even the Revelation of St John, whose pictures contemptuously sweep the old creation away, still seeks to replace the old creation with a new heaven and a new earth – using very physical pictures of the completion of God's plan (Rev. 21, 22).

Above all the individual references, the whole tenor of the New Testament, which we sum up in the doctrine of the incarnation, tells of God choosing to be inseparably involved with his creation.

Dominion and domination

One biblical verse in particular, however, has contributed to the dangerous view of humanity over and against the remainder of God's creation:

> God blessed them, and God said to them, 'Be fruitful and multiply, and fill the earth and subdue it; and have dominion over the fish of the sea and the birds of the air and over every living thing that moves upon the earth' (Gen. 1.28).

The first two chapters of Genesis contain two accounts of the creation of the world. The first is of the magnificent sweep of development, from the creation of light to the creation of the earth, its creatures and then humanity. Humanity at the apex of creation, given God's blessing and charged to fill and subdue and dominate. Then immediately following comes a second account. This account has humanity at its centre. A story of relationships (man is created quite early on and names the animals; is allowed to give them their place; gains a partner); an account of human behaviour and of sin.

Interestingly, it is only fairly recently that we have begun to read the first chapters of Genesis as two separate accounts. Despite the obvious fact that the creation is recounted twice, and in two different ways, traditionally the differences did not bother people who simply read the whole as one story. This approach has much to commend it. At the end of chapter one humanity is blessed and given dominion, in chapter two the meaning of our dominion is spelt out. We name and give our order to the world, but our power has its limits: 'You may eat freely from the fruit of every tree, except . . .' God gives dominion over the world, but as soon becomes clear, this is not an absolute monarchy. Men and women may sin, and must bear the consequences of their actions. Not monarchs so much as stewards; and the difference is crucial. Absolute monarchs can do as they please, because by definition their word is law; their actions right. Stewards will, at some time, have to give an account of their stewardship.

We might see a useful analogy in the apocalyptic idea of Christ ruling on earth, but under God's authority and, at the end, delivering his power to God, from whom it derives (I Cor. 15.24–28). As Christ is a steward, so we too are also called to stewardship.

The integrity of creation

Historically the understanding which God's people have of creation is likely to have spread out from their understanding of themselves as redeemed by God, but we have attempted to demonstrate that this does not mean that creation is only the background against which the drama of human salvation is played. Rather, a greater understanding has allowed God's people to see themselves as a part, stewards or priests of God's total creation which includes much else besides humanity, the whole of which God has created and continues to love even in its fallenness.

A few years ago the World Council of Churches held a consultation process on the theme of Justice, Peace and the Integrity of Creation. For all the suspicion that the World Council was simply following current fashions, and jumping on board the ecological bandwagon, the process did ask many important questions about the responsibility of the churches and their response to the challenges facing the world. The consultation process criticized the past role of theology and the churches. It was claimed that:

> Theologians have been too eager to separate in a simplistic way history and creation, as if God acts only in the history of humanity, and not also in the whole of creation.

> We have made a misleading distinction between creation at the beginning and redemption at the end, denying the biblical links between the two.

> Some churches have created theologies of power based on a patriarchal understanding of God's sovereignty. Behind the World Council jargon here lies an important truth: we have often lazily fallen back on the assumption that God is an

absolute monarch up in the sky; and therefore we can be absolute despots lording it over the earth.

We have been guilty of a narrow concentration on the salvation of the individual person by Jesus Christ at the expense of realizing that God is bringing forth a new creation.

According to the World Council, the distinctive task of the churches is to challenge the secular ways of thinking and living which lead to the threat recognized by the ecological movement. We need to recover our faith in God as creator, our faith in the world as belonging to God, and our faith in a reconciled relationship, through Christ, between humanity and the created world.

God's overflowing love for creation

Throughout this discussion of creation we have stressed the links between God and God's creation, and between humanity and the rest of the created order. These are biblical truths which have sometimes been neglected in our human arrogance. The second, at least, is also, as we have seen time and again, a fundamental scientific insight. We must not expect too much from the suggestive convergence of scientific and theological trends. The necessity for a confession of faith can never be removed, but perhaps we can move beyond the defensive apologetic that has so often characterized the subject. If God is the Trinitarian God of overflowing love, sacrificial giving and constant presence, then the world that we see around us is in fact, and despite appearances to the contrary, precisely the world that we would expect this God to have created. The provisionality of all scientific description will impose a certain diffidence, but a summary is possible. The rigid straightjacket of design and cause which characterized the clockwork universe has been replaced by purpose and persuasion, both of which imply vulnerability and suffering. The models of natural theology, for the first time, do not seek to dictate to those drawn from revelation, but to compliment them. Cross and creation combine to speak of a God who suffers. To repeat Paul Fiddes' comment: 'God has made the world as it is *because* he chooses to suffer with it.'[10]

To finish this section let us look at two visions of the creation, the first from a book by two of the most respected popular commentators on today's science, Paul Davies and John Gribbin:

> The matter myth is built on the fiction that the physical universe consists of nothing but a collection of inert particles pulling and pushing each other like cogs in a deterministic machine. We have seen how in their various ways the different branches of the new physics have outdated this idea. Quantum physics especially pulls the rug out from under this simple mechanistic image ... In contrast to this philosophy, the new viewpoint recognizes the creative and progressive nature of most physical processes. No sharp division is drawn between living and non-living systems. The origin of life is regarded as just one more step (albeit a significant one) along the path of the progressive complexification and organization of matter.[11]

Davies and Gribbin's vision of the universe replaces the isolated and individualistic pictures of earlier science with the possibility of a connected universe, and of the relatedness of all its parts. Although written two and a half thousand years earlier, the vision of the prophet Hosea makes many of the same claims:

> I will make for you a covenant on that day with the beasts of the field, the birds of the air, and the creeping things of the ground; and I will abolish the bow, the sword, and war from the land; and I will make you lie down in safety ... I will betroth you to me in righteousness and in justice, in steadfast love, and in mercy ...
>
> And in that day, says the Lord, I will answer the heavens and they shall answer the earth; and the earth shall answer the grain, the wheat and the oil ... and I will say to 'Not-my-people', 'You are my people'; and they shall say, 'Thou art my God.'[12]

The Fall and Original Sin

The place of humanity within a unified cosmos provides a beguiling vision. This is what God intended for creation, this is what humanity is capable of becoming. Why is it that the state of humanity at least is so very different from God's intention? To answer that question we must turn to the doctrines of the Fall and Original Sin.[13]

The Fall and Original Sin have had a bad press. Oliver Lodge was one of those who attempted the reconstruction of religion in the light of science at the beginning of the twentieth century, and his dismissal of Original Sin catches all the disdain and misunderstanding that surround the issue: 'As a matter of fact it is non-existent, and no one but a monk could have invented it.'

Augustine (354–430) was no monk, which may be part of the problem, for he sought to bring together several centuries of Christian tradition with the dominant Platonic philosophy of his age, whilst at the same time taking perfectly seriously his own experience of temptation, sin and guilt. The early theologians of the church attempted to hold together different Christian insights which were easily pulled apart. On the one hand God was the creator of the world, the one true God responsible for the whole created order, who in Genesis is pictured as looking at what he has made and pronouncing it good. On the other hand the world as humans know it is broken by evil, an evil which continues to play an important, perhaps dominant, role in each individual life. If the chains of evil were freely chosen then presumably men and women were free to make different and better choices? Or were the chains imposed upon us, in which case the creation was not after all good, but rather a cosmic battleground between good and evil? If this was the case, then humans were presumably merely spectators and innocent victims of this great cosmic battle.

The paradoxes and seeming contradictions of the classic account of Sin and the Fall do not spring from any scientific understanding of the world. They lie at the heart of a doctrine which wrestles with the paradoxes of human nature and freedom, and the relationship of God to the creatures which God has made.

Augustine, for example, in his systematic attempt to define the human condition through these doctrines, is careful to tread a line between the less than helpful versions set out by the Gnostics and Manichees at one extreme and by Pelagius at the other. The Gnostics dissolved the problem of the place of evil by simply arguing that the material world was bound to be evil. To be human was to engage in a tragic struggle to escape from the prison of the flesh, and rise to the pure freedom of the spirit. Reinhold Niebuhr sums up their view of humanity: the body is a tomb. Such pessimism could not seem adequate to mainstream churches. If the material is inherently evil, why did God pronounce the creation good? Why did Christ become incarnate in a human, material, body? Why did the New Testament celebrate the resurrection of the body, when victory, according to the Gnostics and the Manichees, was gained by escape from the flesh?

But if evil is not an inevitable consequence of living in a material world, does this mean that we are free to choose between good and evil? The British monk, Pelagius, with arguments that sound just as convincing to modern ears as they did to the contemporaries of Augustine, claimed that indeed human freedom implies exactly this freedom to choose between good and evil. Augustine, with greater realism and greater compassion, understood that in practice there was no free choice. Looking around him, Augustine saw that in the everyday world the choices made by women and men are distorted and tend towards evil.

These are the paradoxes which the doctrine sought to address. Can we preserve the truth of the original goodness of God's creation, alongside our experience of the existence and the attractiveness of evil? Augustine thought that he could bridge the paradox through his concept of Original Righteousness, which reiterated the insight of Genesis that the created universe in itself *is* good, and his concepts of Original Sin and guilt. According to Augustine the sinful human situation is not simply the result of our own individual failed choices. Instead we need to appreciate the power of the bias towards evil, which makes those wrong choices possible, and which lies deep within us.

Original Sin and the optimism of science

The great modern unease over the doctrine of Original Sin is in fact not modern or novel at all. After the Enlightenment it seemed important to stress both the essential goodness of humanity and the supreme value of human freedom and autonomy. Both of these ideas were well known to Augustine and his adversaries. At the start of the new millennium both ideas seem as attractive and as questionable now, given the history of humanity, as they did to Augustine. The fundamental battle here is a philosophical and theological one over the nature of humanity; it is not a scientific one.

The study of how we have become what we are is, however, not simply a philosophical problem. It has practical, material and therefore scientific implications too. Nor can we blame Augustine for all the misunderstandings. In composing his synthesis Augustine draws deeply upon biblical texts. In particular the early chapters of Genesis and Paul's interpretation of them in Romans 5.12–21 are his foundations.

In Genesis 1, after many of the individual acts of creation are recounted, there follows the refrain 'And God saw that it was good' (e.g. Gen. 1.10, 18, 25), with the final refrain: 'God saw everything that he had made, and indeed, it was very good' (Gen. 1.31). One of the intractable problems which all religions face is why the creation in which we exist is not wholly good. The great creation myths of primordial struggles between good and evil suggest one answer to the question. Jewish tradition insists on another, that the creation is made by God alone and is good. The Hebrew Bible then tells a series of complex and nuanced stories, including the whole of the book of Job, with its inclusion of Satan in the heavenly court and its refusal of simplistic answers, in order to explore the existence of evil without ever formally locating the solution in a doctrine of the Fall. By contrast Christian reflection on the same material has traditionally seen the broken state of the creation as intimately linked to the Fall of humanity (see especially Rom. 8.18–25).

We can now see the extent of the conflict between Augustine's understanding of human origins, and hence the explanation of the paradoxical power of sin, which relies on these biblical foundations, and modern scientific understandings:

1. In order to safeguard the goodness of God's creation in the face of its contemporary evil brokenness, Augustine claims that it was created in a state of original righteousness from which it has since fallen. The whole understanding of science is of an evolving complexity from which human consciousness has gradually emerged.

2. Paul and Augustine seem to explain the brokenness of the physical world, natural disasters and 'nature red in tooth and claw', in terms of human sin. How can we demonstrate any serious connections between the physical condition of the world and human sinfulness?

3. One of the specific consequences of this, which Paul spells

out in Romans – taking his lead from many hints in the Old Testament – is that death is something unnatural which has entered the world through Adam's sin, and which literally and physically then infects not simply humanity, but also the whole of creation. We have already noted Arthur Peacocke's robust comment:

> Biological death was present on the earth long before human beings arrived on the scene . . . So when St Paul says that 'sin pays a wage, and the wage is death' that cannot possibly mean for us now *biological* death and can only mean 'death' in some other sense. Biological death can no longer be regarded as in any way the *consequence* of anything human beings might have done in the past, for evolutionary history shows it to be the very *means* whereby they appear and so, for the theist, are created by God.[14]

Even more than this, in biological terms, more complex animals like ourselves need to feed upon slightly less complex organisms in order to survive and develop. Our very success is founded upon the death of other organisms.[15]

4. Finally, Paul pictures the origin of sin and death: 'sin came into the world through one man, and death came through sin' (Rom. 5.12). Augustine builds a very physical theory upon this, his model almost anticipates modern genetics and the inheritance of characteristics. According to Augustine, we have one common ancestor, Adam, from whom all our problems flow. The idea of the inheritance of sin in this way offends all modern understandings of justice and fair play as well as our assumptions of human freedom. It also raises scientific problems: does humanity have one common ancestor, and is it conceivable that a characteristic such as the tendency to sin can be inherited?

Is the 'Fall' necessary?

Before seeking to engage with the specific questions, it is important to be clear that Augustine's comprehensive picture is not necessarily the only way to understand the meaning of the biblical narratives. Jewish teachers have not traditionally interpreted Genesis in the light of a universal Fall and Paul can be read very differently.

For example, it is possible to see Paul confronted with the universality of human sin, and using the image of disease and infection to explain the inexorable spread of sin throughout humanity. He makes the very powerful equation of death and sin in order to force home the seriousness of humanity's problem. Again, and in keeping with the medical analogy, Paul presents Christ as the cure for the disease of sin and its consequence, death. As the infection begins through one man, Adam, so its antidote will come through the new man, Jesus Christ.

It is not necessary to demonstrate a mechanical connection between my sin and Adam's for me to be persuaded both of the universality of sin, and of the fact that it has trapped me in its web, from which I cannot escape unaided. Adam is my type, quite simply because I am Adam; in the tragedy of Adam I recognize myself and my situation. Sin is not exciting and new, it is dreary, monotonous and boring, deadly in its sameness. As Adam is the type, so Christ is the anti-type, the new creation, surprising, different and exciting, bringing the antidote, the cure, to my sin and Adam's.

The essential features of the biblical understanding which Augustine seeks to safeguard are the goodness of God's original intention in creation, the present less-than-perfect state of God's creation, the responsibility of humankind for their own wrong choices and, finally, the intimate links between human sin and the fallen state of the world.

Can we safeguard this whole complex of concepts, remaining true to the Bible and the understandings of science at the same time?

Biblical insights and scientific complexity

Science will not allow us to picture – literally – an original creation perfect in all its parts. A simple, perfect creation, however, is not quite the picture given in Genesis. It has often been noticed that in Genesis 1 we find a series of distinct acts of creation which sweep from the simple and inorganic to the more complex organic world and finally to humanity. This is certainly not precisely the picture of natural selection, but the broad outline is of an evolutionary development in creation. Nonetheless, it is only after the creation and disgrace of humanity that death and decay are mentioned in the stories of Genesis. The clear implication is that a perfect world created by God has been marred by humanity. Paul and the early theologians of the church then use this picture to make the explicit connection between human sin and the entry of death into the world.

If we are to keep faith with science, we need to insist that the literal correspondence of the disordered state of the world, which includes the presence of death in any form, and human sin cannot be maintained. The very long history of the world and its development guarantees this. Death is a natural part of any evolutionary scheme, present from the beginning, and not, in itself, a sign of disorder. Nonetheless, humanity does live in a world which has been broken by its sin. Everyone *could* die as the fulfilment of a ripe old age, but in reality everyone *must* die; death, as we know it, is unnatural, a curse.[16]

The biblical picture is of the fate of the whole creation intimately wrapped up with the fate of humanity – from the gift of dominion and Adam's naming of the animals through creation's groaning in Romans 8 to the final resolution of Revelation. From the time of Augustine, the church began to insist that these biblical truths could only be maintained through doctrines of Original Righteousness and Original Sin, understood in an unambiguously physical way. Irenaeus (*c*.130–200), who lived two hundred years before Augustine, had painted a very different picture of the world as 'a vale of soul making', the place where human beings grew into a knowledge of good and evil through experience, and through experience understood how to resist the attractions of evil:

> The tongue experiences sweet and sour by tasting; the eye distinguishes black for white by seeing . . . In this same way, by experiencing good and evil, the mind comes to understand good and is strengthened to preserve it by obeying God.[17]

In addition, as modern commentators have pointed out, the book of Genesis pictures a complex world even before the first sins of Adam and Eve. In Paul Ricoeur's memorable phrase: 'The serpent is already there.'[18] Evil is present in creation before human sin. It is far more deeply rooted than Augustine's picture of Original Righteousness will allow. We need to be careful to read the text of the Bible, alongside traditional interpretations.

Biblical pictures of the complexity of the creation before humans had the opportunity to sin may allow us to make common ground once again with scientific understanding. Generalizations are dangerous, but it may be that a creation complex enough to lead to the emergence of human beings and human consciousness must also be complex enough to be unpredictable. What we can only regard of the negative and evil aspects of the world around us, the destruction of earthquakes and storms, for example, may inevitably follow from the sheer complexity of any creation in which we can exist to ponder these things. Certainly we have already seen that 'chance' in one form or another is implicit in our understanding of quantum mechanics, which underlies the whole material world, natural selection, which underlies the living world, and chaos theory which underlies the science of complex systems. Brian Wren's picture may indeed paint an important truth:

> Are you the gambler-God, spinning the wheel of creation,
> giving it randomness, willing to be surprised,
> taking a million chances, hopeful, agonized,
> greeting our stumbling faith with celebration?[19]

Augustine wished to safeguard the biblical insight that the material creation as God had created it was good, and that it was not inevitably – by its very material nature – evil. A modern picture would be more hesitant about claiming the self-evident goodness of the original creation, claiming instead that human consciousness and choice is only possible within the ambiguities of a complex world.

The statistics of sin

Augustine's concept of Original Righteousness reaffirms the goodness of God's creation: the material world is not necessarily evil. The doctrine of Original Sin explores the presence of evil and sin in God's creation. It seeks to emphasize both human responsibility for sin, and at the same time, the fact that our choices are tainted by the sinfulness of the world around us and our common human inheritance. Augustine paints a powerful picture of the strong man Adam, broken for ever by his choice of evil over good, and transmitting that brokenness to all his descendants. Adam's sinfulness is both summarized by and neatly transmitted through humanity's disordered sexual desire. Psalm 51.5: 'Indeed, I was born guilty, a sinner when my mother conceived me,' was misunderstood to refer to the sinfulness of all human sexual activity since the Fall, rather than to be a comment on the universality of human guilt, which was probably the psalmist's intention.

Again, the problems raised here are not merely scientific. The notion that we are conceived in sin strikes a blow at the autonomy of the individual: where is my free choice in this? It also questions the modern understanding of sexuality as a natural part of human life. Scientifically, two issues are raised. However powerful the picture, does it make any sense to think of sin, or the disordered disposition to sin, as something physical transmitted like our genes? And, even if it does, will the idea of physical transmission from a common ancestor survive modern enquiries into human origins?

Modern genetics might offer the possibility of a genetic disposition towards sin. From time to time reports surface of the identification of a 'violence' gene or of a genetic basis for psychopathic behaviour. The problem for theology is that the most that science might be able to offer if such reports prove correct is a physical basis for the removal of normal inhibitions, or for a tendency towards extreme behaviour. Augustine was picturing something rather different: the disposition to behave in a sinful way, to make the wrong choices. It anyway seems more likely that in all but a few clear-cut cases of psychiatric illness, the human genetic make-up is far too complex to be used in this simplistic way. All the scientific indications also suggest that humanity will not prove to have one single ancestor, which undermines any literal interpretation of the whole picture.

Modern science might provide us with an alternative understanding, however. Many of the great advances in science of the last one hundred and fifty years rely on our understanding of statistics. From statistical mechanics which was invented in the late nineteenth century to help understand the behaviour of gases, through the attempts of Durkheim and other pioneering sociologists to explain the behaviour of whole societies, to quantum mechanics itself, much of modern science understands and predicts the behaviour of the world through statistical laws. Famously, Durkheim showed that when war or other large events affected the whole of a society, then the suicide rates would go up or down. No one could predict which individuals would commit suicide, but the overall rate could be predicted with some accuracy. In quantum mechanics, the large-scale outcome of any event, for instance the radio-active decay of atoms, can be known with absolute precision, but no physicist can predict whether any particular atom will decay.

We could offer something similar as an analogy to the important truth which lies behind the doctrine of Original Sin. The material world which God has created is not evil. The present condition of human beings is. We each make our own choices, but these choices are enmeshed in the structure of the families and networks of friends and colleagues in which we live, and in society. Our choices are free, but bound, and lead inevitably to the normality of human life as we know it, which is accurately described as fallen.

Augustine's picture safeguards the goodness of God's creation, and attempts to hold together the irreconcilabilities of human entrapment and human responsibility. His scheme is comprehensive, but at the cost of a physical view of the transmission of sin and a negative view of human sexuality. The scientific alternative links my sin and Adam's not mechanically but statistically, which may sound less certain but in fact guarantees precisely the same outcome. Using this picture we know what will happen just as surely as did Augustine.

'For the creation waits with eager longing...'

Picturing the inevitability of human sin is one thing; making the links between the broken human condition and the state of the whole of creation is another. On one level the links are trivial. Human greed and thoughtlessness have exploited and polluted the world we live in and the space around this planet. In the last century human ingenuity has brought this exploitation to the point where the whole planet is threatened. Our world, however, is only a tiny part of the universe. Whatever the scale of human mistakes they cannot threaten the whole of creation. Nonetheless, the picture is serious enough for humanity and our sphere of influence.

On the wider scale we have suggested earlier that it may indeed be the case that a universe of the sort in which we live is necessary in scale and length of existence in order to produce creatures like ourselves. We exist in our limited freedom because the laws of quantum mechanics and the rest of physics operate in the way they do. We are not simply one isolated part of the universe, but are creatures of the evolution of the whole created order. In this sense, Paul's picture in Romans 8 rings true. For God, the fate of humanity and the whole of creation is intimately linked.

Before leaving the topic of the brokenness of creation, it is vital to make one final point. Christians from Paul onwards have wrestled with this subject because they understood how wrong was the state of the world and of humanity which they saw around them. This was not what God intended.

It may have been inevitable that God's love flowing into the creation and giving space for the possibility of humanity and human choice would lead to this, but this fallen world is not what God desires. God's grace brought the creation into being. God in his grace shared dominion and stewardship of the world with humanity. God in his grace grieved over the sin of men and women and sought their salvation. Commentators have often noticed and regretted the church's concentration on sin and the Fall. In fact it marks the church's understanding that something has gone very wrong here. The natural state of the world filled with the overflowing love of God does not need such detailed explanation – without God's love there would be no creation. The brokenness of creation rightly attracts the attention of theologians, but in our concern to understand the scandal of the brokenness of God's good gift, and human culpability, we must take care never to forget the love which makes all existence possible.

'The silence of their equations'

In the same way that physicists dream that a Theory of Everything may carry within itself the scientific explanation of the whole physical world, some theologians claim that the doctrines of creation and Fall, by setting out our understanding of God's purposes in creation and the human condition, contain within themselves the whole of theology. Just as a physical Theory of Everything is not yet complete, so much more work would need to be done before a theological Theory of Everything carried conviction. However, the last few sections may serve to sketch the possibilities and pitfalls of taking science into serious partnership with Christian theology as we seek to understand the implications of God's love in creation.

We must not conclude, however, without remembering that such a partnership is only part of a wider vision. Earlier we quoted the hymnwriter, Brian Wren, and the poet, Michael O'Sidhail, both of whom attempt to allow science to inform their poetry. Pre-eminent among those poets who have attempted to come to terms with the scientific world picture is R. S. Thomas. Thomas is also a priest of the Anglican Church in Wales, and consciously makes the attempt to relate Christianity and science in his poetry. Two of his books are called *Frequencies* and *Laboratories of the Spirit*. In a characteristic short poem, 'Dialectic', Thomas retells the history of Western culture's relationship with God:

> They spoke to him in Hebrew and he understood
> them; in Latin and Italian and
> he understood them. Speech palled
> on them and they turned to the silence
> of their equations.

'The silence of their equations' sounds at first hearing like a condemnation of the scientific method, but as usual with Thomas all is not quite how it seems:

> But God listened to them . . .
> They are speaking to me still,
> he decided, in the geometry
> I delight in, in the figures
> that beget more figures.

'Dialectic' combines two of Thomas' great preoccupations, his immersion in the contemporary language of science and his attempt to probe deeply into scientific understanding. In an interview he stated succinctly: 'In a world dominated by physics and mathematics the cross remains contemporary . . . If poetry can't cope with what God means in the late twentieth century then it doesn't deserve to remain a major art form.'[20]

Hence the first few lines of 'Dialectic' where Thomas notes, just as we have, the change in dominant world view from the Graeco-Hebrew to that of science. Thomas asserts that here is the natural place of God, just as much as in the old languages. Whilst in the last three lines of the poem Thomas' pessimism reasserts itself, the dominant tone is, for once, of the presence of God:

> I will answer
> them as of old with the infinity
> I feed on. If there were words once
> they could not understand, I will show
> them now space that is bounded
> but without end, time that is where
> they were or will be . . .[21]

Philosophical propositions or scientific equations, language or silence, it is all the same. More than that, the God with whom Thomas wrestles is more faithfully described, more at home, more concretely represented by the sparseness and the silences, which Thomas' poetry shares with the equations than by the old, verbose languages. The bleak hill farm and the functional laboratory speak of the same 'great absence/ that is like a presence'.

We have seen in the course of this book that the relation of religion or theology and science is always complex and often leads to ambiguous results. We have attempted to learn how studying science, both the results of science and also the implications of the study of the history, philosophy and sociology of science, can affect theology. The results of science can be important as we have seen in this chapter, but the philosophical implications of science, and the lessons learnt by the rise of modern science will also have implications for the study of theology.

Perhaps only in something like poetry can we fully appreciate this ambiguity. A phrase such as 'the silence of their equations' sounds as if it is delivering a negative verdict on the scientific enterprise, but that it not Thomas' business. Nor does he seek a too easy reconciliation. The silence really is a genuine and profound silence; the time for words has past, and there is no going back. And yet the silence is the silence of 'the geometry that I delight in'. Thomas wrestles with this truth in his poetry; in this book I have tried to suggest solid theological reasons why the endeavour is so important.

Notes

Preface

1. Joseph McCabe, *The Religion of Sir Oliver Lodge*, The Rationalist Press Association, Watts and Co. 1914, p. 45. Admittedly, Lodge's additional interest in psychical research did not make it any easier for either rationalist scientists or orthodox Christians to accept his views.
2. W. H. Mallock, 'Oliver Lodge on Religion and Science', *Fortnightly Review*, New Series, LXXVIII, 1905, p. 839.
3. Published as 'The Silence of their Equations – The Study of Science and the Practice of Theology', *Epworth Review,* Vol. 22, No. 2, May 1995, pp. 43–52.

1 A Large Map

1. There is a full discussion of the Oxford debate in ch.3. For Canon Tristram, see I. Bernard Cohen, *Revolution in Science*, Harvard University Press 1985, pp. 289–90.
2. Peter Atkins, *Creation Revisited*, Penguin 1994, p. 145.
3. Quoted by Brian Appleyard in *The Independent*, 23 January 1995. The following quotations are from the same article. For a discussion of Theories of Everything, see pp. 145f. below.
4. See also p. 172 below.
5. Hans Küng, *Does God Exist?* Collins 1980; SCM Press 1991, p. xxiii.
6. Mary Midgley, 'Strange contest: science versus religion' in Hugh Montefiore (ed), *The Gospel and Contemporary Culture*, Mowbray 1992, p. 41.
7. Ibid., pp. 41, 51.
8. Ibid., p. 54.
9. Stephen Hawking, *A Brief History of Time*, Bantam 1988, pp. 140–41. For a full discussion, see pp. 146, 231 below.
10. John Drury, *The Burning Bush*, Fount 1990, p. 88.
11. Ibid., p. 89.

2 Religion and the Rise of Science

1. John Hedley Brooke, *Science and Religion: Some Historical Perspectives*, CUP 1991, p. 321.
2. William Kingdom Clifford, *Lectures and Essays*, Macmillan 1879, Vol. 1, p. 238.

3. David C. Lindberg and Ronald L. Numbers (eds), *God and Nature: Historical Essays on the Encounter between Christianity and Science*, University of California Press 1986, p. 6. The issue is discussed in detail in James R. Moore, *The Post-Darwinian Controversies*, CUP 1979. For a different, more belligerent, interpretation see, Adrian Desmond, *Huxley*, Penguin 1998, pp. xv-xviii.

4. Brooke, op. cit., pp. 42–43.

5. Roy Wallis (ed), *On the Margins of Science: The Social Construction of Rejected Knowledge*, Sociological Review Monograph 27, University of Keele Press 1979.

6. Knight is quoted by Colin A. Russell, *Crosscurrents: Interactions between Science and Faith*, IVP 1985, p. 18. For Hooykaas, see R. Hooykaas, *Religion and the Rise of Science*, Scottish Academic Press 1972, pp. 85, 161.

7. Brooke, op. cit., pp. 6–10.

8. Christopher Kaiser, *Creation and the History of Science*, Marshall Pickering 1991, pp. 53–94.

9. Stanley L. Jaki, *The Road of Science and the Ways to God*, Scottish Academic Press 1978, pp. 38–39; for a contrary view see Hooykaas, op. cit., p. 34. For a discussion of the importance of the doctrine of creation, see especially, Kaiser, op. cit.

10. Hooykaas, op. cit., p. 50; Russell, op. cit., ch. 2. A. N. Whitehead was one of the first people to suggest positive links, see A. N. Whitehead, *Science and the Modern World*, London 1925.

11. Kaiser, op. cit., *passim*, Jaki, op. cit., pp. 13–14.

12. Hooykaas, op. cit., pp. 1–12.

13. Ps. 34.8; see also I Thess.5.21. Both are noted by Russell, op. cit., p. 70.

14. See, for example, John Polkinghorne, *Reason and Reality*, SPCK 1991.

15. Kaiser, op. cit., ch. 1; Jaki, op. cit., pp. 15–18.

16. Kaiser, op. cit., pp. 36–49.

17. See especially Robert K. Merton, 'Science, Technology and Society in Seventeenth Century England', *Osiris*, Vol. 4, 1938.

18. From Robert K. Merton, 'Puritanism, Pietism and Science' (1936) reprinted in C. A. Russell (ed), *Science and Religious Belief: A Selection of Recent Historical Studies*, University of London Press 1973, p. 25. My summary of Merton's argument follows Lindberg and Numbers, op. cit., p. 4.

19. Hooykaas, op. cit., p. 162.

20. Jaki, op. cit., p. 160.

21. Brooke, op. cit., p. 113; Lindberg, op. cit., p. 5.

22. Brooke, op. cit., pp. 44, 51.

23. Harold P. Nebelsick, *Circles of God: Theology and Science from the Greeks to Copernicus*, Scottish Academic Press 1985, p. xiii.

24. Brooke, op. cit., p. 83, Jaki, op. cit., p. 46. Michael Fuller, *Atoms and Icons*, Mowbray 1995, pp. 104–6, provides a useful introduction to this debate.

25. Brooke, op. cit., p. 90.

26. Ibid., pp. 90–94.

27. Kaiser, op. cit., p. 149.

28. Brooke, op. cit., p. 100.

29. Hooykaas, op. cit., p. 123; Brooke, op. cit., p. 97.

30. Russell, *Crosscurrents*, p. 47; Brooke, op. cit., pp. 78–80. As Michael Fuller notes, op. cit., pp. 104–6, Galileo has became so much of an icon

that it has become almost impossible to reconstruct his motivations, or even the factual circumstances of his trial. Two accessible modern biographies of Galileo are: Stillman Drake, *Galileo*, OUP 1980 (in the Past Masters series) and Michael Sharratt, *Galileo: Decisive Innovator*, Blackwell 1994 (by a Roman Catholic priest and teacher). For Galileo's use of the Bible see Ernan McMullin, 'Galileo on science and Scripture' in Peter Machamer (ed), *The Cambridge Companion to Galileo*, CUP 1998, pp. 271–347, and for the myth of Galileo see Michael Segre, 'The never-ending Galileo story', ibid., pp. 388–416.

31. Brooke, *Science and Religion*, p. 108.
32. Ibid., pp. 80–84; Russell, *Crosscurrents*, pp. 50–52, 76.
33. Cf. Jaki's comment, Jaki, op. cit., p. 70; see also ibid., pp. 68–75 and Kaiser, op. cit., pp. 162–64.
34. This paragraph and the next section are especially indebted to Brooke, op. cit., pp. 137–48.
35. Newton remains a subject of fascination for historians and biographers, not least because so much is still uncertain about his life and beliefs. To take the apple as a small example: A Rupert Hall, in *Isaac Newton, Adventurer in Thought*, CUP 1997, p. 380, claims that 'Really, the oddest thing in Newton's life is the fact that the story of the apple, known to everyone, is true.' On the other hand, Michael White, in *Isaac Newton, the Last Sorcerer*, Fourth Estate 1997, pp. 85–87, very much doubts the story, believing that Newton himself invented, or at least exaggerated, it.
36. This is an important consideration for the debate begun by T. S. Kuhn in *The Structure of Scientific Revolutions*, University of Chicago Press 1962, which centres on concepts such as *incommensurability* and *paradigm shift*. We discuss the debate in chs 4 and 5.
37. Kaiser, op. cit., p. 71.
38. See, for example, Hooykaas, op. cit., pp. 15, 50.
39. Mary Midgley, *Science as Salvation: A Modern Myth and its Meaning*, Routledge 1992, chs 7 and 8. Ch. 7 is entitled 'Putting Nature in her Place'.
40. Brooke, op. cit., p. 121.

3 Darwin's Century

1. Owen Chadwick, *The Secularisation of the European Mind in the Nineteenth Century*, CUP 1975, p. 161.
2. John Durant, *Darwinism and Divinity*, Blackwell 1985, p. 15, quoting earlier sources.
3. Ibid.
4. Thomas Henry Huxley, *Lay Sermons*, Macmillan 1874, p. 201.
5. Adrian Desmond, *Huxley*, Penguin 1998, p. 366, quoting from a letter by Huxley.
6. Colin A. Russell, *Crosscurrents*, IVP 1985, p. 112.
7. Owen Chadwick, *The Victorian Church*, Part I, A. & C. Black (3rd edn) 1971; SCM Press 1987, p. 561.
8. William Derham, quoted by Russell, *Crosscurrents*, p. 113. For Dawkins' comment, see Richard Dawkins, *The Blind Watchmaker*, Longman 1986; Penguin 1988, p. 5.
9. Russell, *Crosscurrents*, p. 115.

10. John Hedley Brooke, *Science and Religion*, CUP 1991, pp. 193–94.
11. Ibid., pp. 198ff.
12. The agnostic Dawkins makes the same point; Dawkins, op. cit., p. 6.
13. Charles Coulson Gillispie, *Genesis and Geology*, Harper, NY 1959, p. xi; Anthony M. Alioto, *A History of Western Science*, Prentice Hall, Englewood Cliffs, NJ 1993, p. 290.
14. This anyway was the best Victorian estimate; Chadwick, *The Victorian Church*, Part I, p. 560.
15. Gillispie, op. cit., p. 222.
16. Alioto, op. cit., pp. 294–95.
17. Brooke, op. cit., p. 227.
18. Alioto, op. cit., p. 294; I. Bernard Cohen, *Revolution in Science*, Harvard University Press, pp. 285ff.
19. Adrian Desmond, *The Politics of Evolution*, University of Chicago Press 1989, pp. 1–8.
20. See, for example, Alioto, op. cit., p. 294.
21. Brooke, op. cit., p. 232; Russell, *Crosscurrents*, p. 132.
22. Adrian Desmond and James Moore, *Darwin*, Michael Joseph 1991.
23. Ibid., pp. 220, 227–28.
24. Ibid., pp. 221, 230.
25. Ibid., pp. 229–39.
26. Ibid., p. 293.
27. See below, chapter 4.
28. For a summary of critical comments, see Russell, *Crosscurrents*, pp. 160–61. See also, Alvar Ellegård, *Darwin and the General Reader*, Götebergs Universities Arsshrift, Vol. 64, 1958.
29. James R. Moore, *The Post-Darwinian Controversies*, CUP 1979, p. 45.
30. See Desmond, *Huxley*, pp. xv-xxii.
31. Moore, op. cit., p. 338. For Drummond, see Brooke, op. cit., pp. 16–17. David N. Livingstone, *Darwin's Forgotten Defenders*, Eerdmans, Grand Rapids 1987, gives an account of the positive reception of Darwin by many nineteenth-century evangelical theologians.
32. Moore, op. cit., p. 268.
33. Desmond and Moore, op. cit., p. 314.
34. Quoted by Russell, *Crosscurrents*, pp. 142–43.
35. Quoted by Desmond, *Huxley*, p. 262.
36. Brooke, op. cit., p. 219; cf. pp. 275–76.
37. John Tyndall, *Fragments of Science*, Longman Green (6th edn) 1879, Vol. II, p. 179. Tyndall was a physicist and later passages in the Belfast address reveal his own less than perfect understanding of natural selection.
38. Ibid., p. 199.
39. John Durant, 'A Critical-Historical Perspective' in Svend Andersen and Arthur Peacocke (eds), *Evolution and Creation – A European Perspective*, Aarhus University Press 1987, p. 22; Brooke, op. cit., *passim*, shows just how complex the disentanglement was.
40. See above, p. x; Cohen, op. cit., pp. 289–90.
41. Desmond, *Huxley*, pp. 275–81.
42. Andrew White, *A History of the Warfare of Science with Theology in Christendom* [1895], ARCO 1955, p. 70. John Durant discusses the changes in evolutionary theories from early demythologizing to its own myths in

Durant, *Darwinism and Divinity*, pp. 32–34. See also Mary Midgley, *Evolution as a Religion*, Methuen 1985. The Oxford meeting has generated a large literature of its own. For the background see my brief article in *Epworth Review*, Vol. 12, No. 3, 1985, pp. 47–49, and Michael Fuller, *Atoms and Icons*, Mowbray 1995, pp. 107–9. Although part of his sympathetic biography of Huxley, Adrian Desmond's discussion (see the previous note) is carefully balanced.

4 What is Science?

1. For a good introduction see, Anthony O'Hear, *Introduction to the Philosophy of Science*, Clarendon Press 1989, pp. 12ff.
2. See Harry M. Collins, *Changing Order*, University of Chicago Press 1992, p. 131 for a long discussion of this point.
3. Karl R. Popper, *The Logic of Scientific Discovery*, ET 1959, revd edn Hutchinson 1972, p. 33.
4. In Imre Lakatos and Alan Musgrave (eds), *Criticism and the Growth of Knowledge*, CUP 1970, pp. 91–196.
5. Nancey Murphy, *Theology in the Age of Scientific Reasoning*, Cornell University Press, Ithaca 1990.
6. Thomas S. Kuhn, *The Structure of Scientific Revolutions*, University of Chicago Press 1962; greatly amended 2nd edn 1970.
7. M. Masterman in Lakatos and Musgrave (eds), op. cit., p. 61, claims to have discovered twenty-two different uses of the term in Kuhn's short original essay.
8. Kuhn, op. cit., p. 117.
9. O'Hear, op. cit., pp. 75–79.
10. For a detailed discussion, see Hans Küng and David Tracy, *Paradigm Shift in Theology*, Crossroad, NY 1989.
11. Kuhn, op. cit., 1970 edn, p. 175.
12. See Ian G. Barbour, *Myths, Models and Paradigms*, SCM Press 1974.
13. Thomas S. Kuhn, *The Essential Tension*, University of Chicago Press 1977.
14. For an extended discussion of the issues involved, see W. H. Newton-Smith, *The Rationality of Science*, Routledge 1981, pp. 112ff.
15. Michael Polanyi, *Personal Knowledge*, Routledge 1958, Preface.
16. For more details, see Ian Hacking, *Representing and Intervening*, CUP 1983, ch. 3. The list below is also derived from Hacking.
17. Quoted by Hacking, op. cit., p. 48.
18. Nancy Cartwright, *How the Laws of Physics Lie*, Clarendon Press 1983.
19. For lengthy discussions of this point from very different perspectives see Hacking, op. cit., ch. 11 and Paul Feyerabend, *Against Method*, New Left Books 1975, chs 9–11.
20. Bas C. van Fraassen, *The Scientific Image*, Clarendon Press 1980, pp. 6–7. Van Fraassen offers this definition as an anti-realist attempting to be fair to the opposition.
21. See David Papineau in Nicholas Bunnin and E. P. Tsui-James (eds), *The Blackwell Companion to Philosophy*, Blackwell 1996, p. 306.
22. For the philosophical arguments, see Newton-Smith, op. cit., ch. 8.
23. O'Hear, op. cit., pp. 111ff.

24. Van Fraassen, op. cit., p. 39.
25. Michael C. Banner, *The Justification of Science and the Rationality of Religious Belief*, OUP 1990, pp. 125–30.
26. This point is discussed in more detail in the concluding part of the next chapter.
27. Hacking, op. cit., pp. 262 and 274.
28. See Mary Hesse in Robert J. Russell et al., *Physics, Philosophy, and Theology: A Common Quest for Understanding*, Vatican Observatory 1988, pp. 188ff. and Paul Avis, review in *Science and Religion Reviews*, 21, July 1992, pp. 37–38.

5 Making Science

1. Joseph McCabe, *The Religion of Sir Oliver Lodge*, The Rationalist Press Association, Watts and Co. 1914, p. 176.
2. See Frank Miller Turner, *Between Science and Religion*, Yale University Press 1974, pp. 176–78, 173. Turner's was a pioneering study of opposition to Victorian science.
3. David Bloor, *Knowledge and Social Imagery*, 2nd edn University of Chicago Press 1991, pp. 183–85. The so-called 'Strong Programme' of the sociology of science is discussed in detail later in this chapter.
4. The criticisms are listed by Bloor himself, *Knowledge and Social Imagery*, p. 163. For the 'science wars' controversy, see the section 'Science wars' below.
5. Stanley J. Grenz, *A Primer on Postmodernism*, Eerdmans, Grand Rapids 1996, p. 47.
6. For details of Merton's work see ch. 2, notes 17 and 18.
7. Dava Sobel, *Longitude*, Fourth Estate 1996.
8. Barry Barnes and David Edge, *Science in Context – Readings in the Sociology of Science*, Open University Press 1982, p. 3.
9. Sobel, op. cit.
10. Stephen Cole, *Making Science – Between Nature and Society*, Harvard University Press 1992, pp. 82–101.
11. Harry Collins and Trevor Pinch, *The Golem – what everyone should know about science*, CUP 1993, pp. 43–55.
12. Ibid., p. 52.
13. Kurt Gottfried and Kenneth G. Wilson, 'Science as a cultural construct', *Nature*, Vol. 389, 10 April 1997, pp. 546–47. For more details, see the section 'Science wars' below.
14. The words are quoted by Cole, op. cit., pp. 78, 79. Cole himself disagrees with this view.
15. Harry M. Collins, *Changing Order*, University of Chicago Press 1992, pp. 51–76.
16. Ibid., p. 56.
17. Ibid., p. 74.
18. Ibid., p. 76
19. Ibid., pp. 79–106.
20. For a photograph of the apparatus see Oliver Lodge, *Past Years*, Hodder 1931, p. 200.
21. Michael Mulkay, *The Sociology of Science*, Open University Press 1991,

pp. 109–30. See Michael Fuller, *Atoms and Icons*, Mowbray 1995, p. 20, for a former scientist's comments on Popper.

22. John L. Casti, *Paradigms Lost – Images of Man in the Mirror of Science*, Scribners 1990, p. 48.

23. Collins, op. cit.

24. T. Bilton et al., *Introductory Sociology*, Macmillan 1996.

25. Confusingly, in different writings Kuhn makes this point with more or less force.

26. For details of the 'Strong Programme' see especially, Bloor, op. cit. On Heisenberg and Uncertainty see Paul Forman 'Weimar culture, causality, and quantum theory, 1918–1927', *Historical Studies in the Physical Sciences*, Vol. 3, 1971, pp. 1–115 and Steven Shapin, 'History of Science and its Sociological Reconstructions', *History of Science*, Vol. 20, 1982, pp. 179–80. Shapin's article has been immensely influential in establishing both the validity and the usefulness of the modern sociology of science.

27. For a detailed discussion, see Michael Mulkay, *Science and the Sociology of Knowledge*, Allen and Unwin 1979, pp. 109–10.

28. David Bloor *Knowledge and Social Imagery*, 1st edn Routledge 1976. In the 2nd edn (see note 3 above) Bloor robustly defends the Principle of Symmetry, albeit with a certain ambiguity, pp. 175–79. The debate continues, see *Nature*, Vol. 386, 5 June 1997, pp. 543–46.

29. Mulkay, *Science and the Sociology of Knowledge*, p. 22.

30. Barry Barnes and David Bloor, 'Relativism, Rationality and the Sociology of Knowledge' in M. Hollis and S. Lukes *Rationality and Relativism*, Blackwell 1982, pp. 21–47.

31. Robert Scholes, *Textual Power*, Yale University Press 1985, p. 99. Quoted by Daniel W. Hardy, *God's Ways with the World*, T & T Clark 1996, p. 135, note 9.

32. Stephen Cole, *Making Science – Between Nature and Society*, Harvard University Press 1992, p. 230.

33. The article was originally published in *Social Text* (Duke University Press), Vol. 46/47, Spring/Summer 1996, pp. 217–52. It is reproduced in Alan Sokal and Jean Bricmont, *Intellectual Impostures*, Profile Books 1998, pp. 199–240. The quotation is from p. 200.

34. *Nature*, Vol. 387, 22 May 1997, p. 332.

35. This section closely follows Gottfried and Wilson's response to the debate in *Nature*, Vol. 387, pp. 445–46.

36. Allan Franklin, *The Neglect of Experiment*, CUP 1986 and *Experiment, Right or Wrong*, CUP 1990.

37. Franklin, *The Neglect of Experiment*, p. 244.

38. Michael C. Banner, *The Justification of Science and the Rationality of Religious Belief*, OUP 1990, p. 36.

39. In later chapters we shall discuss the so-called Anthropic Principle and other possible responses to such insights.

6 Scientific Views of the World

1. The details of the books mentioned in this section are as follows (in alphabetical order of author):
Harry Collins and Trevor Pinch, *The Golem – what everyone should know*

about science, CUP1993.

Paul (P.C.W.) Davies and John Gribbin, *The Matter Myth*, Simon and Schuster, NY 1992.

Richard Dawkins, *The Blind Watchmaker*, Longman 1986; Penguin 1988.

Richard Dawkins, *Climbing Mount Improbable*, Viking 1996.

Daniel Dennett, *Darwin's Dangerous Idea*, Simon and Schuster, NY 1995; Penguin 1996.

Stephen Jay Gould, *Wonderful Life*, Hutchinson 1989; Penguin 1991.

Robert Hazen and James Trefil, *Science Matters*, Cassell 1993.

John Houghton, *The Search for God*, Lion 1995.

Arthur Peacocke, *Creation and the World of Science*, Clarendon Press 1979.

Arthur Peacocke, *Theology for a Scientific Age*, Enlarged 2nd edn SCM Press 1993.

Russell Stannard, *The Time and Space of Uncle Albert*, Faber 1989.

John Wright, *Designer Universe*, Monarch 1994.

Other useful introductory books are mentioned in the relevant sections of the text.

2. Introductory books on relativity include Russell Stannard's *The Time and Space of Uncle Albert*, which has already been mentioned and Nigel Calder, *Einstein's Universe*, Penguin 1982.

3. A much praised recent book on quantum mechanics is David Lindley, *Where Does the Weirdness Go?* Vintage 1997. John Gribbin, *In Search of Schrödinger's Cat*, Wildwood House 1984, is also helpful.

4. Arthur Schuster, *The Progress of Physics during 33 years (1875–1908)*, CUP 1911, p. 112.

5. Richard Healey, *The Philosophy of Quantum Mechanics*, CUP 1989, p. 9 (emphasis added).

6. See John Gribbin, *Schrödinger's Kittens*, Weidenfeld and Nicholson 1995, for a popular discussion of the properties of light.

7. P. C. W. Davies and J. R. Brown, *The Ghost in the Atom*, CUP 1986, provides a good introduction to many of the issues which we shall mention in this section. See also, Gribbin, *In Search of Schrödinger's Cat*.

8. For a good, philosophical discussion of the many worlds interpretation see John Leslie, *Universes*, Routledge 1989.

9. Quoted by Healey, op. cit., pp. 1–2.

10. For further details see, Davies and Gribbin, op. cit. Useful introductions to modern cosmology include: Steven Weinberg, *The First Three Minutes*, André Deutsch 1977 and John D. Barrow, *The Origin of the Universe*, Weidenfeld and Nicholson 1994.

11. Stephen Hawking, *A Brief History of Time*, Bantam 1988. David Wilkinson, *God, The Big Bang and Stephen Hawking*, Monarch 1993, provides an informed and level-headed Christian commentary on the significance of Hawking's speculations.

12. Hawking, op. cit., pp. 140–41. Hawking's inaugural lecture is reproduced in Stephen Hawking, *Black Holes and Baby Universes*, Bantam 1993, pp. 49–68.

13. John D. Barrow, *Theories of Everything*, OUP 1990; Vintage 1992, is critical of the assumptions sometimes made about Theories of Everything. He reminds readers that the full complexity of the universe involves laws, conditions, constants and several other factors, and that no simple Theory

of Everything could ever easily or adequately describe the whole universe.

14. Dennett, op. cit.

15. Ibid., p. 47.

16. It may be possible to pass on the *capacity* to learn, but emphatically not to pass on particular learnt characteristics; see ibid., pp. 77–80.

17. Ibid., pp. 48–60.

18. We have seen how Aubrey Moore, and others, pointed this out soon after Darwin's work was published; see above, ch. 3.

19. Dawkins discusses these 'games' in great detail in *The Blind Watchmaker*.

20. For a detailed discussion see Paul Davies, *The Mind of God*, Simon and Schuster 1992; Penguin 1993 and Roger Penrose, *The Emperor's New Mind*, OUP1992. Penrose's book (and its sequels) have stimulated a major debate on the place of mind in the universe. He writes as a mathematician and physicist, and believes that physical quantum mechanical processes can explain the possibility of choice and free will. Few biological scientists would endorse his approach.

21. Richard Dawkins, *The Selfish Gene*, OUP 1976.

22. Peter Atkins, *Creation Revisited*, Penguin 1994, p. 3.

23. For example, Wright, op. cit., p. 31.

24. In both *Theology for a Scientific Age*, and *God and Science*, SCM Press 1996.

25. Dennett, op. cit., p. 212.

26. 'Top down' and 'Bottom up' causation are discussed by Peacocke, *Theology for a Scientific Age*, pp. 53–63, 157–65, 210–11. For a different perspective see John Polkinghorne, *Science and Christian Belief*, SPCK 1994. Polkinghorne subtitles the book 'Theological reflections of a bottom-up thinker'.

27. Peacocke, *Theology for a Scientific Age*, pp. 51–55; Ilya Prigogine and Isabelle Stengers, *Order out of Chaos*, Heinemann 1984.

28. Peacocke reproduces a detailed diagram of possible different levels and the place of different sciences within them in both *Theology for a Scientific Age*, p. 217 and *God and Science*, p. 49.

29. Dennett, op. cit., ch. 1.

30. Davies and Gribbin, op. cit., pp. 308–9. For a helpful introduction to the relation of dualism and Christian thought from the perspective of a scientist, see Michael Fuller, *Atoms and Icons*, Mowbray 1995, ch. 3, 'The Believer/Knower'.

31. Angela Tilby, *Science and the Soul*, SPCK 1992, pp. 20–21, 96, 130ff.

32. Peacocke, *Creation and the World of Science*, p. 169.

33. Wright, op. cit., pp. 96–105.

34. Jacques Monod, *Chance and Necessity*, Collins 1972, p. 110.

35. Stephen Jay Gould, *Wonderful Life*, *passim*, but especially ch. 3. Dennett has no time for guided evolution, but disputes Gould's picture of the universality of chance. Dennett believes that once life had begun on earth it was very likely to follow a fairly fixed pattern of development. Dennett, op. cit, ch. 10.

36. For details see e.g., Ian Stewart, *Does God Play Dice?*, Blackwell 1989; 2nd edn Penguin 1997.

37. David J. Bartholomew, *God of Chance*, SCM Press 1984.

38. G.D. Yarnold, *Christianity and Physical Science,* Mowbray 1950, pp. 100f.

39. John Polkinghorne in Robert J. Russell, *Physics, Philosophy, and Theology*,

Vatican Observatory 1988, p. 340. Keith Ward discusses the details in *Divine Action*, Collins Flame 1990.

40. Peacocke, *Creation and the World of Science*, ch. 3.
41. Russell Stannard, *Doing away with God?*, Marshall Pickering 1993, p. 89. For more details of the 'cosmic coincidences' discussed in the next paragraph, see pp. 90–104.
42. John Leslie in Robert J. Russell, op. cit., pp. 297ff.
43. A comprehensive 'scientific' treatment of the subject is given by John Barrow and Frank Tipler, *The Anthropic Cosmological Principle*, OUP 1986. Among its enthusiastic advocates is Hugh Montefiore, *The Probability of God*, SCM Press 1985. Mary Midgley is a fierce critic; see *Science as Salvation*, Routledge 1992, especially ch. 17.
44. Tilby, op. cit., p. 111.
45. Davies and Brown, *The Ghost in the Atom*, is a useful introduction here.
46. Brian Wren, hymn no. 5 in *Bring Many Names*, OUP 1989.

7 Relating Science and Religion

1. There are similarities with Acts 14.15–17 where again Paul is speaking to a non-Jewish audience.
2. Mary Midgley, 'Strange contest: science versus religion' in Hugh Montefiore (ed), *The Gospel and Contemporary Culture*, Mowbray 1992, p. 40. See above, p. 5 for a detailed discussion.
3. Ian Barbour, *Religion in an Age of Science*, SCM Press 1990, pp. 3–30.
4. Monod, op. cit, p. 110. The second quotation is given in Bartholomew, op. cit., SCM Press 1984, p. 16.
5. *The Independent*, 19 March 1993 ff.; *The Sunday Telegraph*, 28 March 1993. For Dawkins, see also *The Selfish Gene* and *The Blind Watchmaker*.
6. For a comparatively sympathetic study see, Ronald L. Numbers, *The Creationists*, University of California Press 1992.
7. Ian Barbour, op. cit, p. 4.
8. Quoted in Arthur Peacocke, *Creation and the World of Science*, p. 2.
9. The title of an essay in A. R. Vidler (ed), *Soundings*, CUP 1963.
10. This is similar to Calvin's Doctrine of Accommodation; see above, p. 26.
11. Martin Buber, *I and Thou*, revd edn Charles Scribner's Sons, NY 1958.
12. See, for example, Thomas F. Torrance, *Theological Science*, OUP 1969. There is a more detailed discussion of Torrance's work in the next chapter in the section 'The science of theology'.
13. Ibid., pp. 106–8, 103. Torrance has been deeply influenced by the theology of Karl Barth.
14. Robert Scholes, *Textual Power*, Yale University Press 1985, p. 99. See above, p. 119.
15. Ian Barbour, op. cit., p. 15.
16. J. R. Carnes, *Axiomatics and Dogmatics*, Christian Journals, Belfast 1982. In *Theology in the Age of Scientific Reasoning*, Cornell University Press 1990, Nancey Murphy comes to more optimistic conclusions.
17. See, for example, A. Thomson, *Tradition and Authority in Science and Religion*, Scottish Academic Press 1987, and Nancey Murphy, op. cit.
18. See ch. 4 above and, especially, Michael C. Banner, op. cit. and Robert Prevost, *Probability and Theistic Explanation*, Clarendon Press 1990.

19. David Pailin, *Groundwork of Philosophy of Religion*, Epworth Press 1986, ch. 8, 'Faith and the Existence of God'.

20. See above, p. 9.

21. The terms 'design' and 'teleology' are sometimes used interchangeably; see, for example, John Tyndall's comment on Darwin, above, p. 63.

22. We explored similar possibilities at the end of the previous chapter.

23. See especially, Banner and Prevost, op. cit.

24. Peacocke, *Theology for a Scientific Age*, p. 99.

25. Ibid., pp. 274ff.

26. John Polkinghorne, *Science and Christian Belief*, SPCK 1994, p. 1. Polkinghorne himself discusses this issue in *Scientists as Theologians*, SPCK 1996, pp. 78–79.

27. Polkinghorne, *Science and Christian Belief*, pp. 143–45.

28. See Polkinghorne, *Scientists as Theologians*, pp. 8, 80, 83. In the next chapter, we shall see several instances of theologians making extensive use of these three writers.

29. John Habgood, *Religion and Science*, Mills and Boon 1964 and *Being a Person: Where Faith and Science Meet*, Hodder 1998.

30. Ian Barbour, op. cit., p. 27.

31. Ibid., p. 29. The concepts of Process Thought are expounded sympathetically by David Pailin in *God and the Processes of Reality*, Routledge 1989.

32. See the section 'Do we need metaphysics?' in the next chapter.

33. For a brief account of this scheme see, Arthur Peacocke (ed) *The Sciences and Theology in the Twentieth-Century*, Oriel Press 1981, pp. xiii-xv.

34. Thomas Henry Huxley, *Collected Essays*, Macmillan 1893–94, Vol. V, pp. vii-viii.

35. *Science and Religion Forum Reviews*, No. 13, November 1988, p. 30.

36. Midgley, *Science as Salvation*, p. 223.

37. Paul Davies, *God and the New Physics*, Penguin 1984, p. ix.

38. Hawking, *A Brief History of Time*, p. 175.

39. *Theology*, Vol. 93, Sept/Oct 1990, p. 406.

40. Midgley, *Science as Salvation*, p. 34.

41. Chris Isham in Robert J. Russell, *Physics, Philosophy and Theoogy*, Vatican Observatory 1988, p. 404.

8 Doing Theology in a World of Science

1. John Polkinghorne, *Science and Creation*, SPCK 1988, p. 2.

2. Polkinghorne, *Scientists as Theologians*, p. 8; for a detailed discussion see John Polkinghorne, *Reason and Reality*, SPCK 1991, pp. 92–94.

3. Michael Sharratt, *Galileo*, Blackwell 1994, p. 209. In Peter Machamer (ed), *The Cambridge Companion to Galileo*, CUP 1998, pp. 348–66, Richard Blackwell takes a much more pessimistic view than that taken by Sharratt or myself.

4. *The Times*, 25 October 1996, p. 16.

5. Hawking, *A Brief History of Time*, pp. 115–16.

6. 'Message of His Holiness Pope John Paul II' to the Conference organized by the Vatican Observatory to celebrate the three hundredth anniversary of the publication of Newton's *Principia*, reproduced in Robert J. Russell, op. cit., pp. 10–12.

7. *Science and Religion Forum Reviews*, No. 22, 1993, p. 8.
8. T. F. Torrance, *Reality and Scientific Theology*, Scottish Academic Press 1985, p. ix.
9. Thomas F. Torrance, *Theological Science*, OUP 1969, p. 26.
10. See Daniel W. Hardy, 'Thomas F. Torrance' in David F. Ford, *The Modern Theologians*, Blackwell 1989, Vol. One, pp. 71–91.
11. Ibid., pp. 77–79.
12. See above, p. 174.
13. Colin Weightman, *Theology in an Polanyian Universe: The Theology of Thomas Torrance*, Peter Lang, NY 1994, pp. 281–91.
14. Torrance, *Theological Science*, pp. 106–8, 103.
15. Thomas F. Torrance, *Divine and Contingent Order*, OUP 1981, p. 34. See also the discussion above, p. 20.
16. Jürgen Moltmann, *God in Creation*, SCM Press 1985, ch. 2.
17. Paul Fiddes, *The Creative Suffering of God*, Clarendon Press 1988, p. 35.
18. Torrance, *Theological Science*, p. ix.
19. Wolfhart Pannenberg, *Systematic Theology*, T & T Clark 1991–98, Vol. I, p. 49.
20. Wolfhart Pannenberg, *Theology and the Philosophy of Science*, Darton, Longman and Todd 1976, p. 127.
21. Ibid., p. 45.
22. Ibid., pp. 126–54.
23. For the questions to scientists see Wolfhart Pannenberg, *Towards a Theology of Nature*, Westminster John Knox Press, Louisville 1993. For the other discussions see Pannenberg's *Systematic Theology*, Vol. II, pp. 50–52 (inertia), pp. 119ff. (evolution) and pp. 81ff., 154–55 (space and relativity).
24. See ibid., pp. 79ff.
25. Pannenberg, *Towards a Theology of Nature*, p.1 4.
26. See Langdon Gilkey, *Nature, Reality, and the Sacred*, Fortress Press, Minneapolis 1993, p. 1.
27. Ibid., p. 20.
28. Ibid., p. 26.
29. Ibid., p. 51.
30. Ibid., pp. 193ff.
31. Ibid., p. 89.
32. Ibid., p. 203.
33. Daniel W. Hardy, *God's Ways with the World*, T & T Clark 1996, p. 1.
34. Micheal O'Sidhail. 'Cosmos' in *Hail! Madam Jazz*, Bloodaxe Books 1992. Reproduced by Hardy, op. cit., p. 141.
35. Hardy, op. cit., p. 133.
36. Ibid., pp. 134, 136.
37. Ibid., p. 234.
38. Ibid., p. 102–3.
39. Ibid., p. 105.
40. Ibid., pp. 156–57. Hardy is commenting on Frank Tipler, *The Physics of Immortality*, Macmillan 1995. Pannenberg is also sympathetic, at least to Tipler's earlier work; see his *Systematic Theology*, Vol. II, pp. 160–61.
41. Hardy, op. cit., p. 145.
42. Peter Hodgson, *Winds of the Spirit: A Constructive Christian Theology*, SCM Press 1994, p. 8.

43. Sallie McFague, *The Body of God: An Ecological Theology*, SCM Press 1993, p. 74.
44. Hodgson, op. cit., pp. 53ff; McFague, op. cit., pp. 91ff. Both follow closely the work of Ian Barbour, Arthur Peacocke and John Polkinghorne, although none of these writers would emphasize the postmodern aspect of the changes.
45. Hodgson, op. cit., p. 185; McFague, op. cit., p. 91.
46. McFague, op. cit., p. 95.
47. Hodgson, op. cit., p. 87.
48. Sallie McFague, *Models of God*, SCM Press 1987, p. 27. Cf. *The Body of God*, p. 84.
49. McFague, *Models of God*, p. 14.
50. Hodgson, op. cit., p. 113–14.
51. Ibid., p. 142.
52. Polkinghorne, *Scientists as Theologians*, pp. 1, 6.
53. Ibid., p. 29.
54. Peacocke, *Theology for a Scientific Age*, p. ix.
55. Hardy, op. cit., p. 145.
56. In Robert J. Russell, op. cit., pp. 205–6.
57. Ibid., p. 213.
58. For example, two of the best textbooks of systematic theology, Alister McGrath, *Christian Theology*, Blackwell 1994 and Daniel L. Migliori, *Faith Seeking Understanding*, Eerdmans, Grand Rapids 1991, only mention science in the context of natural theology, and make no attempt to engage directly with the implications of scientific thought. Similarly, Stanley J. Grenz has written a superb introduction to postmodernism (*A Primer on Postmodernism*, Eerdmans, Grand Rapids 1996), which deals well with its roots in contemporary science, but his lengthy, *Theology for the Community of God*, Paternoster 1994, ignored this material entirely.
59. Peacocke, op. cit., pp. 221–22.
60. We shall take up this theme in detail in the final chapter.
61. Daniel Dennett, *Darwin's Dangerous Idea*, Simon and Schuster, NY 1995, p. 212.

9 Creation Waits

1. *The Times*, 22 July 1994.
2. Paul Davies and John Gribbin, *The Matter Myth*, Simon and Schuster, NY 1992, p. 21–22.
3. For Tilby, see ch.6 note 44, and for Tyndall see ch. 3, note 38.
4. Peter Selby, *Grace and Mortgage*, Darton, Longman and Todd 1997, p. 4; Dietrich Bonhoeffer's theology is articulated in *Letters and Papers from Prison*, SCM Press 1971.
5. Wayne Meeks, *The Moral World of the First Christians*, SPCK 1987, pp. 145–46.
6. Karl Barth, *Church Dogmatics*, T & T Clark 1936–69, III/1, Preface.
7. Hawking, *A Brief History of Time*, pp. 140–41.
8. For a detailed discussion, see, p. 202 above.
9. Jürgen Moltmann, *God in Creation*, SCM Press 1985, p. 76. The criticism by Polkinghorne is found in *Science and Creation*, p. 2.

10. Fiddes, op. cit., p. 35.
11. Davies and Gribbin, op. cit., pp. 235, 285.
12. A paraphrase of passages from the prophecy of Hosea, prepared as part of the *Justice, Peace and the Integrity of Creation* Project for the World Council of Churches.
13. A useful introduction to the topic, with generous extracts from key documents, is J. Patout Burns, *Theological Anthropology*, Fortress Press, Philadelphia 1981.
14. Peacocke, *Theology for a Scientific Age*, pp. 221–22.
15. Ibid., pp. 62–63.
16. See Eberhart Jüngel, *Death the Riddle and the Mystery*, Westminster Press, Philadelphia 1975, p. 74.
17. Irenaeus, *Against Heresies*, ch. 39, quoted in Burns, op. cit., pp. 26–27.
18. Robert R. Williams gives a good summary of the work of Ricoeur and others in 'Sin and Evil' in Peter Hodgson and Robert King (eds), *Christian Theology: An Introduction to its Traditions and Tasks*, SPCK 1983, pp. 179–83.
19. Brian Wren, hymn no. 5 in *Bring Many Names*, OUP 1989. See ch. 6 for a detailed discussion of the issue.
20. *The Independent*, 27 February 1993.
21. R. S. Thomas, 'Dialectic' in *Collected Poems,* J. M. Dent 1993, p. 342. Used by permission.

Index